PREDICTIVE ANALYTICS FOR BUSINESS FORECASTING & PLANNING

BY J. ERIC WILSON, CPF

Graceway Publishing Company, Inc.

BOOK EDITOR
Andrew Scuoler, CPF

GRAPHIC DESIGNER
Judy Chan

Copyright © 2021 By Graceway Publishing Company, Inc.

Manufactured in the United States of America
Library of Congress Control Card Number: 2020925218
ISBN: 978-0-9839413-8-5
(Softcover)

1st Edition 2021

Published by:
Graceway Publishing Company, Inc.
350 Northern Boulevard
Great Neck, New York 11021 U.S.A.
+1.516.504.7576
info@ibf.org
www.ibf.org

All rights reserved. No part of this book may be used or reproduced in any manner without written permission except in case of brief quotations embedded in critical articles and reviews.

TABLE OF CONTENTS

FOREWORD BY JOHN LLEWELLYN ix
FOREWORD BY CHAMAN L. JAIN, PH.D. xii
ABOUT THE AUTHOR xiv

PART I—THE PREDICTIVE ANALYTICS FOUNDATION 1

The Role of Artificial Intelligence in Demand Planning 3
Demand Planning Evolution 6
What Is Business Forecasting? 8
What Is Predictive Analytics? 12
Business Benefits of Predictive Analytics 15
What If? (Scenario Planning with Predictive Analytics) 19
Laws of Predictive Analytics and Business Forecasting 22
The Intersection of Business Forecasting, Machine Learning, and Business Intelligence ...25
Types of Analytics 29
Machine Learning as a Cause and Effect 34
Traditional Business Forecasting vs. Predictive Analytics 38
New Models and Methods 41
SPOTLIGHT—How Starbucks Uses Predictive Analytics and Your Loyalty Card Data ...43
Brave New World 45
Summary—A New Experience 47
Section Review 49

PART II—PREDICTIVE ANALYTICS AS A PROCESS 51

The Journey from Data to Insights 53
Principles and Considerations in Predictive Analysis 55
Predictive Analysis Process 59
Define the Need 64
Gather Inputs 66
Clean and Explore Data 69
Dealing with Dirty Data 72

Predictive Modeling 75
Training Your Model 78
Choosing the Right Model 81
Monitoring and Evaluating Models 84
Five Tips to Avoid Under and Over Fitting 87
Avoiding Bias 89
Managing Outputs 93
SPOTLIGHT—RSI and Burger King Try to Forecast the Impossible 97
Collaboration in Predictive Analytics 100
Consensus—One Number Attitude 102
Summary—All About the Process 105
Section Review 107

PART III—PREDICTIVE ANALYTICS AS DATA ANALYSIS 109

Data Analysis and Data Mining 111
What Is Data Mining Used For? 113
Types of Data 116
What is Big Data? 120
N=All (How Much Data Do You Use?) 124
Data Mining Techniques 127
Reconciliation of Time, Space, and Item/Location 130
Clustering Analysis and Segmentation 134
Constraint-Based Clustering (Rule-Based Methods) 137
Connectivity-Based Clustering (Hierarchical Clustering) 142
Centroid-Based Clustering (K-Means) 146
SPOTLIGHT—How Volvo Mobility Used Clustering to Improve Their Car Sharing Experience 150
Summary—Finding Answers in Data 153
Section Review 156

PART IV—PREDICTIVE ANALYTICS AS AN APPROACH 159

- Consumer-Driven Forecasting 161
- Predictive Analytics Toolbox 163
- Advanced Statistical Methods and Data Models 169
- Naïve Bayes 172
- Regression 177
- Logistic Regression 183
- Artificial Neural Networks 188
- Decision Trees 194
- ARIMA and ARIMAX 200
- AI and Deep Learning 208
- SPOTLIGHT—How Walmart Uses Kaggle to Find the Best Method 211
- Summary—Strategies Using All of the Above 214
- Section Review 216

PART V—PREDICTIVE ANALYTICS AS A FUNCTION 219

- A Predictive Analytics Culture 221
- A Good Planner 223
- Seven Habits of a Highly Effective Demand Planner 225
- Talent Management 228
- Core Competencies of Success 232
- Behavior/Personal Competencies 236
- Functional/Technical Competencies 239
- Enterprise/Professional Competencies 241
- Imagination and Storytelling 243
- Why Should I Send My Team to That Conference? 246
- The Future of the Predictive Analytics Function 249
- Transforming Your Predictive Analytics Function 252
- Structuring Predictive Analytics Departments and Roles 255

  SPOTLIGHT—Lowe's Data Interpreter/Analytics Translator 260
  Winning Support and Executive Buy-In 263
  Summary—Data Science or Demand Planning 266
  Section Review 268

PART VI—PREDICTIVE ANALYTICS AS A SYSTEM 271

  Rise of the Machine 273
  Open-Source Tools Available for Forecasting 275
  How to Choose a System That's Right for You 279
  System Requirements 283
  System Cost and Resources 287
  Building a Business Case 290
  Should You Use a Consultant? 294
  Digital Transformation 297
  Five Pitfalls of Transformation Projects 300
  Building the Right Training and Development Program 304
  Cloud 307
  Data Visualization and BI 310
  SPOTLIGHT—Escalade Sports Transformation 314
  Summary—Building the Perfect System 317
  Section Review 320

SECTION REVIEW ANSWERS 323

PREDICTIVE ANALYTICS GLOSSARY OF TERMS 331

SUGGESTED READING FOR IBF CERTIFICATION 343

  Suggested Reading for Certified Professional Forecaster (CPF) 345
  Suggested Reading for Advanced Certified Professional Forecaster (ACPF) 347

REFERENCES AND ENDNOTES 349

FOREWORD

The gap between what one is taught at university or college and what is necessary to do one's job is almost always wide and sometimes it is a gulf. That is not to say that what one has been taught is wrong. On the contrary, it is the essential first step. But it is only the beginning. That has certainly been my experience having spent most of my professional life as a quantitative economic and financial researcher and forecaster.

I got my first taste of this reality when I arrived at Oxford as a young man to embark on my doctorate. I felt that I understood a good bit of the statistical and econometric theory on which I would need to draw in the empirical part of my thesis. And I even knew, in principle at least, how to perform many of the specific statistical and econometric operations. But, as I soon found out, I did not know how to do the actual analysis. In short, I had read many recipe books; I knew what most of the utensils in the kitchen were for; but I did not know how to cook.

Progressively, and like most people who work in this area, I did most of my real learning on the job: building components for a macroeconomic forecasting model at Cambridge; leading a division at the OECD that constructed a global economic 'linkage' model; heading a team at Lehman Brothers forecasting exchange rates, interest rates, bond yields and many other financial variables; and now in my own firm trying to predict what will happen in all sorts of areas both financial and economic. In a world that was already experiencing rapid change before Covid-19 hit, I am still learning on the job. For economic forecasters and Demand Planners alike, forecasting in such a volatile environment is, and will continue to be, a major challenge.

Almost everyone I have talked to you over the years—analysts, supply chain planners, data scientists, economists, statisticians—agrees that experience teaches some broad lessons. Here are a few. People need forecasts for almost every action that they undertake, be that in business, policymaking, or indeed in personal life. But forecasting is difficult—far more so than those who have not done it realize. Managers often put more weight on a forecast than the forecaster who made it would. It is essential that users of forecasts understand the limitations inherent in any forecast. Explaining a forecast along with its assumptions is therefore a critical part of a forecaster's job.

But that is only the beginning: there are layers and layers of more detailed issues. A forecasting method can work well for a period, and then suddenly go off. The biggest mistakes tend to be made when something novel hits the system being forecast, usually something external to the forecasting model. Forecasters, therefore, have to try to take account of how what they are forecasting stands to be affected by the world outside—and yet it is impossible to include all potential influences. Just as a map drawn to a scale must trade detail for usefulness, a forecasting method must trade content for usability.

These points barely scratch the surface of all the issues that a professional forecaster has to address every day. There is so much to be learned.

In addition to the myriad technical aspects of forecasting, there is another important element in forecasting, one that I have learned repeatedly and was taught more forcefully the more senior the person I was interacting with. And that is the need, once the research has been done, and the forecasts made, to "tell a story". Eric emphasises the importance of this in this excellent book. It is all very well to find a good relationship between variables; to subject them to tests of statistical significance; to satisfy oneself that one has done a good technical job. But if anyone—generally one's boss—is to be persuaded to act upon these results, they must understand what they mean, in straightforward language. No boss worth their salt will act based on a black box projection alone.

The question I ask myself today is, could I, for my part, have acquired what I know today quicker, and with less pain? And the answer is that, had I had access to Eric Wilson's book back then, it would have set me on my path faster. For Eric is a highly experienced analyst with over 25 years' experience working in a variety of industries and large organizations, in demand planning and predictive analytics. Eric has "been there and done it". So, of course, have others but the uniquely valuable thing about Eric's book is that he has pitched it, with commendable aim and impressive clarity, at forecasters who, having undergone their requisite formal training, are now tasked with doing the job.

If you engage seriously with this book, you stand to benefit considerably. Eric does not so much tell you how to do it—there are already books for that—rather, he tells you how to do it right. And in the process he gives you confidence, so necessary when you find yourself plagued with doubts about the data you are using, the appropriateness of the technique you have adopted, the assumptions you are making, or the conclusions that you are considering reaching.

I would recommend reading this book in two stages: first, a fast skim-read to take note of the wide range of research topics covered; then a slow and careful re-reading of the part(s) relevant to your present need. Proceed in that way and Eric will serve as your 'guide, counsellor and friend' and will hold your hand, teach you a lot, make you feel more comfortable, lead you to produce better analysis, and help you tell a more compelling story.

I certainly wish that Eric's book had been available when I started out.

John Llewellyn
Llewellyn Consulting

FOREWORD

Having been involved in demand planning and forecasting since the early 1980s, I have witnessed the shift in market dynamics from supply-driven to demand-driven, and, more recently, the upheaval caused by the proliferation of eCommerce and omnichannel. Add to that decreased customer loyalty and the need to constantly launch new products, companies are having to fight harder than ever to gain and defend market share. To survive and grow in these markets, we need a proactive demand planning process which responds to market changes quickly and intelligently. The author of this groundbreaking book provides a roadmap for how to do exactly that.

As with many new technologies, events occur that drastically speed up adoption—one event can drive an acute need for a whole approach. This book comes at a time when Covid-19 has caused unprecedented supply and demand shocks. It has changed consumer behavior in ways we could not have imagined, rendering our demand assumptions obsolete. Not only has it highlighted the importance of effective demand planning and forecasting, but it has also revealed that simply extrapolating sales history isn't enough to paint a picture of future demand. Forward-thinking companies are diving into to their data and leveraging predictive analytics to understand their customers, their buying behaviors, and how they are reacting to changing events. These are the companies who can weather whatever storms lie on the horizon and enjoy significant growth when the clouds clear.

The future of our field is predictive analytics, machine learning, and data mining. To support these new techniques we need to improve our data, processes and technology, and change company culture. In the age of predictive analytics, data is King; Data when processed becomes information, when analyzed becomes knowledge, and when knowledge is put into action, it becomes a value-adding business plan. Predictive analytics provides an opportunity to use both historical data as well as the unstructured data that truly represents what is in the heart and mind of consumers. Identifying causal relationships in such data takes us beyond simply knowing what happened, to drawing inferences about customers and markets to know why things happened, and what will happen and why. This is nothing short of a revolution for business. Take the example of social listening, which collects and analyzes what consumers are saying about our products and brands. This is accomplished by deploying tools such as natural language processing to analyze social media posts and gives us the ability to better plan new products, understand product life cycles and identify opportunities for our sales, marketing and product teams.

That is not all predictive analytics is capable of. One Midwest grocery chain, for example, discovered that when men buy diapers on Thursdays and Saturdays, they also buy beer. Predictive analytics, then, not only generates forecasts to build out demand plans that support supply chain and production but identifies valuable business opportunities that sales and marketing can exploit. That is game-changing and, as Eric Wilson reveals in this book, represents both a new responsibility and opportunity for demand planners. The Demand Planner of tomorrow will drive insight across the organization to not only create demand plans, but to optimize business processes and identify commercial opportunities. When reading this book, you'll learn that demand planning will go beyond being an operational function (typically housed in supply chain) to a centralized, enterprise-wide driver of insights.

Even as cause-and-effect modeling adds a whole new string to the Demand Planner's bow, forecasts and demand plans remain crucial to any business. The unprecedented insight provided by predictive analytics greatly improves our forecasting efforts. Data mining techniques including clustering analysis, decision tree, and K-Nearest Neighbors to determine associations and classifications are all tools we can use to improve forecast accuracy, all of which Eric explains how to use in easy-to-understand language. Since data is now increasing exponentially and from ever-increasing sources, we require technology to acquire, store and process it. After reading this book, you'll know what tools are available to turn data into actionable insight, as well how to build the culture, processes and skills to support a sustainable predictive analytics function.

You'll find no shortage of books about predictive analytics, but none shows how to use it to drive demand planning and forecasting, making this book a must-read for anyone involved in demand planning, forecasting, S&OP, or analytics. Demand planning and forecasting are changing and if you learn the valuable lessons of this book, you can be part of this exciting, new, data-driven era. As ever, early adopters will reap the biggest rewards; companies still applying traditional statistical modeling to sales or shipment data will struggle to compete with the forward-thinking companies that are employing advanced predictive analytics techniques.

Chaman L. Jain, Ph.D.
Editor-in-Chief, Journal of Business Forecasting (JBF)
Founder, Institute of Business Forecasting
Professor, St. John's University

ABOUT THE AUTHOR

 J. Eric Wilson, like many Demand Planners, didn't plan on a career in forecasting and planning but it would turn into a lifelong passion. It was when he set up his first business buying and selling books at the age of just 18 that he first discovered the importance of using forecasting to balance supply and demand. Struggling with stockouts of popular titles on the one hand and surpluses of less popular books on the other, he realized he needed a way to predict likely sales volumes. He learnt the basics of inventory modeling, inputting sales history and overlaying moving averages, seasonal indices, and life cycle models.

Eric directly credits these forecasting models with the success of the business, and the key reason he was able to pay his way through college. He experienced firsthand the power of business forecasting and he was hooked.

In the years after winding up his successful book selling business, he found his first formal demand planning role, taking up a position as a Forecasting & CPFR Manager for Rittal Corp. From there, over the next 25 years, he would assume a series of Demand Planning leadership roles including Director level positions at several multinational companies including Berry Plastics, Tempur, Sealy and Escalade Sports.

Eric is an award-winning demand planning professional, recognized for his work in both demand planning and predictive analytics. He was recognized as a Top 20 Pro to Know by Supply & Demand Chain Executive in 2015 and was awarded the Excellence in Business Forecasting & Planning award by the Institute of Business Forecasting in 2016. Eric sits on the advisory board of the University of Kentucky - Gatton College of Business Supply Chain Forum.

A prolific writer, he has been published in multiple trade journals and newspapers, including The Journal of Business Forecasting, The Wall Street Journal, The Financial Times, and The Washington Post. Eric is also the author of the book, Cultural Cycles, and the host of the IBF On-Demand podcast. He is currently the Director of Thought Leadership at The Institute of Business Forecasting (IBF).

Eric is a proud father of three and calls Kentucky home.

PART I

THE PREDICTIVE ANALYTICS FOUNDATION

After reading this section, you should be able to:

- Define AI and understand how it fits with demand planning.
- Understand the differences between traditional and more advanced methods of demand planning.
- Clarify the current and future role of predictive analytics in business forecasting and demand planning.
- Explain the differences between descriptive, diagnostic, predictive, prescriptive, and cognititive analytics.
- Recognize the similarities and differences between business forecasting and business intelligence.

The Role of Artificial Intelligence in Demand Planning

We hear a lot of buzzwords about Artificial Intelligence (AI) and its potential impact on business forecasting and demand planning. This is a hot topic and a significant amount of interest and attention should be given to it so we may better understand its impact. However, there is also quite a bit of confusion as to how exactly we may benefit and what the future holds.

In the book to come, we will provide an overview of some AI-related technologies, more specifically, predictive analytics and how it is being utilized today. We will underscore the critical role that it is playing and will play going forward, as well as explain how you and your team can be prepared.

While the basic concepts of Machine Learning and AI are not new to forecasting and demand planning, there has been an obvious renewed interest. For years, forecasters have used algorithms including artificial neural networks, association rules, decision trees, and Bayesian networks—all of which are common methods in machine learning. I guess you can say we were data scientists before data science was cool!

But this is not your daddy's AI, in part because definitions change over time. AI is the concept of machines being able to carry out tasks in a way that we would consider "smart." There was a time when a machine adding 2+2 without humans providing the answer was considered to be smart. Now machines can decipher unstructured text in almost real-time, tell us directions, make predictions on our purchase preferences, and even talk to us.

Artificial Intelligence in Demand Planning Has Hit a Tipping Point

Another reason we are seeing this hype about machine learning and AI is we have also hit a tipping point. For a while, forecasting and demand planning processes and capabilities were greater than the technology that could support it. Now, we are no longer playing catch up and technology has surpassed planners' abilities. Because of new technologies, the machine learning we see today is different from the type of machine learning we saw in the past. While many machine learning algorithms have been around for a long time, the ability to automatically apply complex mathematical calculations to big data—over and over, and at faster speeds—is fairly recent, and is now far, far more advanced.[1]

Artificial Intelligence (AI): *the capability of a machine or system to augment or automate any process or output that normally requires human intelligence or intervention.* By system we mean a collection of algorithms, hardware, software and/or connect ware. It represents a significant advance in how we can forecast and plan. It is extremely important for us because the technologies it uses automate and augment the processes that we use most. For example, regression, which requires very complex calculations, is now easily performed through AI-related technologies. Before AI, we could only work with a minimal number of variables. With AI, we can now calculate millions of variables in seconds.

In 2018, the Institute of Business Forecasting (IBF) conducted research asking demand planning and forecasting professionals how they imagined their role evolving in the coming years. These questions were to measure how practitioners saw the discipline of demand planning in the year 2025 regarding people, process, and technology. Not surprisingly, 70% of respondents predicted that, by 2025, AI and machine learning will provide the industry's most important technological advancements.[2]

There is an arms race to leverage both machine learning and AI in demand planning solutions more effectively and in new ways. One software provider interviewed by IBF stated that almost every single one of their research dollars going forward is tied to these technologies. All of this makes one pause

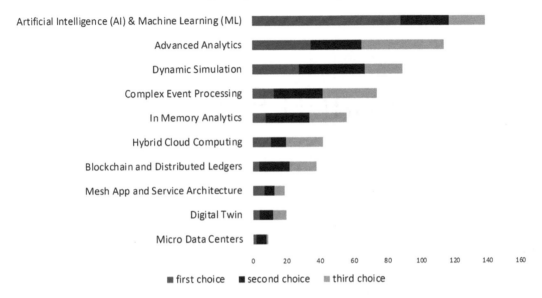

Fig a | IBF survey results: Technologies chosen as each respondent's top choice.

and wonder—if we have come this far today, where will we be tomorrow?

AI-related technologies represent the future of advanced business forecasting. Predictive Analytics is a key component of that journey. While most of AI is focused on applying data, we see predictive analytics as an enabler of insights and actions today. To be honest, this is not a book about AI or a deep technical dive into sophisticated modeling and coding. Rather, it is about the next logical progression of demand planning today into predictive analytics and providing you with the next level of information so you can act today and be prepared for tomorrow.

Demand Planning Evolution

If you think about it, virtually every business decision and process is based on a forecast. Anything you plan is generally based on an assumption of something else happening in the future. By definition, that is a forecast. Mind you, not all forecasts are derived from sophisticated methods and even educated guesses about the future are more valuable than no forecast at all.

It does not matter which industry you are in, whether your company manufactures products or offers services, whether your company is small or large, or whether it is a prediction several years in advance or only a few minutes beforehand—whatever the circumstances or time horizons involved, forecasting is an important aid in effective and efficient planning.

Of course, the more accurate the forecasts, the better the plans. If we know what happened in the past and why, or have some intelligence about what may occur next, we can then predict what is likely to happen in the future. With this information, we can potentially alter the future to the company's advantage.

The importance of demand planning and predictive analytics to an organization will mean it becomes a top priority for investment over the next few years. The sheer volume and complexity of today's data are challenging enough, but the top organizations of tomorrow will need to turn this data into useful insights quicker and for better decision-making to create a competitive advantage.

Is it possible to rethink the traditional approaches to predicting demand or are we stuck in the past? For the most part, forecasting roles, processes, and technology have not changed much in years. Unfortunately, the way some companies look at and use data has not changed either.

There are a select few businesses, though, that are not only breaking new ground but are creating a revolution in the demand planning field. This new wave of predictive analytics often challenges the status quo and, if done well, can reform an organization and becomes a game-changer within an industry. It will handicap companies that are left behind or retain the status quo, and they will eventually see their competitors pass them by.

Companies need a new breed of talent, deployment models, and technologies. We cannot simply cobble together existing pieces. What we need is an evolution—and maybe a revolution—in how to look at and use demand planning and predictive analytics. In the chapters to come, we will describe strategies to understand the basics of demand planning and predictive analytics, and how to navigate the potential of tomorrow's demand planning.

What Is Business Forecasting?

Forecasting may not be what comes to mind when you hear the phrase "the oldest profession," but it is one of them. For thousands of years, people have been making predictions by interpreting the stars and other signs, trying to either gain an advantage or survive. It was the early 1900s, a time of financial panic, that brought this discipline to the forefront in business.[3] For those who had suffered through financial panics, forecasting offered the idea that economic activity was not simply random but followed discernible patterns that could be predicted.

Dr. Chaman Jain founded the Institute of Business Forecasting (IBF) in 1981, in part to help define the role and function of forecasting.[4] Since then, the processes, approaches, and activities have continued to evolve. Dr. Jain used business forecasting as a broad all-encompassing term covering the people, processes, systems, and technology needed for demand planning, forecasting, business analytics, and collaborative planning. As business has become even more competitive and the financial environment even more uncertain, the role of the business forecaster has become critical in most organizations today, allowing companies to either gain an advantage over competitors or keep pace with them.

Business Forecasting

Business Forecasting: *The process of using analytics, data, insights, and experience to make predictions* *and answer questions for various business needs.* The insight gained by business forecasting enables companies to automate and optimize their business processes. Their goal is to go beyond knowing what has happened and provide the best assessment of what will happen in the future to drive better decision-making.

In business, many people think of a forecast as how many of something we will sell next week, and that may be a part of it. But business forecasting can encompass anything that identifies the likelihood of a future outcome, provides comparative information using analytics, and drives data-driven business decisions. Business forecasting can be used in:

- Strategic Planning and decision-making (long-range planning),
- Finance and accounting (budgets and cost controls),
- Marketing (consumer behavior, life cycle management, pricing), and
- Operations and Supply Chain (resource planning, production, logistics, inventory).

At the heart of business process decisions is the forecast, which involves techniques including a combination of the following:

- Qualitative knowledge-based forecasting: The use of opinion or educated guesses in developing forecasts,
- Quantitative deductive forecasting: Used to develop a future forecast using past data and often for statistical or mathematical models, and
- Machine inductive learning forecasting: Takes information from a previous iteration or training data set and applies it to help build the current or future model.

These techniques—along with analyzing data and use of statistical algorithms—can also be the foundation of and input into a demand plan.

Demand Plan

A demand plan is a subset and is most often a primary output of business forecasting. **A Demand Plan:** *Is a projection of the future that combines the knowledge of the past with the best assessment of future* *need of a product or service.* The demand plan, or sales forecast, most frequently displays the likely sales (demand) a company will experience, regardless of actual ability to meet demand (hence it is often called the unconstrained forecast). Best practice is to build a demand plan through a structured forecasting process to develop a consensus forecast that includes a baseline demand forecast along with other inputs and variables, resulting in a demand plan that is jointly agreed upon by the different functions of the organization.

Demand Planning

Demand Planning: *Is the process and techniques used to create a demand plan and other data analytic outputs used in the planning process or to enable business decisions.* If the demand plan is the output, this is the process that uses various inputs, principles, methods, and models to generate the output of a prediction of a future event or need for a product or service. In addition to this, some include—and we suggest adding to the planning process—not only what may happen but also what we can make happen. Planning demand looks holistically at demand and what can happen, what we want to happen, and what we can do to make it happen. Demand planning may include:

- **Demand Sensing:** *The sensing of demand signals and then predicting demand.* Demand signals include who is buying the product or service and how the sales and marketing activities are influencing the demand.
- **Demand Translation:** *Translating demand from the market to each role within the organization.*
- **Demand Shaping:** *Manipulating the demand for a product to achieve the desired goal.* If the demand for a product is expected to be greater than supply, the manufacturer/customer may shape (more appropriately, re-shape) the demand by increasing its price and/or by cutting down the promotion.
- **Demand Orchestration:** *Determines the best solution or outcome among various choices, given the known parameters.* It is actually creating demand and influencing behavior but also about finding the right balance to improve forecasts, reduce costs, minimize risks, and increase sales and profit.

Demand planning and business forecasting are not standalone processes. Forecasting is a key process and demand planning is a critical driver for business processes such as Business Efficiency Planning

(BEP), Finance and Financial Planning and Analysis (FP&A), Product Management and Marketing, Product Lifecycle Management (PLM), Operations and Supply Chain, and Sales and Operation Planning (S&OP), to name a few.

Demand Planner

This is and should be much more than just someone who plans demand. Demand planners are storytellers who use numbers as their language. The role of demand planning uses data and forecasts to help highlight opportunities and threats; tells us ahead of time what we expect sales of a product to be; and identifies which markets or channels of distribution are likely to expand, and which ones may contract.

Words have meaning and even though it may be semantics, it is important to understand what we create, how we create it, who creates it, and what we can do with it to help provide those advantages mentioned above inside an organization.

> *"The great enemy of clear language is insincerity. When there is a gap between one's real and one's declared aims, one turns, as it were, instinctively to long words and exhausted idioms, like a cuttlefish squirting out ink."*
> —George Orwell[5]

What Is Predictive Analytics?

As a discipline, predictive analytics has been around for many decades and has been a hot topic in academia for many years. Its application in the field of demand planning, though, is still relatively untapped. Its effective use in business is more an exception than a rule. Despite the mass of information available to us, and machine learning algorithms that can model the supply chain for insights, companies have barely scratched the surface with data analytics.

Part of the reason for this may be confusion surrounding traditional demand planning and predictive analytics. Demand is for "something" and can be for a product or service. It manifests itself as a sale to an end-user, an order, a shipment, inter-plant transfer, distribution requirement, etc. Broadly speaking, there are two approaches to demand forecasting: one is to obtain information or make assumptions about patterns of past purchases, the other is to obtain information or make assumptions about external factors or the likely purchase behavior of the buyer.

While predictive analytics can be utilized to develop a demand plan, Demand Planners using traditional approaches often only use the past sales to forecast demand. Predictive analytics not only forecasts the demand itself but also uses a systematic computational analysis of data or analytics to try to determine "why" demand occurs. Demand planning only creates an estimate of demand; predictive analytics creates an evaluation of what the future may be "if."

Predictive Analytics: *A process and strategy that uses a variety of advanced statistical algorithms to detect patterns and conditions that may occur in the future for insights into what will happen.* The goal is to go beyond knowing what has happened to provide the best assessment of why it occurred or what drivers will impact something occurring in the future. Predictive analytics takes a more humanistic and sometimes intuitive logical approach. Instead of relying on past historical activities, predictive analytics analyzes the influencers, interactions, and activities of the actors (consumers) in demand.

With this, predictive analytics generally uses more and different data. It uses external variables to try to understand the forecast drivers better and, as a result, can provide a more accurate prediction. Compared to traditional time-series methods, predictive analytics is more forward-looking and proactive in its approach. And typically, predictive analytics uses more advanced methods including machine learning techniques.

The algorithms used in predictive analytics are considered advanced because they integrate external information, such as customer-buying behaviors and multiple other drivers, with internal data. They do this with multiple, sometimes hundreds, of variables using learning algorithms. Doing this helps us understand behaviors and drivers and how they might impact and predict the future. The result is that it helps organizations to achieve their business goals.

In other words, predictive analytics enables us to learn much more about consumers and the underlying data. By doing so, we're able to predict their buying choices with greater accuracy. Predictive analytics enables us to observe consumers closely, along with markets and other conditions such as the economy, the weather, etc., making it possible for us to go beyond looking at the past when we forecast.

Traditional demand planning asks, "What did the item do last year?"

The new era of predictive analytics asks, "What does the consumer do when this happens?"

The predictive analytics approach does not replace traditional demand planning or an organization's need for a demand plan. What we are doing today is adding to it with different techniques and processes to gain even greater insights and improve the demand plan and demand planning process.

It is not replacing but augmenting and advancing the field to keep up with the market and business needs.

Because of this, predictive analytics is more than just a forecast of how much of an item we will sell next month. Instead, it opens the door to many more insights. The world beyond that door is not limited to just supply chain either but brings the predictive analytics professional into every function and can add value to every business decision.

Applied to business, predictive models are used to analyze current data and historical facts to better understand customers, products, and partners and to identify potential risks and opportunities for a company. They can be used for micro-targeting campaigns to gain strategic advantages or to determine the color and font on a website that drives the most traffic. For retailers, this translates to consumer loyalty, less churn of customers, and customized experiences to make a higher probability of sales. For online sellers, with predictive analytics, you can understand how your page ranking, number of comments, ratings, and "winning the buy box" on Amazon.com impact your sales on any given day.

Revealing the future by getting into the head of the consumers, rather than by analyzing the history of the item, can pay enormous dividends. And, with the abundance of real-time consumer data available today, future demand for your organization's products and services may be more precisely determined using predictive analytics rather than relying solely on traditional demand planning processes.

Predictive analytics has grown in prominence alongside the emergence of big data systems. As enterprises have amassed larger pools of data, they have created increased data mining opportunities to gain predictive insights. Heightened development and commercialization of machine learning tools have also helped expand predictive analytics capabilities. Because of this and the changing business environment, professionals in our field will continue to migrate to new ways of modeling and planning and start to see crossover of these predictive models into traditional forecasting and planning.

Business Benefits of Predictive Analytics

The need for forecasting stems from the time lag between knowing an event is coming and the occurrence of that event. Most people in business recognize this process as sales forecasting or demand forecasting, where the impending event is the future orders of an estimated quantity. This is just one example of forecasting. Business forecasting and predictive analytics can also be used for insights into the causal factors connecting events. You can use it to better identify risk and opportunities before the event, or the driving factors behind a sale, to enable or shape the sale before it would have naturally occurred.

There are all types of business decisions that use some type of prediction or insight for guidance. People generally think of decisions only in terms of the big ones. However, decisions are made daily at every level in an organization. All decisions have an input and judgment and if there is any time lag between that judgment and the result of the decision, it also requires a prediction or forecast. More often than not, our predictions are hidden as inputs into decision-making. The underlying truth is that better predictions mean better information, which means better decision-making.

Strategically, forecasts allow for a quantitative foundation for quick identification and objective, unbiased evaluation of information to help pursue new opportunities. These are long-term forecasts that can help organizations to adapt. When forecasts covering long periods are made, the probability of error may be high. Hence, competent forecasting is an essential requirement for this type.

Tactically, forecasts can allow companies to micro-target a market with precise accuracy, as well as help to determine whom to reach and when, and how to shape demand. These are mid-term forecasts that help business to anticipate and prepare. When forecasting is used to allocate resources, order product, and provide the insights to deliver business performance, precision, and an understanding of the strengths and limitations of forecasting are essential requirements.

Operationally, in almost real-time, forecasts allow you to sense and react immediately to signals and changes across an entire supply chain. These are very short-term or even reactive forecasts that help business respond effectively and efficiently. When forecasting is used operationally, you need to be agile and react in almost real-time. Hence, experience in a demand planning/supply chain environment and using analytics are essential requirements for this type.

You may not realize it, but predictions are everywhere and are a crucial foundation input into every business decision and outcome. Here are only 11 of many business questions that may be answered more effectively with better predictive analytics:[6,7]

- **Can we service our customers?** With accurate forecasting, you can achieve a higher rate of on-time in-full (OTIF) delivery. The information from demand forecasts can not only help to achieve these targets but also provide a clearer picture of what future service may look like for customers.
- **What should we carry in inventory?** The more accurate the demand forecast, the better prepared your company will be to manage its inventory and resources. With a more consistent demand plan, you can factor in and reduce uncertainty, which means better management of cash.
- **What does the customer want?** Consumers are far more likely to make a purchase when your site provides relevant recommendations. When they see content or products that appeal to their interests, they'll naturally want to learn more about your offerings. The application of predictive analytics has made this possible, even common.
- **Are we going to keep that customer?** Every business wants to predict which customers are about to leave, and for what reasons, so they can manage churn and target their retention efforts. **Churn Analysis:** *The evaluation of a company's customer loss rate with the aim of reducing it. Also referred to as customer attrition rate, churn can be minimized by assessing how people use your product.* Without predictive analytics, a retention campaign may be a lot costlier.

- **What does the customer really think of our product?** When predictive analytics is combined with linguistic rules, companies can scan social media to determine what customers are saying about their brand and their products. It can even find hidden, underlying patterns that might indicate excitement or frustration with a particular product. Samsung used this to detect and counteract dissatisfaction concerning a red tint on the screen of a new phone by text-mining comments on the web.
- **Should we discontinue this item?** Business forecasting can look at what future sales and market share may be for a particular item, along with segmenting based on other items, as well as helping to identify which product features are not working. **Conjoint Analysis:** *A survey-based statistical technique and optimal market research approach for measuring the value that consumers place on features of a product or service.*
- **Should I lower the price?** Price elasticity models are based on analysis data that can be converted into predictions. Even better though, solid forecasting may help increase sales and profits. Better predictions ahead of time may prevent the need for panic sales to rid your business of excess merchandise.
- **Who should we target?** Predictive analytics may be used by Marketing departments to micro-target campaigns for a narrowly defined audience. **Market Basket Analysis:** *A type of analysis that helps companies cross-sell and up-sell products based upon the theory that if you buy a certain group of items, you are more (or less) likely to buy another group of items.* Understanding the correlations, relationships, clusters, and probabilities or outcomes with different variables are predictions that need to be made.
- **Where do our customers come from**? Using predictive analytics, we can better understand demographics, geography, socioeconomics, and other key attributes. On the web, you can use data and analytics to understand how things are connected. **Social Network Analysis (SNA):** *A process of mapping and measuring relationships and flows between various attributes, locations, and information/knowledge entities to understand social structures.*
- **How much of this new product will we sell?** Predictive analytics and deep learning are uniquely well-suited for forecasting new products. They act as a long-term memory function and are better than traditional approaches at learning patterns over time and finding like products to forecast. A well-known shoe company, for example, used this for a new product by identifying a similar product using images and attributes like design and color. They put together initial sales projections based on this hybrid of other shoes that the system determined were similar in appearance.

- **How much is this customer worth? Customer Lifetime Value (CLV):** *Represents the value of a customer to your business over the entire length of your relationship with that customer.* With predictive analytics, companies can calculate probabilities better and forecast potential sales more accurately, allowing you more precise insight into CLV and a better understanding of your customers.
- **What color should the banner be on our website?** Another way predictive analytics helps companies is with understanding how price, placement, wording, and even color schemes on websites impact sales. Online retailers can use the tons of data they gather on the behavior of their customers to make adjustments based on what appeals to them the most.

What If? (Scenario Planning with Predictive Analytics)

What if we not only knew what the forecast will be for an item for the next period but also understood a range of potential outcomes for that item?

What if we didn't just have a number but also had a list of drivers that contributed to many possible numbers?

What if we not only had an outcome but could use probabilities to discover unseen outcomes?

What if, instead of a single plan, we gave the business alternative scenarios that could play out?

What if we didn't just forecast numbers but used predictive analytics to understand drivers, paint scenarios, and drive the demand you want?

"What if?" is the question that underpins predictive analytics.

"What if?" is perhaps one of the more critical and important aspects of predictive analytics. Predictive analytics and scenario planning allow a business to respond to alternative situations more quickly and effectively. Predictive analytics, using simulation techniques, can increase our knowledge and confidence in making informed decisions. Predictive analytics focused on forecast drivers is information that helps us shape our future by telling us what actions should be taken that will lead to desired business conditions.

The most basic part of forecasting is the assumption. As Demand Planners, assumptions are more important than numbers. Much of our job is managing them, interpreting them, and turning them into insights. Assumptions are numerous and help us break down complexity and uncertainty. Every business forecast contains assumptions.

Another term for assumption may be "scenario." A scenario, in this context, is a potential circumstance or combination of assumptions that could have a significant impact (whether good or ill) on an organization. In the messy world of people and behavior, there can be no forecast without a scenario. The only question is whether to make your assumptions explicit (known) or implicit (unknown). You have a choice: pick a single assumption (usually a single number) or use predictive analytics to understand more variables and therefore more assumptions. The latter choice makes the variables known and allows us to forecast more accurately.

Scenario planning and predictive analytics are based on the premise that, for every choice taken, there are several possible outcomes. By accurately identifying multiple variables that contribute to the forecast and preparing for each of these alternative scenarios, it is possible to be reasonably sure that the initial action was the correct one. This level of strategic foresight also allows for the creation of contingency plans that can be activated immediately, if the situation calls for action of that type.

By using predictive analytics and making the assumption known, it is possible to prepare in advance for several potential outcomes rather than simply meeting them as they come along. The preparation can often save a great deal of time and money, as well as provide the company with intelligence that helps to defuse negative situations while maximizing the benefit from positive ones.

At the core, this is what demand planning and predictive analytics do. Their job is to take the questions that seem almost unanswerable (due to their complexity and the many unknowns) and try to manage the assumptions and develop answers. Each of the questions involves dozens of factors that can change the outcome. To help, there may be some good analytical approaches to addressing the unknowns and breaking down the complexity posed by such tough forecasting questions.

As Demand Planners, we live in the world of ambiguity and uncertainty and transform it into insights the business can use. More than managing numbers, we manage assumptions and need to understand their contribution. We use weighting and ratios and work towards the best fit of our data sets to the right model to minimize uncertainty and provide answers.

Our world is changing as well, and we need to adapt. Predictive analytics and probabilities just may be the train that is taking us into the future. We have already seen a shift from traditional time-series modeling to predictive analytics due to omnichannel and e-planning, much of which is driven by regression models or even more sophisticated machine learning and probabilistic forecasting.

One of the primary goals of predictive analytics is to assign a probability to forecast drivers. With these probabilities, you can understand (as unlikely as it may be) the likelihood of the Black Swan event occurring, or indeed a variety of other more day-to-day outcomes. Predictive analytics can be used to create several different what-if scenarios, especially in the areas of risk assessment, customer-buying trends, and business. For example, it can be used with a business's sales history to determine when customers are most likely to make large purchases or which products will perform best. It can also be used in a market as a whole to get an idea of when a business could safely try to expand without taking unnecessary risks.

Most importantly, whether the business knows it or not, they need predictive analytics and probabilities and to better understand likelihoods along with uncertainty. Black Swans are real, and we need to understand what we can mitigate and what we will accept. While this is being done already by many companies, data-driven organizations are using probabilities, demand planning, and, most of all predictive analytics to drive advanced decision-making.

Laws of Predictive Analytics and Business Forecasting

Predictive analytics, business forecasting, and most everything that you do have principles that you must know if you want to implement successful forecasting for your business. Use these principles as your guiding star to move from the basic world of forecasting into the advanced analytics world.

Here, I would like to present the five basic and most important principles of predictive analytics. Those principles are something that must be in front of the eyes of every planner and that every executive must be reminded of often.

Predictive Analytics Includes Uncertainty

Remember that you still want to forecast the future, which is something unknown. So, you cannot expect that you will predict the future reality with 100% accuracy. Because it is expected that your forecasting will be wrong, the real question is, "by how much?" Forecasts can be wrong and demand plans can be accurate if you include probability and/or an estimate of error.

Predictive Analytics Is Less Precise and Accurate as You Get More Detailed

A group of products or aggregation of an attribute or feature will have less uncertainty and more accuracy than at a very granular or item-level detail. For the dimension of time, forecasts will deteriorate and have more errors as you go from months to weeks to days. It also stands to reason that if we can combine features, we may be able to get a better view or more insights. The way you forecast and plan demand is unique to what question you would like the forecast to answer.

Predictive Analytics is More Precise and Accurate the Closer You are to the Signal

Tomorrow is more predictable than three months from today or one year from now. It also stands to reason that point of sale (actual customer demand) is closer to real demand than retailer or distributor orders are. Consumer behavior or leading indicators, in turn, may be closer to real demand than shipments. The objective is to get closer to consumer sentiment and true demand. Recognize that the closer you get to the true demand signal and why the demand is occurring, the better the forecast will be.

Predictive Analytics Improves with the More You Know or Can See

Predictive analytics relies on historical data and external environmental factors. Historical data are an important starting point for many forecasts. At the same time, you can't expect to have the same results from forecasting if you do not have enough history or if there is some change in environmental conditions. We want as big and complete a picture as possible—this will be better than a narrow picture from a small sample. Lots of interlocking weak information may be vastly more trustworthy than a point or two of strong information.

Predictive Analytics Is a Process

With that, it does not matter if you need to estimate the result of 2+2 or predict the future impact of a Taylor Swift tweet in real-time, it uses the same basic steps and principles. It will require collection, transformation, modeling, and analysis of data to gain consensus for a future forecast. Most importantly though, demand planning is a collaborative process, not a test of statistical algorithms. In many ways, we manage assumptions and expectations more than we manage numbers. The analytics provide a solid foundation with which to work, but the real value comes from answering questions or enabling others to make decisions.

The Intersection of Business Forecasting, Machine Learning, and Business Intelligence

Most of what we have discussed around predictive analytics is in terms of a new way to forecast where you are not just looking at your internal sales history, but also you are bringing in more data, different drivers, and other external variables to improve your forecast. We have focused on using predictive analytics to help in discovering "Why do things happen?" and the benefits of translating this into "What could happen if…?" With advances in technology, we now have advanced models and methods that can better enable predictive analytics.

The Demand Planner or predictive analytics professional blends forecasting and business intelligence. They merge techniques and methods including machine learning to support the business's needs.

A common misconception is that machine learning, business forecasting, advanced business intelligence, and all things predictive analytics are synonymous. The diversity of opinion reflects the fluidity of how we understand the defining language of the field. Business forecasting is the *process* to extract information and provide insights. Machine learning is a subset or application of AI and is more

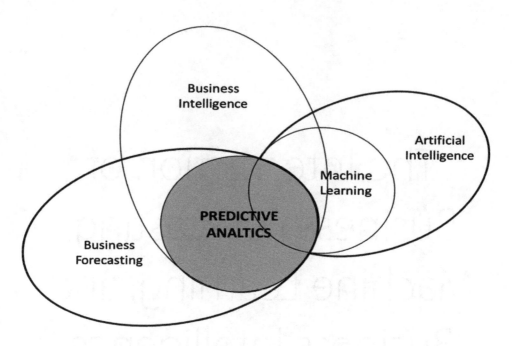

Fig b | Infographic depicting intersection of AI, BI, and business forecasting

of an *approach* than a *process*. Business intelligence is the different types of analytics and outputs. Where they overlap is the intersection of process, approach, and insights of predictive analytics.

Business Intelligence

Business Intelligence or BI focuses on infrastructure and output. The use of the term business intelligence can be traced to the mid- to late-1860s, but it would be a century later before consultant Howard Dresner was credited with coining the term. His definition was, "**Business Intelligence:** *An umbrella term that covers architectures, databases, analytical tools, applications, and methodologies used for applying data analysis techniques to support business decision-making.*"[8] Despite this definition, historically, when people thought of business intelligence, most considered it as a fancy way of talking about data reporting. It has always been much bigger than just a dashboard and, through the years, people have begun to better understand the breadth and uses of BI to inform data-driven business decisions.

Predictive analytics in BI has become a natural and needed progression of decision-making capabilities and insights. Where most of BI focused on visualization of data and descriptive type analytics, with predictive analytics we are asking more what could happen or even what we can make happen as an organization. Predictive analytics helps in presenting actionable information to help executives, managers, and other corporate end-users to make informed business decisions. Overall, predictive analytics can help discover why things happen and use this knowledge to reveal what could happen in future.

Business Forecasting

Business Forecasting: *The process of using analytics, data, insights, and experience to make predictions and answer questions for various business needs.* It is a process of breaking something down into its constituent elements to understand the whole and make predictions.[9] Where BI is about the tools and representation, business forecasting is the analysis and procedures.

Predictive analytics in business forecasting has become a more advanced process that encompasses more and different types of data, more forward-looking causal type models, and more advanced algorithms and technology. It uses several tools, data mining methodologies, forecasting methods, analytical models (including machine learning approaches), and descriptive and predictive variables to analyze historical and current data, assess risk and opportunities, and make predictions. Instead of just historical sales, we are trying to better understand the factors or the likely purchase behavior of the buyer. Predictive analytics is a new way to forecast where you are not just looking at your internal sales history, but you are bringing in more data, different drivers, and other external variables to improve your forecast.

Machine Learning

Machine Learning involves different approaches and methodologies. It is a subset of AI and is a collection of different techniques, methods, modeling, and programming that allow systems to learn automatically.[10] **Machine Learning:** *An algorithm or technique that enables systems to be "trained" and to learn patterns from inputs and subsequently recalibrate from experience without being explicitly programmed.* Unlike other approaches, these techniques and algorithms strive to learn as they are presented with new data and can forecast and mine data independently.

For predictive analytics, machine learning has opened new opportunities and provides more advanced methods for it to use. Predictive analytics in machine learning is a category of approaches to achieve better forecasts, improved intelligence, automation of processes, and a path to AI. Some new advanced models and methods can be incorporated to further enable predictive analytics.

Predictive Analytics

At the intersection of advanced business forecasting, mature business intelligence, and some machine learning techniques, is predictive analytics. **Predictive Analytics:** *A process and strategy that uses a variety of advanced statistical algorithms to detect patterns and conditions that may occur in the future for insights into what will happen.*

Predictive analytics used to be out of reach for most organizations. However, recent advances in professional skills, increased data, and new technologies, including machine learning and AI techniques, have made it much more accessible. Predictive analytics utilizes many advanced business and planning processes to provide more information with less latency and improved efficiency. This is not just about advanced analytics outputs and business intelligence; it also offers more mature organizations a view of what and why things occur. Finally, while predictive analytics may use some machine learning techniques, it is only a portion of the planner's toolbox, along with other statistical and data mining techniques.

Types of Analytics

What a business knows, and the strategy with which it uses information to make business decisions, may be best described as the organization's business intelligence. Business intelligence includes the data, infostructure, and the culture to convert data into meaningful information. The maturity of the company will depend on if they are merely generating reports, understanding causes, predicting outcomes, or orchestrating results.

Thanks to big data, computational leaps, and the business playing field undergoing radical changes, a revolution in planning has been sparked that has given birth to new data analysis of which predictive analytics is a part. With the explosion of data and using this increase to stay competitive, companies are gradually moving from looking in the rear-view mirror to looking at what is in front of them to even charting their own course.

In their book, *Competing on Analytics*, Thomas Davenport and Jeanne Harris describe the competitive advantage to degrees of information, or what they call intelligence.[11] The authors divide these into two quadrants: those that are descriptive, or what I would call traditional or reactive, and those that are predictive, or what I would call revolutionary and proactive. Building on this we can further look at the progression as a continuum from pure descriptive to past predictive to prescriptive, or even what others are calling cognitive. As shown in the graph below, by asking particular types of questions and answering them, we can implement different methodologies and, consequently, attain specific types

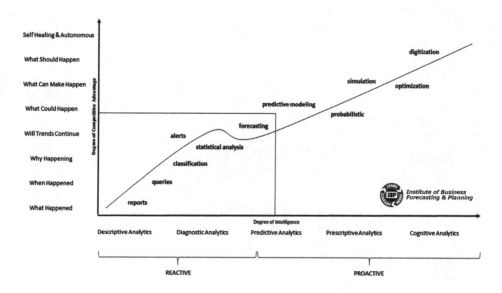

Fig c | Infographic demonstrating types of analytics and outputs

of outputs as we progress toward more mature analytics (fig c).

Ultimately, while we see competitive advantage as we go up the y axis, all the processes along the x axis are required to support some decision-making. While some companies are struggling to get to predictive modeling, probabilistic forecasting, or simulating and orchestrating responses, most companies likely have some elements of each kind of analytics.[12] Whether it be descriptive, diagnostic, predictive, prescriptive or cognitive—the five types of analytics are usually implemented in stages and no one type of analytics is better than the other. They are interrelated and sometimes even additive and each of these offers a different insight.

Success is gained by reconciling all of these approaches within the same strategic framework. It is important to understand that all levels of analytics provide value, whether it is descriptive or predictive, and all are used in different applications. That said, those that are truly using analytics for competitive advantage can strongly leverage the future of predictive analytics and the revolution that is taking place today in demand planning.

Descriptive Analytics

This is the simplest stage of analytics and, for this reason, most organizations today use some type of descriptive analytics. **Descriptive Analytics:** *A process and strategy of gathering and interpreting data to describe insights into the past and what has occurred.* For the most part, the majority of reports that businesses generate are descriptive, trying to summarize historical data or trying to explain why one event in the past differed from another. In addition to reports, some queries and classification processes can fall into and be used for descriptive analytics. We can even use more advanced machine learning algorithms at this level for more complex data mining and clustering. The purpose of all these can be to understand what went on or prepare data for other types of analysis.

Descriptive analytics takes the raw data and, through data aggregation or data mining, provides valuable insights into the past. However, these findings simply signal that something is wrong or right, without explaining why. For this reason, more mature demand planning functions do not content themselves with descriptive analytics alone and prefer combining it with other types of data analytics.

Diagnostic Analytics

At this stage, you can begin to answer some of those "why" questions. Historical data can begin to be measured against other data to answer the question of why something happened in the past. **Diagnostic Analytics:** *A process and strategy of gathering and interpreting different data sets to identify anomalies, detect patterns, and determine relational insights into the data and what is occurring.* Some approaches that use diagnostic analytics include alerts, drill-down, data discovery, data mining, and correlations. This may include some traditional forecasting techniques that use ratios, likelihoods, and the distribution of outcomes for the analysis. Supervised machine learning training algorithms for classification and regression also fall in this type of analytics.

Most BI stops short of this stage and only reports key performance indicators (KPI's) or historical data. Companies gain a competitive advantage with seasoned Demand Planners' use of diagnostic analytics, as it gives in-depth insights into a problem and more information for business decisions. At the same time, we are still reactive; even with forecasting, we can only answer what trends may continue.

Predictive Analytics

Predictive analytics is about capturing relationships among a large amount of descriptive and predictive variables from the past and using them to predict unknown outcomes. As a strategy, **predictive analytics:** *A process and strategy that uses a variety of advanced statistical algorithms to detect patterns and conditions that may occur in the future for insights into what will happen.* This book refers to predictive analytics as a more advanced forecasting process that factors why something occurred into its projections. However, when distinguishing types of analytics, most people think of it more broadly as a term encompassing most techniques that provide any forward-looking projection.

By successfully applying many traditional forecasting techniques to more advanced machine learning predictive algorithms, businesses can effectively interpret big data to gain huge competitive advantages. Unfortunately, most companies are still scratching the surface of the capabilities of this stage and operate solely in the green-shaded area of figure c between "what happened" to "what could happen," and therefore, only implement traditional forecasting methods. They miss the bigger picture of "what we can make happen" using what we now understand.

Prescriptive Analytics

Prescriptive analytics is the next step in the progression of analytics. It takes the data we gathered in descriptive analytics that told us 'what' and combines with the diagnostic analytics that told us 'why'. Then we get insights about when it may occur again and progresses to highlight what you can now make happen. **Prescriptive Analytics:** *A process and strategy combining data, mathematical models, probability of future events, and various business rules to infer actions to influence future desired outcomes.* Some refer to this as demand shaping, but it can also include simulation, probability maximization, and optimization.

Prescriptive analytics is complex when compared to traditional analytics and many companies are not yet using it in day-to-day business activities. Admittedly, to consistently operate at this level of maturity takes people, process, technology, and an analytics-driven culture across the entire organization. That said, if implemented properly, it can have a major impact on business growth and be a competitive game-changer. Large-scale organizations like Amazon, Target, and McDonalds are already using prescriptive analytics in their demand planning to optimize customer experience and maximize sales.

Cognitive Analytics

Wouldn't it be nice if we could take all of the analytics and data and allow the system to teach us or even operate semi-autonomously? Welcome to cognitive analytics. **Cognitive Analytics:** *A process and strategy that brings together several intelligent technologies including semantics, AI algorithms, and many learning techniques such as deep learning and machine learning to accomplish self-healing or semi-autonomous analytical cognition.*

By applying such techniques, a cognitive application can become smarter and self-heal. It can become more effective over time by learning from its interactions with data and with humans. Through this, we may even begin to blur the boundary between the physical and the virtual worlds and automate processes to bring new capabilities and possibilities to demand planning.

Machine Learning as a Cause and Effect

Machine learning is an integral part of predictive analytics. Many of its techniques have been adopted by advanced business forecasting and many other areas. Machine learning elements are part of every category of data analytics or business intelligence from descriptive to cognitive.

Machine learning is being used in a wide array of applications today. Just visit Netflix, YouTube, or Amazon and see a recommendation for other content; behind the scenes, machine learning is working hard to understand your preferences and behaviors. Like something on social media and algorithms are building your feed and what you see using predictive analytics to identify patterns. Business intelligence applications are using machine learning to help identify useful data. We are even seeing machine learning as the underpinning of self-driving cars and other autonomous operations that use deep learning neural networks.

Machine learning as an approach overlaps with predictive analytics, business forecasting, and business intelligence. It is not just about advanced algorithms for prediction but is also used for data mining, clustering, classification, and identification. Machine learning evolved from the study of pattern recognition and explores the notion that algorithms can learn from and make predictions on data.[13]

As these algorithms begin to become more "'intelligent,'" they can overcome program instructions to make highly accurate, data-driven decisions.

With machine learning algorithms and techniques, we can:

- **Enable processes better**: Machine learning is a type of algorithm or technique that deals with how you may better enable processes.
- **Forecast and mine data**: A difference between machine learning and other tools is that machine learning and algorithms strive to forecast and mine data on their own.
- **Provide more advanced methods for data mining and predictive analytics to use**: Machine learning has opened new opportunities for both data mining and predictive analytics by providing more advanced methods for these processes to use.

Many approaches can be taken when conducting machine learning to achieve these three outcomes. They are usually grouped into the categories of supervised or unsupervised learning.

Supervised Learning Algorithms: *Algorithms that try to model relationships and dependencies between the target prediction output and the input features such that we can predict the output values for new data based on the relationships that it learned from the previous data sets.* With Supervised Learning Algorithms, we rely on experts who act as teachers to feed the training data, which helps the model to know what the right answers should be. In this way, it learns and improves.

Unsupervised Learning Algorithms: *Algorithms that learn from plain examples without any associated response, leaving the algorithm to determine the data patterns on its own.* Whereas with Supervised Learning Algorithms where we provide a good data set to use to compare to future inputs, Unsupervised Learning Algorithms look at the data set provided and find structures in that dataset on their own.

Machine Learning Used in Descriptive Analytics

Machine learning and data mining often employ the same methods for descriptive analytics and overlap significantly. Many of the quantitative methods that utilize unsupervised learning can be used to gather and interpret data. This includes many clustering algorithms and association rule learning as well. A clustering problem is one where you want to discover the inherent groupings in the data, such as grouping customers by purchasing behavior. An association rule learning problem is one where you want to discover rules that describe large portions of your data, such as "people that buy X also tend to buy Y."

Machine Learning Used in Diagnostic Analytics

Machine learning models that are more supervised, such as Bayesian or Random Forest, are typically used for classification and diagnostic purposes. Machine learning can be used to help identify anomalies with fraud detention or discover outliers in historical data for pattern detection and to determine relationships. While many of these may be the first step in a process to cleanse or organize data for further use in predictive models, on their own they are all part of diagnostic analytics. Diagnostic analytics includes the most common methods for classification problems when the output variable is a category, such as "red" or "blue," or "sale" and "no sale," and for regression problems when the output variable is a real value, such as "dollars" or "volume."

Machine Learning Used in Predictive Analytics

Of course, there is machine learning that uses these and other descriptive variables for predictive modeling such as ARIMAX, neural networks, extrapolation of regression models, and tying multiple weaker diagnostic and predictive models together in an ensemble algorithm. By learning the "why" and "if" from prior methods and techniques, we can now operate at the convergence of predictive analytics and machine learning. With a neural system, you can take data sets from previous marketing campaigns with input variables such as "age," "income," "price," and "date." The model will determine the risk and opportunity associated with a new campaign. For time-series based patterns, ARIMAX can not only project trends and seasonal patterns but also include or exclude drivers.

Machine Learning Used in Prescriptive and Cognitive Analytics

Machine learning does not stop there; it may also be found in prescriptive and cognitive analytics. **Deep Learning:** *A subset of machine learning based on algorithms that attempt to emulate human thought and behavior to solve complex problems.* Instead of organizing data to run through predefined equations, deep learning sets up basic parameters about the data and trains the computer to learn on its own by using many layers of processing to recognize patterns. At this level, there is a more than significant overlap between machine learning and prescriptive and cognitive analytics. Due to the larger data sets and computational requirements involved, machine learning plays a larger role in these more advanced categories of business intelligence than other methods. Machine learning has intimate ties to optimization and, as a subpart of AI, can help drive an organization to automate or augment processes.

Traditional Business Forecasting vs. Predictive Analytics

For many companies and many Demand Planners, predictive analytics may seem revolutionary. To others with a traditional mindset, advanced predictive analytics may appear to be simply a more powerful or advanced version of regular demand planning. In fact, the concepts of behavior predictions can be traced back to 1689 and many of the new machine learning algorithms—like neural networks and ARIMAX—have already been around for decades. How new and revolutionary are these concepts really? It's difficult to say, but I do know we are seeing them slowly replace more traditional methods typically used by Demand Planners.

This is partly because—despite these concepts being over 40 years old—we are seeing a renaissance in demand planning brought on by more data, technology advancements, and the shift toward a more consumer-centric and consumer-driven marketplace. This is changing traditional business practices, making us look at consumers in different ways and driving a whole new approach to planning.

Traditional forecasting was all about the numbers and using levels, trends, and seasonality observations to characterize expected outcomes. Conversely, predictive analytics as a philosophy is more about behavior; further, it may also use explanatory variables to characterize expected outcomes

Traditional	Revolutionary
Demand Planning Forecasting • Requirements based • Limited factors • Forecasts sales • Tells you what to order • Used when relationship between variables is strong • Provides an output or answer	**Predictive Analytics** • Opportunity oriented • Limitless factors • Predicts drivers • Tells why consumer orders • Can be used to find relationships between unknown variables • Provides insights and solutions

Fig d | Table showing traditional vs. revolutionary approaches to demand planning

or expected responses. This is just the tip of the proverbial iceberg and this comparison between the two approaches reveals the many differences (fig d).

Traditional demand planning primarily uses time-series and only a few demand factors. Even causal modeling, for the most part, consists of simple ratios and/or single variables that are used to extrapolate out.

Advanced predictive analytics uses a combination of models and techniques. That can include using machine learning algorithms to evaluate larger data sets with many more attributes and limitless amounts of fundamental factors at once.

Traditional demand planning is somewhat limited in its approaches and inputs. It uses predefined or static hierarchies to find a best fit single model and only forecasts those same items.

With advanced predictive analytics, we can predict sales of items and use similar algorithms and approaches to predict pricing, market share, weather, conversion rates, advertising, in-store merchandising, and a host of other variables with a multitude of dynamic hierarchies.

Historically, traditional demand planning has been used for a reliable single point signal to produce or purchase products and manage inventory levels by providing a sales estimate for items.

Advanced predictive analytics is being adopted not only by supply chains but also by marketing departments for promotional planning and by sales departments for targeting customers or even customer retention and product management for portfolio optimization. It is accomplishing more by exposing why demand may occur and providing what-if capabilities and drivers that may be used to influence demand.

Traditional demand planning typically works to a requirements-based model, answering clearly defined business questions regarding what will happen or what to order.

Meanwhile, advanced predictive analytics is a new type of analysis that demands a different approach. It uses opportunistic analytics and explores answers to ill-formed or even nonexistent questions.

Traditional Demand Planners have taken a strategic approach to managing forecasts and data (with varying degrees of success) for decades. They know how to acquire and house all relevant information and then build models to anticipate future results. Traditional information managers have taken a deductive approach by looking at their sales history, going through several rounds of collaboration and judgmental inputs, and working toward achieving one version of the truth.

The newer avant-garde big data professionals understand the corporate strategy or a concrete business question as the starting point; however, they look at it with a bottom-up approach. They believe that the innovation is in the data themselves and that exploring this will lead to new answers, new drivers of their business, and new business strategies. Inside these innovative demand planning functions, a revolution is brewing, and a new generation of radical data junkies coming up through the ranks is looking at information, forecasting, and demand-driven networks differently.

Yet many Demand Planners are still stuck in the past. Base-Lift continues to be widely used for forecasting due to the historical perception of sustainability challenges with predictive analytics. Techniques have not changed—or companies are reluctant to change—and thus they operate in the same way they always have. Whether it's because they want to remain in their comfort zone or some other reason, they fail to realize the potential of predictive analytics.

New Models and Methods

Time-series and many traditional forecasting models come with limitations. These fall primarily into three areas: data, assumptions, and difficulties.

- **Data:** Several seasons of data are needed to forecast when using time-series models. Also, both time-series and regression techniques typically consider either a single—or at most, a few—variables such as trend, seasonality, and cycle. The data sources for these models come primarily from demand history.
- **Assumption:** Traditional models assume that current and past patterns will continue. They do not take into account that radical changes might occur.
- **Difficulties:** With traditional models, it's difficult to handle exogenous factors, non-numeric data, or big data.

Just think about many of today's drivers that are not necessarily time-related or interval-structured type data. The Internet of Things (IoT) and the sensor data of connected devices, including geo-spatial data (such as the distance to the nearest rival store), can be used to predict sales, weather, and macroeconomic and demographic trends. Consider the wealth of eCommerce information available today that wasn't available before: website clicks, page rankings, cart abandonment, and other metadata. Finally, think of the plethora of unstructured data yet to be tapped on social media and in the text and comment sections of web pages. This is where predictive analytics, machine learning, and data mining add value in a way that traditional models cannot.

Thankfully, we have excellent AI-related advanced models that can go beyond what time-series and other types of models offer us. Predictive analytics turns raw materials into forward-looking insights. It processes these data using different statistical methods such as extrapolation, regression, neural networks, and machine learning to detect data patterns and derive the forecast.

Predictive analytics and machine learning enables us to:

- **Handle more and different data:** Predictive analytics enables us to work with many more variables than time-series models. Just a few of these variables are consumer data, website clicks, and weather. Machine learning techniques can process an unlimited number of predictor variables.
- **Cope with big data:** Big data is information that goes beyond normal processing and storage capacities.
- **Determine significance:** They can determine which variables are significant.
- **Be more forward looking and identify causal factors:** For example, predictive analytics allows us to consider changing leading indicators. As they change, so do our predictions.
- **Use more advanced algorithms and technology:** Compared to traditional methods, we can access more sophisticated mathematical calculations by using algorithms such as artificial neural networks, ARIMAX, and ensemble models.

Caveat: Machine learning and many advanced methods are more reliant on the availability of data than time-series and some regression models. Common sense tells us that the more data there are, the better the learning will be. However, be careful. You can end up with an overly complex model that can lead to worse results. So, all the data you use must be relevant.

SPOTLIGHT

How Starbucks Uses Predictive Analytics and Your Loyalty Card Data

In the era of big data and growing competition, it's no longer enough for Starbucks baristas to know you like a tall skinny vanilla latte. The iconic Seattle coffee brand is relying on Demand Planners and data scientists behind the scenes to increase market share. They are using software and predictive analytics to learn more about you and boost sales in the process.

Micro-targeting and personalized sales are fast becoming the Holy Grail for retailers, as this attention to detail is key to keeping consumers coming through their doors or visiting their websites. This involves recording and analyzing every physical and digital touchpoint, allowing companies to understand what customers want and then allocate resources to better meet this demand. Most companies now routinely log every visit to a product page, every call made to an inquiry response center, and every email received.

How Starbucks Collects Your Data

Of course, to gain insight from predictive analytics, you need data. For Starbucks, the key to this digitalization of consumer insights is the Starbucks loyalty card, the likes of which were first made popular by grocery and mass merchant stores. With this kind of card, consumers can now go to a grocery store's website, enter their loyalty card number, and retrieve a record of everything they have purchased from that store in the past twelve months. Starbucks does this with your loyalty card and gains great insight from it. They also analyze data captured by their mobile app, which customers use to pay for drinks and accrue loyalty points.

Using what Starbucks calls its "digital-flywheel program," it correlates data from customer purchases and preferences, to store location, meteorological data, and internal inventory levels to better predict what is driving sales. Data scientists at Starbucks know what coffee you drink, where you buy it, and at what time of day. Pairing this with data from millions of other users, along with other correlating data, they have very real and actionable insights.

Gerri Martin-Flickinger, the Chief Technology Officer and EVP at Starbucks explained this in 2016: "With about 90 million transactions a week, we know a lot about what people are buying, where they're buying, how they're buying. And if we combine this information with other data, like weather, promotions, inventory, insights into local events, we can actually deliver better personalized service to other customers."[14]

Starbucks Uses Predictive Analytics to Personalize Your Experience

Starbucks, along with many other retailers, is moving from just forecasting what may happen, to using predictive analytics and AI to deliver a more personal experience. And this goes beyond sending customers emails on their birthdays—it sets the groundwork for merging digital marketing and physical stores. Starbucks now generates recommendations for customers approaching their stores, using location data to know when customers are nearby. Starbucks segments its customers with data and machine learning, then sets up rules based on decision trees mapping their purchase behavior. The customer is then sent personalized offers, usually on their smartphones.

The data shows them how much you spend on average. They know, for example, that on a Thursday you are most likely not alone and spend a little extra, buying a blueberry muffin and two venti lattes. From your purchase habits, along with other insights, they work on targeting you so that you increase that average spend and buy a cupcake crème Frappuccino and a chocolate chip cookie on Monday to treat yourself.

Brave New World

Traditionally, forecasting techniques were based on historical demand and the assumption that history repeats itself. While these methods and principles generally hold, with e-planning, many traditional forecasting models—and the technology of the past—struggle to keep up. It is a brave new world for Demand Planners in which predictive analytics encompasses various new statistical techniques like probabilistic modeling, machine learning, and data mining, which analyze current and historical facts to make predictions.

In today's business environment, changes in the marketplace are swift, sudden, and may not follow the historical pattern. Just looking at historical shipments will not tell the whole picture. Instead, we must look at patterns of consumer behaviors and other attributes. In this way, we can not only predict the sale but also understand the "why" behind the purchase. The new e-planning environment is dynamic, and it operates on the power and speed of technology and innovation. Prediction is becoming more about behavior than history. This is powerful because, once you understand the drivers, you can influence demand like never before.

With new modeling comes new inputs and the means of collecting the data you need. Previously, third-party syndicated data from Nielsen and others could help you better understand markets and competitors in traditional retail stores. Now we have web crawlers that traverse multiple sites and bring us relevant data whenever we want. Instead of looking at just shipments or sales history, we have access to website clicks, rankings, and the number and sentiment of customer reviews. We have a new wealth of information, all of which needs to be understood, modeled, and translated into real-time forecasts.

In this e-commerce environment, planning now means you collect data, plan demand, and micro-target at much lower levels of aggregation and time. Consequently, we may no longer have weeks to put together the next demand plan; instead, we may be dealing with changing prices or the impact of new reviews hourly. With e-commerce, you are competing almost in real-time for price, features, and delivery promises. Feedback comes just as quickly in the form of reviews and competitive responses. To be more agile, companies are looking at technology and demand sensing techniques to translate the drivers into rule-based or machine-learned responses.[15]

This brings us closer not only to the level of demand but also to demand intent. Traditional demand sensing focuses purely on information from customer relations management (CRM) or point of sale (POS) data from retailers that are aggregated weekly. Today, advanced Demand Planners are absorbing sales directly on an hourly basis or even quicker. At the same time, companies that aren't Google, Amazon, Facebook, or Starbucks are struggling to take advantage of consumer insights and this digital revolution.

Some businesses still perceive forecasting and demand planning as only a supply chain problem; they generate a discrete demand signal to assist Operations and miss the opportunities this new world is offering. While AI and machine learning are buzzwords, many technology providers persist with their old methods and struggle to adapt to this new e-planning environment. Also, for some companies, big data is considered as much a problem as it is an asset.

We need to better understand this new environment and to forecast and plan differently—the winners in this new era will be the ones that can see, interpret, and act most efficiently.

Summary— A New Experience

Companies that understand what drives the consumer can plan their business strategy to take advantage of the significant impact of e-commerce. By working with Demand Planners and focusing on new models, sources of data, and technology, companies can learn how to provide customers with what they want: a personalized shopping experience, affordable prices, and a wide variety of available products.

Amazon has totally revolutionized the marketplace and, with it, demand forecasting and demand planning. The question may not be *if* the Amazon effect will filter into your planning but *when*. Remember, though, that this just happens to be the newest disruption. More than just impacting retail sales, is it also changing the way demand planning and forecasting are done (and doing business generally). Research from the Institute of Business Forecasting (IBF) shows that this is just the beginning and the role of the Demand Planner will continue to transform. It stands to reason that, in a changing landscape that contains the IoT, AI, and unstructured data, things will continue to change, and we will need to innovate and adapt. Those left in its wake have no choice but to embrace change, technology, and innovation, and find new ways to forecast and plan.

Companies that unlock the potential of predictive analytics will make smarter and faster decisions in the future, as well as redefine business operations.

Is it possible to re-think the traditional approaches to predicting demand or will we remain stuck in the past? Every indication is that, yes, we must evolve and we are evolving. In the immortal words of Bob Dylan, "These times, they are changing." For Demand Planners, supply chain executives, and those at the forefront of predictive analytics, we must adapt and change. Entire companies—not just demand planning—must leverage predictive analytics, which requires both revolutionary and evolutionary approaches.

There is a new generation coming into the workforce with new ideas. We are at a precipice of change. Recent improvements have made it easier to implement predictive analytics as well as making it sustainable. Technology is developing quickly and its cost is decreasing. New in-memory technologies easily store large amounts of data for quick processing. Sophisticated models can now run in a shorter amount of time and be easily modularized to integrate with existing enterprise software solutions. As a result, business units can now collaborate with user-friendly interfaces and make corporate decisions quickly. We truly have reached an inflection point in addressing key challenges for implementing predictive analytics and demand-driven forecasting.

So, ask yourself the following questions: Are you ready? Are you embracing disruptive innovation? Are you challenging the status quo and the processes that exist in your organization? Do you have a swift and agile workforce that can embrace the change? Are you leveraging big data and predictive analytics to the fullest extent? Do you know where and how true analytics will play out inside your organization? The tools are there and the time is now. The companies that will succeed and thrive are the ones that not only master descriptive analytics but revolutionize their companies by embracing predictive analytics.

Section Review

Multiple Choice: Identify the choice that best completes the statement or answers the question.

1. Which is a stated principle of predictive analytics?

    a) Predictive analytics is always more accurate.
    b) Predictive analytics can operate with little to no data.
    c) Predictive analytics is a process.
    d) All of the above.

2. Business intelligence is:

    a) A system for data and reporting.
    b) A methodology used for supporting business decision-making processes.
    c) The architecture of databases and analytical tools.
    d) All of the above.

3. What type of analytics does machine learning support?

    a) Diagnostic analytics.
    b) Predictive analytics.
    c) Cognitive analytics.
    d) All of the above.

4. If I am trying to understand what we can make happen, what type of analytics is this?

   a) Descriptive analytics.
   b) Prescriptive analytics.
   c) Predictive analytics.
   d) Cognitive analytics.

5. Predictive analytics and machine learning help enable us to:

   a) Understand why sales occurred and the drivers of demand.
   b) Handle more and different types of data.
   c) Help determine which variables we should use.
   d) All of the above.

True or False

6. ☐ Diagnostic analytics is used to help understand what should happen.

7. ☐ Predictive analytics only uses machine learning, whereas traditional planning uses time-series methods.

8. ☐ Predictive analytics is more forward-looking based on attributes whereas traditional planning is more static and based on the past.

9. ☐ Machine learning works to automate the traditional forecasting process.

10. ☐ Supervised machine learning is characterized by learning a model based on a data set that contains the answer or target.

PART II
PREDICTIVE ANALYTICS AS A PROCESS

After reading this section, you should be able to:

- Understand and be comfortable with the steps in an analytics process.
- Consider and better identify outliers in data and what to do with them.
- Know why and how we split data and how to use the different data sets.
- Determine what to look for when training a model.
- Manage the predictive analytics process and outputs and how to present data.

The Journey from Data to Insights

Most forecast practitioners focus only on a final number—the same error consumers of forecasts make. They miss the nuances and structure, failing to understand that any planner's job is more about managing assumptions than numbers. Others focus first—and sometimes exclusively—on technology and models and ignore the purpose of the forecast and the human elements. Successful practitioners approach every forecast (or analytical project) with a comprehensive understanding of how it fits in the wider business context.

In many ways, business forecasting and predictive analytics processes are more important than the numbers.

Data are crude information and not knowledge by themselves. The sequence from data to insights is:

- Data to information,
- Information to facts, and
- Facts to insights.

Taking this one step further, these insights should be valuable inputs as future data when we start this process again. Data become information when they become relevant to the problem you're trying to solve. Information becomes facts when the data can support it. Facts are what the data reveal.

A business forecasting process or predictive analysis provides a mechanism for gathering appropriate information, soliciting participation from individuals who know about future events and compiling it all into a consistent format to develop a forecast. The process concentrates on defining how the information will be gathered and reconciled into a picture of the future. In cases where a statistical forecast is used, the process will also define how much weight should be given to the mathematical models versus input from participants in the final consensus forecast. Remember, our ultimate objective through this process is to present a concise, accurate, and understandable result that helps the end users of the forecast.

Principles and Considerations in Predictive Analysis

Business forecasting can either be a project or process, and both are approached in similar ways. Before you begin with any project or process, there are common considerations that generally arise. In business forecasting, one of the first questions is whether you are obtaining information to make assumptions about the likely purchase behavior of the buyer or obtaining information to make assumptions about patterns of past purchases. This is one consideration of many that can impact the inputs, process, and results. Here are a few of the most frequent considerations.

Scope

Forecasts for traditional demand plans are generally classified by the length of the forecasting horizon. Time horizons vary from one organization to another and even from one product type to another. Note that different forecast time horizons require their own processes and methods. The three types of forecasting horizons are typically categorized as Strategic (over one year), Tactical (three-months to one year), and Operational (what is happening now or in the immediate future). Mostly, demand plans are tactical. However, it is important to understand the differences between the three types. There are limitations of each model or process according to the time horizon you're forecasting for and Demand Planners must adjust their approaches and methods accordingly.

In predictive analytics, we still look at time horizons (strategic or tactical) but we conceptualize our predictions in slightly different terms. Predictive analytics is less—or even sometimes not at all—about predicting the future. Rather, it is often about predicting behaviors and relationships. These relationships may be dependent on time and projected to a point in the future or independent of time and used to sense or shape demand. Others, like classification or clustering, may be irrespective of time, such as predicting groupings or classes.

- Predictive: The main goal is to predict a discrete or continuous value.
- Classification: The main goal of classification is to predict the target class.
- Clustering: The main goal is to group related data points together.

Schedule

Another consideration is how often this forecast will need to be generated or if it is an *ad hoc* requirement. If this is a recurring forecast output, you should determine the frequency with which the forecast is regenerated. This can be:

- Annually (like for budgets),
- Quarterly or monthly (perhaps for scheduling and resource planning),
- Weekly or daily (for finite planning), or
- Almost real-time (such as demand sensing and response).

A longer duration between forecasts generally means fewer resources required and a higher level of aggregation of data and time buckets being forecasted. Forecasting more frequently may mean more variability with smaller time buckets, a more resource-intensive but fresher data set, and a more agile response. To determine whether to increase the frequency with which we forecast demand, we have to address two important questions:

- What would the benefits be of doing that?
- Would it be cost-effective or even feasible?

Not all forecasts are part of an ongoing forecasting cycle or process; some are a one-time analysis to answer a question, or an input into other processes. Such analyses may still have a frequency. With experimental variables, for example, you may manipulate an independent variable to examine the effect on a later analysis, such as price effect on sales. Or it could be a static variable like an *ad hoc* forecast or looking for an association as with segmentation analysis. Ultimately, it comes down to your business's situation, what insights you need to make the right decisions, and what information end users need.

Structure

Although what you are forecasting may seem obvious, confusion over this question is all too common. It is important to understand the differences between orders, shipments, and scanner data to ensure they are compatible with the anticipated results. Orders and shipments (or sales) are different. Although shipments are typically tracked and easy to access, they are not a true measurement of what your customers want. Shipments tend to be different to orders because of backorders, lost sales, manufacturing delays, and other constraints in the business. If you sell to retail, in many cases even scanner data are not the same as data from orders because of store inventory policies, batching, lot sizes, etc. For these reasons, you should always try to get to consumer intent and as close to true demand as possible.

Sometimes when we talk about analytical variables, they are described as categorical (or nominal), discrete, or continuous (or interval).[16]

Categorical Variables: *Contain a finite number of categories or distinct groups. Categorical data might not have a logical order.* For example, categorical predictors include gender, material type, and payment method.

Discrete Variables: *Numeric variables that have a countable number of values between any two values.* A discrete variable is always numeric. For example, the number of customer complaints or the number of flaws or defects.

Continuous Variables: *Numeric variables that have an infinite number of values between any two values.* A continuous variable can be numeric or date/time. For example, the length of a part or the date and time a payment is received.

In addition to these, there are many other considerations one may have to think about. Understand the resources and constraints you may have. We may need to determine leading indicators or independent and dependent variables. We could be asked to produce forecasts that are constrained or unconstrained. We may look at a single number or multiple numbers. We could be forecasting for budgets, targets, purchase plans, or what-if scenarios. We could have mature products, growth products, new products, or be dealing with end-of-life items. All of the above will require different strategies, methods, and models.

Predictive Analysis Process

Predictive Analysis: *The process of collecting, transforming, cleansing, modeling, and managing data to predict a discrete or continuous value.* This provides the required insights for making informed decisions. This includes anything from an *ad hoc* analysis to your monthly or weekly forecasting cycle. Even if the steps may not be spelled out, they should be implied and understood.

Whatever forecasting cycle you choose, you should define the need, i.e., why you are doing it. This need not be done every time, but should be done at some point to clarify what questions the process needs to answer and what inputs it will analyze. Ongoing, this need is implicit in why you are doing it every week. Even regular forecasting cycles are answering regular questions or inputs for regular decisions being made.

Any predictive analytics or forecasting process consists of the following five iterative phases.[17,18]

Define the Objective and Success Metrics[19]

The very first step consists of understanding the who and the why. This could be as simple as a recurring need that is part of a monthly demand planning cycle, where you generate an item level forecast for operational planning. Something more complex could be an *ad hoc* request for analysis of a potential new product launch or cluster analysis. Whenever we are required to carry out analysis, we first need to know the internal customer, assess the requirement, and determine the required data. Only then can you do your analysis properly.

In this step, we are asking questions to determine what problem our analysis needs to solve or what question needs to be answered and to assess the required resources to perform that analysis. Depending on the situation, this could lead to a quick naïve or judgmental forecast, or a detailed probabilistic analysis. Who is the internal customer (or customers) and what question (or questions) do they want to answer?

- What input or factors should be included? This includes factors like market data, sales input, time-series sales history, and causal inputs.
- What resources and data are already available? This includes different models, software, and time parameters. We need to assess if we can do the analysis and if there are sufficient data.
- What is the objective and how will it be measured? We must be very clear about what the objective is and how success or failure will be measured using specific metrics such as Root Mean Square Error (RMSE) and Mean Absolute Percent Error (MAPE).
- What assumptions are built into the model? If you already have a pre-defined model, such as an artificial neural network or a decision tree, you need to collect data that are relevant to those models. Like other models, they will have different needs, inputs, and structures that should be considered.

While virtually anything can be forecasted, we can only forecast some things well. It is our job as professionals to understand probability, the data available, and the limitations of systems and models. We must be able to weigh this information in light of what the decision-makers are requesting.

Clean and Explore Data

The next step consists of gathering data, whether it be updating historical demand or acquiring new data sets, and preparing and cleansing your data. **Data Set:** *A collection of data organized as a stream of information in logical record and block structures.* We need to select data as per the need, clean it, construct it so useful information can be extracted, and then integrate it all. Cleaning data is one of the most important tasks in the analysis process. Incorrect data leads to incorrect decisions and predictions. This is one of the most important and time-consuming steps. It's estimated that 60% to

80% of a machine learning project involves getting the data right and preparing it for analysis.

As part of a monthly demand cycle, this is often just updating historical demand and possibly pruning outliers or adjusting for promotions. It could also mean having to collect entirely new data sets for new analysis or existing analysis. Whether it is an existing data set you are only updating or entirely new data, a critical step is analyzing and understanding your data, ensuring it is in the correct format, and cleansing your data set.

- Take your time to summarize the data and visualize it as much as possible. Visual understanding can be very important and powerful.
- Before you collect new data, identify what information can be collected from existing databases or sources on hand.
- Align with data you trust. Work on standardizing the data and data sources so that when it's assessed, you can have confidence in its format and usability.
- Clean, clear, and complete data is essential. Make sure that you understand the data and what it represents.
- Take care of anomalies. The axiom "garbage in, garbage out" comes to mind. With the right focus and the right data selected upfront, we will greatly improve the ability and efficiency of our predictive modeling.
- Test early and often. The time to find an error in your data is before you have modeled it and presented your findings.

Data and Predictive Modeling

Predictive Model: *A combination of methods where the primary objective is to predict the probability of a discrete or continuous value using a set of predictor values.* Once data are gathered, we can begin the analysis of the data. In this step you select approaches, develop estimations, generate predictions, add assumptions, and collaborate and develop consensus as needed. In the most basic terms, in business forecasting this could be generating a baseline forecast, reviewing it and adding assumptions, and then developing a consensus demand plan.

- Splitting data: For supervised learning tasks, such as classification and regression, split data into training, validation, and testing data sets.

- Know what goes in: Understand the key factors, variables, and parameters.
- Align the algorithm used with the nature of the data; there is no magic algorithm for every occasion.
- If you can't explain it, then you probably can't use it. Start with what you know and what you can do and then experiment, adjust, and iterate models over time.
- Build consensus: Work with stakeholders to make sure you are meeting their needs and objectives as well as gaining information and inputs along the way.
- Lead with data: Make sure to use quantitative approaches and objective tests of assumptions and models.

Evaluate the Model

Model: *A mathematical representation of a real-world process.* Step four involves understanding the performance, the estimations, and whether the inputs and outputs are meeting the hypotheses of the model. While most see this starting with a statistical forecast, best practice is to begin modeling with an estimate based on the model and requirements from the very first step of defining the need. Then, when the various methods, techniques, algorithms, and analyses are placed together into a model and run, we can review them.

- Don't use all your data and hold some back: This goes back to splitting the data in the previous step and creating a test data set to evaluate your model. Always test against "blind" data (or previously unseen data).
- Iterate, Vary, and Evaluate: Use multiple models and test models against the original objective, each other, and the baseline.
- Evaluate inputs as well as the outputs: Don't just look at the final results, but make sure you look at the data and inputs for collinearity or other issues.
- Understand what inputs and features you can use: Focus on adding and removing features to improve the forecast.
- Beware of overfitting: Remember you are training a model, not teaching it to memorize your data.
- Know when enough is enough and when to use early stopping. Don't spend time chasing the last 5% of accuracy if there is no business benefit.

Manage Results and Apply or Publish the Model

You can create the best predictive analysis and forecast, but it won't matter if it is not properly communicated, utilized, and measured. Our process does not stop at the water's edge; we need to ensure we met the initial need of why we generated the prediction and continually monitor and improve. It starts with being able to communicate findings in the language and output that your audience needs. We must not forget the fact that good Demand Planners are storytellers who use numbers as their language.

- Tell a story: Avoid just presenting numbers and the forecast. You want to present a story that people can follow. Good Demand Planners are storytellers who use numbers as their language. Managing results and communicating clearly with key stakeholders is integral to many business processes such as S&OP, IBP, BEP, and others.
- Find the right canvas: The purpose of the information and the audience that you're communicating with should determine the format of your presentation. Incorporate pictures, graphs, and other visuals that will help your audience understand the results as fully as possible.
- Be honest and open about error margins and the assumptions of a model: Your output can't just be "black box." Your audience needs to understand how you came to your conclusions. They also need to know what risk was involved. That's what error margins will tell them.
- Know your audience: It is critical to understand your audience. Identify what they need, what they need to know, and how to best present that information to them. Take time to format a clear presentation of results for a non-technical audience if necessary.

Good communication is timely, useful, consistent, and formalized. For a monthly process, as the final step, I would recommend a Demand Review that may be standalone or part of a formal S&OP, FP&A, or BEP process. In these meetings, you can develop collaboration for inputs, communicate efficiently the outputs and any uncertainty in the numbers, and measure the success or shortcomings.

To this final point, any good process should be measured and tracked not only to see if it meets the objectives but to improve future predictions. Predictive analysis and forecasting should be viewed as a continuous improvement process and tracking and measuring forecast performance is an essential part of it. If you cannot assess your current process, it is very difficult to improve it.

Define the Need

Have you ever stopped and wondered why the heck are we doing all of this? If not, perhaps you should ask that (and a few other questions) every now and then. Before starting any predictive analytics analysis or a regular forecasting cycle, you should at least know why you're doing it. The exact—or at a minimum, implied—definition of the problem is imperative to obtaining the desired outcomes.

So, what are some of the questions you may need to know?

Let's start with who your customer is. As simple as this is, it still can take on multiple meanings. It is right to consider the consumer and, in predictive analytics for forecasting, a lot of it revolves around understanding the end-users and behaviors that influence demand. However, this may be only part of the definition of your customer. Before you start an analytics project or forecast, you must understand your internal customers and who will be your internal consumers of the work you do.

Every decision requires the input of a prediction. I may be making an assumption, but chances are that your internal customer is using your forecast or analysis as an input to a decision they need to make. In defining the need, you should also describe or understand decisions that may be affected by the forecasts. As analysts, you should examine how decisions might vary depending on the forecast. One approach may be even to ask the decision-maker to describe what forecast inputs will change their decisions. The problem should be structured so the analyst can use knowledge effectively and so that the results are useful for decision-making.

Everything can be forecasted; only some things can be forecasted well. It is our job to understand probability, the data available, and limitations of systems and models—and weigh this against what the decision maker is requesting and when they need the findings. Consider whether the events or series can be forecasted to the level of precision people want. Before you get started, you need to find agreement on methods, data, and limitations and what may be needed. This is your opportunity to propose other information or set expectations.

You must tailor the level of data aggregation (or segmentation) to the decisions. Here, you need to ask or know the critical questions of time, level, geography, and other attributes. One can make forecasts, however, for various components that can then be aggregated or disaggregated to fit the decision needs. Thus, the analyst can focus on the level of aggregation that yields the most accurate forecasts.

Your decision maker may need a certain level of granularity or attribute, but do we have the data and resources to achieve it? The relevant data needed to solve these business decisions are identified at this stage with key questions such as "What data is available?", "How can we use it?", and "Do we have sufficient data?". Before starting out, make sure that all data sources are available, up-to-date, and in the expected format for the analysis.

If you don't know where you are going, no matter what vehicle you use, you will get somewhere, but it may not be where you want. When planning any predictive analytics project or proceeding with a process, you need to start with the end in mind. This is critical for any new project to help understand the who, what, where, and why—particularly for regular forecasting cycles. It is just as important—even if it is not a formal step—that you can answer any of the above questions with confidence before you proceed to avoid making the same mistakes of the past.

Gather Inputs

"Data! Data! Data! I can't make bricks without clay."
—Sherlock Holmes, in Arthur Conan Doyle's The Adventure of the Copper Beeches

Increasingly complex business problems demand not just more data, but more diverse, comprehensive data. And with this comes more quality problems. Poor data quality is enemy number one to the widespread, effective use of predictive analytics. While "garbage in, garbage out" has applied to analytics and decision-making for generations, it carries new weight and a special warning in the digital age.

In this digital age, data are no longer scarce—it's overwhelming. After you understand the objective of your project or analysis, the key is then to shift through the data streams, lakes, and oceans available to organizations and correctly interpret its implications. Unfortunately, for many of us, these data lakes resemble more of a data swamp and most data fail to meet the basic standards we need to forecast. Reasons can range from data creators not understanding what is expected, to poor collection, to overly complex processes, to human error; but they all result in the same thing: poor analysis and poor decisions.

For these reasons, data and inputs are a critical step in any analytics process. Time should be spent on what is going into any model and analysis. Data processing is simply the conversion of raw data to meaningful inputs through a process. This includes collection (and possibly preparation) and ensuring you have the right inputs in the right amounts in the right format.

Collection

Since the quality of data collected will impact heavily on the output, the collection process needs to ensure that the data gathered match the question you are seeking to answer and are properly defined and accurate. When obtaining data, identify data or data sets that might be useful in making forecasts. Ask whether or not you can do anything about the independent variable you're considering, i.e., does the output of your analysis provide actionable insight that will help drive sales? For example, if you can't change the temperature outside, how important is it to understand past correlation between sales and weather to predict the future?

Data can be collected from existing sources like weekly sales data or obtained from new sources. At the high level, types of inputs include quantitative data that deals with numbers you can measure objectively, and qualitative data, which cannot be measured and is subjective.

Other more granular ways to look at data include the times at which data were collected and how many variables were studied. We call these data cross-sectional or longitudinal. Longitudinal data can be categorized as repeated measures or time-series. Finally, we can think about data in terms of how they are organized. It may be structured data, which comprise clearly defined data types whose pattern makes them easily searchable; or unstructured data, which is "everything else" and is usually not easily searchable like audio, video, and social media postings.

Preparation

In the world of data swamps, it may be necessary to manipulate or cleanse data into a form suitable for analysis and processing. Preparation is about constructing a data set from one or more data sources to be used for further exploration and processing. Raw data cannot always be processed and must be checked for accuracy. Analyzing data that has not been carefully screened for problems can produce highly misleading results. In addition to fixing data errors, this phase may also include fixing data formats.

When cleansing data, first ask if they need to be adjusted or not. Remember, just because you may have never seen a Black Swan does not negate their existence. What you may view as an outlier may just be a reoccurring abnormality that needs to be in the data. It is always a good idea, if possible, to visualize your data before adjusting to better assess patterns, to identify mistakes, and to locate unusual events. Be careful though, because even the best of us can be misled by graphs if they extend patterns from the past.

If you do decide to cleanse the data, consider adjusting for mistakes, changing definitions, missing values, and inflation as required by expectations. This can include adjusting intermittent series and aggregating data across time, space, or decision units to avoid zeros; and using statistical techniques and/or domain knowledge to adjust for unsystematic past events.

The final step in this stage is to ensure that the data are in the correct format so that the analytical system can use them. The input is where verified data are coded or converted into machine-readable form so they can be processed through a computer. Data from different source systems may need to be combined via data integration routines and transformed into a common format before being loaded into an analytics system. In other cases, the collection process may consist of pulling a relevant subset out of a stream of raw data or combining streams into a larger pool of data.

This is often taken for granted if the information is part of a larger enterprise system, but understanding what information is going in, at what aggregation, and what filtering will help with the analysis and interpreting outputs later on.

Clean and Explore Data

Preparing data for predictive analytics is only half the battle. Some report that 80% of the work in data analysis is just collecting, preparing, or repairing the data before you even get started. As we continue to find new data sources and our processing and algorithms become more advanced and hungrier for more data, the task of making sure we do not have "garbage in" becomes even more difficult.

Understandably, having more data is a double-edged sword. On one side, it may provide game-changing insights; on the other side, you may be introducing more noise and bad data. For some, being a little messy is just the price of big data and it all washes out, while others are more skeptical of any new data and consider it flawed if it has any errors. The truth is, both sides of this sword can cut and cause pain. You need to proceed with a thoughtful, nuanced approach to including or excluding data, and to cleansing or loading them as is.

Understanding this balance and knowing if you should trust your data allows you to push the data to their limits. Data don't have to be perfect to yield new insights, but you must exercise caution by understanding where the flaws lie, and backing off by either not cleansing or not using the data. How you approach this depends on how large the data set is, the source of the data, the use of the data, and how clean the data already is.

Data Cleansing: *The process of finding and eliminating errors in the completeness, correctness, and timeliness of the data.* Reasons to cleanse include:[20, 21]

Missing Data

If data are missing, there are different options we can consider to be able to use our model:

- We can drop the row or column.
- We can fill in a value with a fixed number.
- We can use a mean, median, or mode with other values around it to come up with a value.

Outliers

Another issue could be outliers. **Outliers:** *Observations or values that are unusually large or small or outside of acceptable tolerances.* However, before we talk about options for working with outliers, it's very important to understand that outliers aren't always outliers. Be careful when pruning or getting rid of an outlier because it may provide more information if left in. If we truly know that something is an outlier:

- We can eliminate it or just get rid of that data point.
- We can clip or prune it using mean, median, or mode with other values around it.
- We can look for different ways of summarizing or aggregating the data to eliminate the outliers.

Duplicate Data

If there are duplicate data, there are three options to consider:

- We can drop the duplicate rows or columns.
- We can concentrate the key fields to make unique identifiers. This will help us to search and find those duplicates.
- We can do visualization, which is a good way to examine the problem and identify where pruning may be needed.

Formatting Issues

Formatting issues can be the most troubling and time-consuming matter. They can come in many forms, maybe including numbers formatted as text and different ways that dates are presented. For example, some systems will add in a timestamp into their dating. In that case, we might end up with a date that is 15 characters long. Other issues include way the names of nation-states are added. For example, do we choose to use an abbreviation for the United States such as U.S. or do we want to spell it out? Some options in these circumstances include:

- Splitting the data and create a new field for the split date and the time stamp. By doing this, we are actually splitting an attribute itself. For example, with a date, we can separate out the date field from a timestamp. We can also separate out a first and last name.
- Ensuring that we have categorical data and numeric values and set them up correctly.
- Concentrating on the key fields and make unique identifiers to help locate these issues as well.

Dealing with Dirty Data

Ultimately, any data that take away from the integrity of the entire data set are considered dirty data. With this in mind, it is no secret that all data are dirty data. This makes our jobs of preparing the data for use in models and gaining insights that much more difficult. I guess you can say demand planning is a dirty job!

Even though all data are dirty and include some mistakes, this does not necessarily mean all data need to be cleansed.[22] You may find that the effort and time to cleanse to perfection does not generate any significant results in the end. Or you may find that you are over-cleansing and removing good data that you think are dirty when they are not. A great example of this is how many people are quick to prune and remove outliers when they are not in fact outliers.

Outliers are one of those issues that everyone knows about but aren't sure how to manage. In many cases, planners are too quick to remove what they believe may be an outlier based on observation of the data they have. The truth is, most times there is a valid reason and although it may be a Black Swan, they do exist and need to be accounted for. Instead of trying to create a more normal distribution and pruning outliers, your first instinct should be to embrace them and consider if they could be the most important data point you have.

Try, if it makes sense, not to remove or over prune your data unless there is a clear external reason or sound modeling purpose. Instead of killing or wounding an observation, it should provoke you to consider why it exists or if your model is correct in dealing with it. If you think your model is appropriate, then such outliers will save you from underestimating the variance (in smaller samples) or they will be negligible (in larger samples).

Even if you never prune for outliers, you cannot avoid some data cleansing. You can consider the following to help you proceed with greater confidence and understand what you may need to focus on to provide cleaner data and better insights.

Know Your Source

Align with data you can trust. Work on standardizing the data and data sources so that when it is accessed you can have confidence in its format and usability. Alignment of units of measure and data definitions like addresses, prices paid, or currency is important. This can and should include external data sources whenever possible. Make sure you trust your data and know where it comes from and how it is managed. You need to know the journey the data has taken from its original source to forecast output.

Profile Your Data

This step entails getting to know the data closely before transforming them. Data profiling reveals data structure, null records, outliers, junk data, and potential data quality issues, etc. A thorough inspection of the data can help determine if a data source is worthy of inclusion in the data transformation effort, identifies possible data quality issues, and reveals the amount of wrangling required to transform the data for business analytics use.

Clean the Data

Even if you fully trust your data source, you will still have to integrate other data sources. And you'll inevitably find some data that do not meet the standards you need. You will need to clean data and adjust for mistakes, changing definitions and missing values, and adjusting for inflation. I recommend that, no matter how much data you have and where it is from, you should always trust but verify. You should scrub a small random sample and assess for usability and errors that may impact your model or results. This method will greatly accelerate data exploration and quickly set the stage for further transformation.

Visualize Source Data

When judgment is involved, graphical displays may allow you to better assess patterns, identify mistakes, and locate unusual events. Common graphing tools and techniques can help bring the "current state" of the data to life. Histograms show distributions; scatter plots help find outliers; pie graphs show percentage to whole; and line graphs can show trends in key fields over time. Showing how data look in visual form is also a great way to explain exploratory findings and needed transformations to non-technical users.

Test Early and Often

The time to find an error in your data is not after you have integrated the data, modeled with it, and presented your findings. The best point to understand and resolve data issues is early in the process. You should have an established business process and business case for data processing and data governance that includes regularly profiling data sources and data variables to ensure reliability.

Predictive Modeling

An algorithm is a procedure or formula for solving a problem based on conducting a sequence of finite operations or specified actions. Generally speaking, when most people talk about algorithms, they're talking about a mathematical formula or something that is happening behind the scenes, like the operations that power our social media news feeds.

While these are indeed algorithms and they are a sequence of steps designed to perform a task, algorithms are more than just math.

Algorithm: *Any detailed operation or set of rules used to carry out an operation, solve a problem, or express an outcome using a finite number of steps.* It can also be as simple and "non-'mathy" as the recipe to bake a cake.

In demand planning, where the cake we are baking is a forecast, our recipe generally entails different prediction methods and approaches, along with layers built from inputs from various sources. The steps and sequence of the inputs, the configuration of the methods, the repeating of steps, and the outputs all come together to form an algorithm.

And this can easily consist of multiple methods and inputs reduced to three logical operations: AND,

OR, and NOT. While these operations can chain together in extraordinarily complex ways, at their core, algorithms are built out of simple rational associations and a limited series of steps.

This means that an algorithm can be anything you like, for example, an exponential smoothing model that takes an input and uses a set of rules, parameters, and steps to deliver an output to your forecasting process. After you have properly defined the need and have the right data in the right format, predictive modeling is the analysis stage that comprises myriad types of algorithms that employ various analytical methods.

Yet, while there are many different algorithms available to us, there's a subset of analysis applied in data mining and predictive analytics that includes:[23,24]

Clustering Analysis

This technique is a way to help understand and analyze data by putting them into smaller manageable subgroups to highlight attributes and make better predictions. The resulting model can be used both to categorize new records and to do predictive modeling against the data for the designated subgroups.

Descriptive Analysis

This helps tell you what has happened in the past and attempts to characterize it, so as to predict similar events in the future. Describing past behavior and then applying predictive models to the resulting data helps to frame opportunities for operational improvement and identify new business opportunities.

Anomaly Analysis

This involves detecting the outlying values in a data set to identify noise and improve prediction and anomalies. A database may contain data objects that do not comply with the general behavior or model of the data. We can isolate these data objects to better understand their impacts and, subsequently, better formulate our response.

Time-Series Analysis

This looks at a collection of values observed sequentially over time and is used to perform time-based predictions. Assuming that past data patterns such as level, trend, and seasonality repeat, this can create models using only the data being forecasted to predict future patterns.

Regression Analysis

This technique is designed to identify meaningful relationships among data variables, specifically looking at the connections between a dependent variable and other independent factors that affect it.

Training Your Model

Most machine learning models have some key aspects in common. All generally have three main components:

- A model and methodology to make predictions or identifications.
- Parameters that are the signals or factors used by the model.
- Learners that cause the system to adjust to create the outcome.

Most models work by finding the relationship between a label or the thing we are predicting and its features or input variables. **Feature:** *An individual measurable property of a characteristic that is being observed.* Models also contain parameters that are estimated from the data (where the machine is learning) and model hyperparameters that are set manually by the Demand Planner.

Traditional business forecasting using time-series data tries to extrapolate forward observed patterns or variables (level, trend, and seasonality) based on the history of that series. The parameters are often assumptions about the form of the data. With time-series though, it is almost always the case that the development data set and the production data set are not from the same distribution because real-world business time-series data are not stationary, and the statistical properties of your distribution will keep shifting as new actuals come in. The only way around this is to retrain your model every time; otherwise, it needs to re-learn each time you get new data or every time you want to generate a new forecast.

Model training is a one-time activity or is done—at most—at periodic intervals to maintain its ability to take into account new information. The model learns from the data. Machine learning, on the other hand, works by finding a relationship between a label and its features. We do this by showing it a model data set that contains the target, along with the manually set hyperparameters to help it estimate its own parameters. We refer to this process as training our model.

There are still different types of learning within this. First, there is Supervised Learning, which is when algorithms try to model relationships and dependencies between the target prediction output and the input features such that we can predict the output values for new data based on those relationships. Then, there is Unsupervised Learning, which is when algorithms learn from plain examples without any associated response, leaving it to the algorithm to determine the data patterns on its own. I am focusing here on supervised learning as it is the one most used in demand planning and is trained on user-generated data for user-facing products. This excludes other domains like image classification or language understanding. Also, I am focusing only on training and testing here, and avoiding many other important issues such as feature engineering, which also affect the process.

One of the most important steps in building a machine learning model is splitting your data. You do not always have this luxury in traditional forecasting models, but it is critical in machine learning algorithms and should not be overlooked. After you understand the modeling need, data structure, and availability, your first step before building the model is splitting the data to be able to get reliable estimates of your model's performance.

Think of your data as a limited resource. You need to split it to perform a different task without using the same data. To do this, you need three sets of data: a training data set to learn from, a validation data set to refine your parameters, and a testing data set or the holdout data to evaluate the model. Each one is a step in your process.[25]

Training Data Set

Training Data Set: *The part of the overall data set used to train the model.* The training data must contain the correct answer, which is known as a target or target variable. The learning algorithm finds patterns in the training data set that map the input data attributes to the target you want to predict. Each type of algorithm has parameter options (weights and biases in the case of a neural network, the number of trees in a Random Forest, etc.). During this step, the decision you must make is to select one option for each algorithm, plus what and how much training data you will use.

Validation Data Set

Validation Data Set: *The part of the overall data set you use for evaluation of a model's fit on the training data set while tuning model hyperparameters.* Some consider this a subset of their training data set. You can divide your training set into training and validation. This new data set sees the data but does not necessarily learn from them. It is important though to help choose the right parameters and hyperparameters for your estimator. Based on the validation data set results, the model can be tuned (for instance, by changing parameters or classifiers). This will help us get the most optimized model.

Testing Data Set

Testing Data Set: *The part of the overall data set you use to provide an unbiased evaluation of a final model fit before putting it into production.* This is data the model has never seen before and is ready to be used to choose or test your final model. The test data set provides the benchmark used to evaluate the model. It is only used once a model is completely trained. If you evaluate your model on the same data you used to train it, your model could very easily have overfitting. This is a major reason we have the three data sets because a model should be judged on its ability to predict new, unseen data. The decision here generally is to evaluate and choose between competing models and/or if the model based on the outputs from the testing data set should be migrated to production.

Now that we have defined the three data sets into which your data should be split, you might be wondering how much data should be in the training, validation, and test sets. That's a great question and, unfortunately, like so many things in our field, it depends. Some models need substantial data to train on while others have few hyperparameters that are easy to validate and need only small validation sets.

How much data and how to split it is completely up to you, but you'll need to consider the number of samples in your data, the type of model you are training, and the task you face. Regarding the proportion to be divided, it is not essential that you use 70% to 80% for training and the rest for testing. It completely depends on the data set being used and the task to be accomplished.

Choosing the Right Model

Selecting the right model plays a very important role in predictive analytics and forecasting. Use the wrong model, and you might as well not have bothered at all. Use the right one, and you have a robust forecast you can plan your business operations around. So how do you choose the right one?

Each model captures a specific data pattern, has a shelf-life of its own, yields unique results, and reacts differently for different time horizons. There are hundreds of variations of baseline methods that can be combined into thousands of models with unlimited steps and inputs you can choose from. Finding or building the perfect one may be a one in a million proposition.

Finding the needle in the haystack—or the best method or model—goes back to all the work we put in before arriving at this step. It is about understanding the problem, categorizing the inputs and outputs, and knowing your information and its limitations. It comes down to a combination of business needs, specification, experimentation, and time available.

Keep the following points in mind when finding, building, using, or analyzing any model or method:

One Size Does Not Fit All

One thing that is certain regarding modeling and predictive algorithms is that, despite all the possibilities available, no one approach caters to all your problems. Even the most experienced data scientists cannot tell you which algorithm will perform the best before experimenting with others. The good news is you don't need to get it right the first time. You can select or build an algorithm that nearly solves your problem and then, over time, customize it for a complete solution.

Keep It Simple

It is easy to get lost in the details or think bigger is better, but it is best to select simple methods initially and use simple procedures unless you can demonstrate that you must add complexity. Complex methods may include errors that propagate through the system or mistakes that are difficult to detect. The more complex and numerous the features, the more specialized techniques you need. If you can't explain it, then you probably can't use it properly. Start with what you know and what you can do, and then experiment, adjust, and iterate models over time.

Models Should Meet the Situation

The predictive or analytical model should provide a realistic representation of the situation. You need the right test of models, inputs, parameters, and situations to match the current problem. You're looking for the right balance between accuracy and the potential for overfitting. You also need enough time to develop and train/tune the model.

There Is No Magic Bullet

Because we know that no model in the world works in every situation, it is important to look at different ones. By combining forecasts, you can incorporate more information than you could with one forecast. Studies have even shown that combining methods reduces error by 12.5% compared with a single method.[26] Combining has the potential to reduce risk due to the effects of bias associated with a single method.

Predictive Models Can Get Old

Just because it worked once does not mean it works every time. Patterns change, data change, features change, and reactions within models change. Update models frequently as the underlying data or environment changes or revise parameters as new information is obtained. Make sure you use quantitative approaches and objective tests of assumptions and models.

There is no "one size fits all" algorithm or model. Choosing the right one depends on several factors including:

- Purpose;
- Data size, quality, and diversity; and
- Resources available.

There are also additional considerations like accuracy, training time, volume, parameters, data points, and much more. This is where we come in—it is the Demand Planner's role to help choose the right model that fits the data and the underlying truths, utilizing our experience and professional knowledge.

Monitoring and Evaluating Models

When it comes to forecasting models, there is no one size fits all. And with different inputs, methods, and parameters, how do you choose the right one, and once you have a model, how do you evaluate it?

Predictive modeling works on a feedback principle. Planners build a model, get feedback, and make improvements and continue until we achieve the necessary outcome. An important aspect of any predictive model or process is the evaluation aspect and the ability to differentiate models and their results.

There are two ways to evaluate a predictive model: examining its inputs and fit or examining its outputs or uncertainty.

Evaluating Inputs

Evaluating the inputs is a backward-looking assessment to see which model fits or learns the best. It looks at how the model generates a prediction before it occurs and describes the relative difference between training or historical data and a hypothetical forecast generated by the model using that same training data. The primary reasons for testing inputs are to learn how to improve a given model and, in the case of causal models, to better assess the effects of policy changes.

Evaluating Outputs

Evaluating the outputs involves assessing the model's output against the actual results that occur and the amount of uncertainty or error. This is weighting and then measuring the results of a prediction against a future observation. The type of error measurement you use depends on the type of model you're evaluating. The major reasons for testing outputs are to determine the precision of a model and to assess uncertainty.

The model should achieve your desired outputs, deliver good prediction performance, and balance the trade-offs of the chosen models and the way you choose to configure them. To balance tradeoffs, be aware that, as a model tries to match data points more closely, or when a more flexible method is used, the bias reduces but variance increases.

Unfortunately, the model with the best fit does not always give you the best results. A model can perform well and be very flexible on the trained data set but does not do well on actual observations or on a data set that it is not trained on. This is overfitting. **Overfitting:** *The use of an overly complex model that describes noise (randomness) in the data set rather than the underlying statistical relationship.* On the other hand, if the model is too simple and does not capture the complexity of data, it is underfitting. **Underfitting:** *Occurs when a model is overly simple, informed by too few features, or regularized too much, which makes it inflexible in learning from the dataset.*

The Goldilocks Zone

The goldilocks zone becomes that sweet spot between complexity and increase in bias, and the flexibility and increase of variance. Generalization is the balancing act, where you shift between models with high bias and those with high variance. This is the point just before the error on the test data set starts to increase where the model has good skill on both the training data set and the unseen test data set.

The skill of the model at making predictions determines the quality of the generalization and can help as a guide during the model selection process. It's always a good idea to try as many models as time and resources permit. The problem then becomes one of selecting the best model for the desired prediction task. Out of the millions of possible models, you should prefer simpler models over complex ones.

Splitting your data and having a Hold-Out process is undoubtedly the simplest model evaluation technique. After we generate a prediction from the training set, we test a model based on test data to which it has never been exposed before to see if we get similar results. It is important though to remember to leave your test data set untouched until a model is built and ready to be deployed. Be careful though, because if you keep tweaking your model based on the same hold out data, then you may be lulled into using the test data to train your model, thereby overfitting the model without realizing it.

Five Tips to Avoid Underfitting and Overfitting

In addition to splitting your data and using a test data set, here are five other helpful tips to assist you in minimizing bias and variance and reduce underfitting and overfitting.[27,28]

Use a Resampling Technique to Estimate Model Accuracy

In machine learning, the most popular resampling technique is k-fold cross-validation. The approach is to split the historical data into training, validation, and test data. You develop a model and validate performance on k-folds (or splits) of the training and validation data sets. This allows you to train and test your model k-times on different subsets of training data and build up an estimate of the performance of a machine learning model on unseen data.

Regularization

Regularization refers to a broad range of techniques for artificially forcing your model to be simpler. The method will depend on the type of learner you're using. For example, you could prune a decision tree, use dropout on a neural network, or add a penalty parameter to the cost function in regression.

Oftentimes, the regularization method is a hyperparameter as well, which means it can be tuned through cross-validation.

Use More Data

Often, with time-series and many machine learning algorithms, adding or training with more data can help algorithms detect the signal better. Of course, caution should be taken here. Adding extra points to the data typically reduces overfitting problems but if you start adding extra dimensions to the data, then you are likely to end-up with overfitting problems even if the models themselves stay unchanged.

Focus on Adding and Removing Features

Feature selection methods can be used to identify and remove unneeded, irrelevant, and redundant attributes from data that do not contribute to the accuracy of a predictive model or may, in fact, decrease the accuracy of the model. For models that do not have built-in feature selection, you can manually improve their generalizability by removing irrelevant input features. An interesting way to do so is to tell a story about how each feature fits into the model. If something doesn't make sense, or if it's hard to justify, consider removing it.

Early Stopping—Knowing When Enough is Enough

Early stopping refers to stopping the training process before the learner passes that point by itself. When you're training a learning algorithm iteratively, you can measure how well each iteration of the model performs. Up to a certain number, new iterations improve the model. After that point, however, the model's ability to generalize can weaken. In the simplest case, training is stopped as soon as the performance on the validation data set decreases as compared to the performance on the validation data set.

Avoiding Bias

Ignorance occurs when the outcomes are not known (or predicted); uncertainty occurs when the outcomes are known (or predicted) but the probabilities are not; and risk occurs when the probabilities of outcomes are thought to be known.[29]

Bias: *In forecasting, bias occurs when there is a consistent difference between actual sales and the forecast, which is manifested as over- or under-forecasting.* Think about a decision you made in the past that you were convinced was right. Or that time you were sure that the forecast was going up or down and the exact opposite occurred. What did you miss? What you missed was the human factor at play. It is an error you created that impacted the accuracy of the forecast.

Irrational behavior can cause consumers to act independently and create variation, but it may also impact you, the forecaster, in creating your own bias. Face it, we can be our own worst enemy and if you want to make the forecast better, you may want to remember these nine mental traps and common biases to avoid.

The Trust Me Bias

This is the tendency to interpret information in a way that confirms one's preconceptions, more commonly known as confirmation bias. It is one of the most common types of bias—and one that we all fall victim to because the data often "feel right." This happens a lot when people have an idea of what should happen, find a way to get the models or data to agree with their ideas, and rationalize it afterward. The misconception is that your predictions or opinions are a result of rational, objective analysis. In truth, your opinions are more often the result of focusing on information that confirmed what you believed, while ignoring information that challenged your preconceived notions.

Overfitting Bias

This involves an overly complex model that describes noise (randomness) in the data set rather than the underlying statistical relationship. You may be surprised how common overfitting is and many people (or their forecasting systems) do it unknowingly every day. This occurs when you allow your system to choose "best-fit" modeling for time-series data. With dozens of models with infinite parameters and enough time, you can fit a model to almost any data set. But there's no guarantee that the model will generate good forecasts or even if it should be used at all.

Anchor Bias

Setting an anchor is used in negotiations where the value of an offer is highly influenced by the first relevant number (the anchor) that starts the negotiation. It can also generate bias when your boss or a sales executive says from the outset, "I think we may be up 10% next period." Anchors, whether on purpose or accidental, are extremely influential. They create subtle psychological cues that influence what results you come up with that just happen to be close to 10% up for the next period.

Innovation Bias

This looks at innovation with a bias that it must be an improvement. Cognitive studies have shown that human beings tend to over-emphasize both similarities and differences between new and old things they are appraising. For our purposes, this can be in evaluating new data or models compared to older ones. Of course, the new ones must be better right? We tend to overvalue a new model and accept new data usefulness and undervalue their shortcomings.

Black Box Bias

This is somewhat the opposite of innovation and it's based on a simple premise: "If I don't understand it, it must be wrong." This is the idea that if you don't understand where the number came from or you didn't add your qualitative judgment to it, then it can't be right. Don't be distracted by your ego—accept that this time you just may not be adding value. In Michael Gilliland's book *Business Forecasting: Practical Problems and Solutions*, he highlights a study by Steve Morlidge. After studying over 300,000 forecasts, Morlidge found that a staggering 52% of the forecasts were worse than using a naïve forecast or random walk.[30]

Complexity Bias

This is the belief that the more elaborate and numerous the inputs, the better the results. You believe that, unless you are forecasting at the customer/item/location level every hour, adding assumptions from every salesperson and factoring in the weather for the next five days etc., you don't have a forecast. The forecasting process can be degraded in various places by the biases and personal agendas of participants. The more elaborate the process, with more human touchpoints, the more opportunity exists for these biases to taint what should be a simple and objective process.

Modeling Bias

This is the tendency to skew data and predictive models by starting with a biased set of assumptions about the problem. This leads to the selection of the wrong variables, the wrong data, the wrong algorithms, and the wrong metrics. This can also be over-trusting a process because it worked well once. The danger here should not be underestimated; analytical processes must be constantly fine-tuned to remain effective. Committing to an analytical process because it once delivered a positive result and forgoing continuous fine-tuning and critical scrutiny of the results is asking for trouble.

(n=all) Bias

This is somewhat obscure, but it happens to the best of us. We can become focused on information, trends or details that do not affect the outcome we are pursuing. This bias is hard to root out because it's often a good thing to use everything we know, or even toss unknowns into the input of a data-mining operation. One problem is that, with enough data to examine, eventually you'll find a statistically significant relationship where no such relationship exists. Another problem is that, even if you find the answer, it becomes difficult to understand what provided the answer.

The "I already know all this" Bias

Finally, if those are not bad enough, we cannot forget the worst one of all, the "I already know all this" bias. This one creates a blind spot and a failure to recognize one's own biases. To solve this, you must admit you don't know what you don't know and that you can fool even the smartest person you know—yourself.

Managing Outputs

When people talk about the forecasting/predictive analytics process, there is one crucial part we tend to miss out—the presentation. It is like running a marathon where we pour our blood, sweat, and tears into 25 miles, then stop at the final mile. Everything you have done up to this point will all be for naught unless you get across the finish line. Similarly, with predictive analytics, our efforts will be fruitless unless our insight is effectively presented to people who can use it.

Of course, the answers predictive analytics provides only create business value if your organization understands and can use them. Whether it's a report, executive dashboard, or meeting presentation, it is very common for insight to be overlooked due to lack of focus, being overly technical, or poor presentation.

Nobody Likes Boring Facts and Figures, So Tell A Story

I have said a couple of times already that Demand Planners are storytellers who use numbers as their language. It is important that you just don't present numbers and a forecast but present a story that people can follow. Some people may think a story around the data is an unnecessary, time-consuming effort. They may feel the facts stand on their own and should influence the right decisions. Unfortunately, this is based on the flawed assumption that business decisions are logical and not emotional.

This is the difference between reading an owner's manual and a novel. While one has the facts, the other is what people actually like to read. And ultimately this is our goal: not to come up with a number, but to influence others to listen so they employ those numbers. To do this we need to present forecasts and data in a way that is simple and easy to understand.

When telling a data story, it is not unlike storytelling in general. Stories have a logical structure containing a beginning, middle, and end. All stories have conflict, which, in our case, is business questions like balancing supply and demand. The protagonist, or hero, is data insight, and he/she will answer those questions. It is the Demand Planner's task to weave a narrative to enlighten the audience about the problems the company is facing and how they can be solved.

Find the Right Format to Present Your Insight

Stories can be told in writing, in art, in a song, or with a one-person monologue. I am not saying you should sing about your data, but you do need to identify the most meaningful format for presenting it. To increase the effectiveness of your communications and presentation, this step should be on your mind throughout the entire data analysis process. The purpose of the information and the type of audience should determine the format of your presentation.

It is important when putting a presentation together to determine what communication format will be most useful to your audience so your data inspires action instead of going unheard. Think about your audience. Would they best respond to an executive summary or one-pager encapsulating your narrative and facts? Or do they need a whole book containing your methods, iterations, assumptions, and data?

They say a picture speaks a thousand words. We live in a visual age, so whenever possible ditch the text and visualize the story. Your data are only as powerful as your visual presentation of it. Graphs are often easier to understand than tables and have a more meaningful impact on the audience. A chart that takes 30 seconds to understand, compared to a visual representation of the forecast or data that takes only 2 seconds, could mean the difference between accepting or rejecting your analysis.

Know Your Audience

Too often when we present our data, they will make sense to those who do the analysis but not to those who might actually use it. Determine what is most important to your audience. It is easy to summarize all the data you're working with, but some pieces of data are more important to your audience than others. Often, large data sets are presented, and the Demand Planner explains only the dominant trend or the one measure of most interest to them personally.

The audience is sometimes left to wonder things like, "Why is that data point there?" or "What caused that point to be low/high/odd?". Try to foretell what questions may come up and consider when presenting if the data adds value, supports your narrative, and provides exactly what the audience needs, rather than raising more questions.

It is important that you also calibrate data altitude optimally. Present forecasts and data in measurements that are meaningful to the decision-makers. Unless you are talking to other planners or data scientists, don't say "statistically significant," "r-squared," or "k-means algorithm," etc., unless you are sure that they understand these terms. You can never assume the audience fully understands what you are saying. Simplicity is critical to getting your message home.

Consolidate Information to Get to The Point as Quickly as Possible

Good data stories include enough information to state a case but not so much information that the audience struggles to understand the point. A common criticism of ineffective data stories is that they fail to get to the point fast enough. The Demand Planner needs to avoid clouding up their story with information and data that do not directly add to the narrative of the analysis and help answer the question at hand. Don't distract your audience—keep your story clear, simple, and impactful.

Typically, far too much time is spent on explaining what went into the analysis. I can understand the tendency to do this. After all the time spent on defining the need, data collection, and analysis, you want to show them all the data process stuff that got you to this point. I get it, you want to demonstrate your value and instill confidence in your findings by dazzling the audience with your skills and techniques. Maybe you want to give the audience all of the information so they can make their own decision because you feel it isn't your job to assume what they need or what they should do. But make no mistake, they're relying on you to point them in the right direction with your insight.

A lot of times, you could take just 10% of what you have done, leaving your audience with the real value of your insight, and you make data (and yourself) the hero. Every piece of data presented on the chart demands a portion of your audience's attention. That is why busy charts with multiple data sets put a lot of stress on your audience. Try to focus not on what you have done, not on what you can do, not on everything you may think they need, but consolidate data and information so your audience can make a good decision.

Statistical data are often presented in a dry, clinical manner. Perhaps the theory is that the audience should naturally be excited about data? Like predictive analytics and forecasting, data storytelling may lack a connection to business outcomes. If an insight isn't understood and isn't compelling, no one will act on it and no change will occur. Try to tell a compelling and exciting data story by finding your narrative and format, understanding your audience, and giving them the right amount of information so they can take action.

SPOTLIGHT

RSI and Burger King Try to Forecast the Impossible

Forecasting new products is difficult enough and has its challenges. Trying to predict an entirely new item in the food and beverage industry for a limited time offer (LTO) is next to impossible. But with the right people and process, one company has shown they can make the impossible happen.

We have all seen the difficulties of forecasting and planning play out in the fast-food industry, especially around new products or LTO. It was in 2018 in the United Kingdom that Kentucky Fried Chicken was forced to close restaurants after running out of chicken. In the summer of 2019, McDonald's introduced a limited time offer, a porker breakfast sandwich. It ended up much more limited than they would have liked, running out of bacon due to excess demand. And we cannot forget the new chicken sandwich from Popeye's in the United States that caused fights because availability was so scarce due to tweets that skyrocketed demand.

In the restaurant industry, LTOs present unique challenges. These are generally planned weeks in advance and can be impacted by external influences such as consumer responses, how stores individually promote, and paid and social media. Fail to forecast enough and we end up with headlines about shortages and irate customers. Forecast too much and you can lose millions of dollars in unsold food.

Restaurant Services, Inc. (RSI), which is an independent Supply Chain and Purchasing Co-op for Burger King, knew these challenges well as they were faced with forecasting and planning for the new Impossible Whopper. The food chain known for its flame-grilled beef hamburgers were introducing a new plant-based burger that looked and tasted like their signature Whopper without the meat. This was not a core item and it wasn't being sold by their competitors. There was no sales history but a lot of publicity and focus, so they had to get it right. At the same time, they had to ensure they did not have excess inventory for which they would be liable.

RSI is a not-for-profit company that is owned by over 450 U. S. Burger King franchisees who operate close to 7,200 stores. For each new item and LTO at Burger King, RSI generates forecasts and analyses of product requirements, collects and interprets menu item sales data, and estimates product demand. They use this to help manage Burger King's suppliers' timelines to produce exactly what the franchise members need and mitigate supply issues as much as possible.

Even though RSI produces forecasts every day and updates plans daily, their first step to plan the new Impossible Whooper was to define the project. While the objective was clear, they still needed to understand who their internal customers were, what the time horizon of this LTO would be, what data and resources they needed, and other critical questions. Before they could start modeling or even collecting data, they wanted to make sure they knew the "who, what, when, and why" of the new item.

After this, they determined what data they would use and where the data would come from. RSI has the advantage of having a very data-rich and analytically driven culture, so getting the right data was not a problem. Finding the relevant data and cleansing it, however, presented a challenge. With the Impossible Whopper being new, they did not have a like item to compare it to, but they did have years of daily point of sales data from hundreds of other menu items from which they could mine insights. From this data, they used clustering algorithms to help identify attributes and profiles that may be used to model this new item better.

In painting a room, 70% of the effort is in the preparation. It is not much different in forecasting and predictive analytics. Thanks to the up-front efforts, providing a forecast of anticipated sales for the new Impossible Whooper simply involved running this new information through their standard multiple regression and other models. The outputs were monitored closely in the three months ahead of the first sale and were updated as new information was made available. As limited test markets were phased in, new data and information were evaluated to either validate assumptions or tweak models to fine-tune parameters and provide even better outputs.

Within the food and beverage industry, forecast error (looking at MAPE at the SKU level lag 1) can be as high as 65% for new products and LTOs. RSI, in forecasting a truly disruptive product with no history, national promotion, and media fanfare, was able to reduce their error to SKU MAPE of 29.5%—almost twice as good as industry benchmarks. With a focus on the process, defining the problem, analyzing the data, and modeling, they were able to improve their average forecast error for promotional items (including many with sales history) by 15%. Most importantly, they were able to meet RSI's core mission to support Burger King franchises and ensure a successful launch of a revolutionary new item while avoiding excess inventory.

Collaboration in Predictive Analytics

Collaboration is not just about asking Sales for a forecast. Yes, Sales have great insight into the latest developments in the market, particularly at a regional level. They know about competitors entering the market and they gauge the sentiment of their clients in real-time. They know what products are accelerating in demand, which accounts are growing, and what client expectations are before anyone else. Sales are the firm's eyes and ears in the market. It should go without saying that forecasting should use their information and assumptions more times than not when creating forecasts.

But collaboration plays a much bigger role than that when it comes to the analytics and analysis process. We can no longer think of collaboration as just incorporating someone's input or having a meeting. Predictive analytics is at the heart of every business decision.

In defining the need, it is imperative to collaborate with decision makers and others who will be impacted by the forecast. When gathering inputs, you may need to collaborate with Sales, Marketing, customers, Finance, and a host of other people for contributions. During analysis, collaboration may be added to the baseline predictive model or incorporated in the forecast process or algorithm.

In this new business environment where we need to be more agile and generate more insights faster than ever before, we need to leverage resources and processes that are responsive and understand the data. As today's culture of 'disruptive' thinking begins to permeate every corner of business, approaches to processes and insight-driven decision-making are also evolving. Being adaptable and collaborative is now the name of the game, and if a company can't do this, the outlook is grim.

In the past, different functions had different goals:

- Product Management and PLM was concerned only with branding and innovation,
- FP&A was concerned only with P&L, and
- S&OP was concerned only with balancing supply and demand.

But what was true then isn't true now. Considering the need for businesses to react faster and more efficiently, we need to collaborate across functions and processes, and consolidate the analytics that supports these functions and processes.

The key objective for all of these processes is an integrated and collaborative planning process driven by a demand planning and analytics function in which everyone participates. No matter what is done, the operative words are "integrated," "planning," and, most important, "collaboration." It is a collaborative process from beginning to end, whether it be an *ad hoc* data analysis, a recurring weekly predictive forecast, or a formalized planning process.

With the collaborative approach, you change focus from pure statistics and modeling to communicating, building relationships, and sharing analytics and demand-related information. Organizations that thrive have learned that they are part of an integrated value chain and are integrating predictive analytics into all of their processes and decisions.

Predictive analytics professionals and Demand Planners who are adding value today have learned that they can no longer work in silos and need to collaborate through the entire process. Collaborative processes—whatever the acronym—that add value are ones in which people have learned to adapt and focus on working together to better meet consumer and business needs as driven by data and analytics.

The benefits are clear: companies need to be more agile and efficient. Sharing the right resources makes sense. Leveraging predictive analytics inside your organization helps every business function to have improved visibility and plan better. Reducing latency in your processes can save time and provide the right information quicker to make better decisions.

Consensus— One Number Attitude

There is an age-old debate in demand planning: Should you strive to be a "one number company" where all functions work to the same forecast or not? The idea is that a one number forecast creates alignment and that the whole company works to the same set of assumptions. Some say this creates more risk, while others say the idea of companies working to one number is just a myth.

I do not understand what the fuss is about and believe there is both a right and wrong answer here. It depends on who you are, where you are in the organization, and what you are doing with the number. Taking these things into consideration, you absolutely need a one number attitude.

I think the debate may stem from not defining what we mean by one number. If you mean that what you purchase matches exactly the unconstrained forecast that matches exactly what we report in financials, or if you mean that you march to a signal point forecast and ignore uncertainty—the answer is no, you don't want that!

If you mean that you are generating the same baseline forecast for the entire company and translating it for other functions using the same set of assumptions or analysis—the answer is yes, you want that!

Besides having everyone singing off the same hymnal, this coordination ensures best practices in data gathering and analysis, modeling, managing assumptions, and, just as important, monitoring performance.

A one number attitude is more than a consensus forecast; it is a mindset that starts from the very beginning. In defining the needs of a forecast or analysis, you need to reach consensus that you are working on the same problem. This root problem can have many tactical decisions related to it, and the analysis created to solve the problem can be used by many different roles and functions. We want to avoid functions defining their own problem in silos, driving different analyses that run counter to other competing analyses from other functions.

A company with a one number attitude has the same data and base assumptions and coordinates best practices on transforming or manipulating the inputs. Data can mean something entirely different depending on where you pull it from, the filters used, when you pulled it, and the level of aggregation. In gathering data and inputs, it is important to not only have a single set of truth, but also consensus on what is being gathered and how.

This can be the difference between looking at shipments, orders, or POS data, and how much data you are looking at to analyze sales sentiment. Problems are sure to arise when different functions operate from their own data sets and inputs are collected in vacuums.

You can have the same set of data and the same set of assumptions and with different techniques come up with very wide-ranging results. Sometimes we see different functions doing different analyses using different principles using different data—even though the analyses serve similar purposes. One of the key things often forgotten is that judgment or expert opinion is used as a forecasting method and is used widely without people realizing the impacts. Some of the best forecasts are derailed or overridden based on someone else looking at the same data and operating off of intuition instead of a one number attitude.

A company with a one number attitude strives for centralized quantitative analysis whenever possible, is analytically driven, and performs analysis using the same principles and systems. They make sure to tie all the modeling and techniques back to the purpose of the forecast.

A one number attitude enables the entire organization to plan based on the same range of possibilities, assumptions, risk, and upsides. It provides the foundation for Finance, Production, Logistics, and Supply Chain to get outside of their silos and connect with each other.

It gives way to meaningful and productive conversations around planning and the impacts each function can have. In this scenario, the same forecast that drives Operations and Sales and Marketing is now driving gross margin, variable cost, and cash flow. While there may be allowances and other financial adjustments to the sales forecast, using the same baseline allows you to understand the drivers and variables better, and how they all connect.

Oftentimes, companies get hung up on the term "one number"; the truth is a train wreck on either side of the tracks is just as bad. Forecasting involves uncertainty and uncertainty is never a single number; planning to a single number guarantees problems.

On the other side, failure to align on the same business goals, assumptions, data, and modeling to better understand and plan for uncertainty is just as dangerous. It is the responsibility of the analyst or Demand Planner to present the risk and assumptions that went into the analysis. It is then incumbent upon the users of those insights to think through all options, combinations, and permutations of potential plans.

This does not come without challenges, however. To develop a one number culture, companies must break down information silos and eliminate multiple versions of the truth. This only happens when stakeholders throughout the organization openly share data and information, and that means the long-standing gap between functions must be bridged.

Everyone in the process has to stay very close to one another in sharing the information and data coming from various parts of the organization. Often, demand planning is central in holding not only the entire process together but also the information to run it. Ultimately, when the forecast is tied to sound predictive analytics and agreed-upon assumptions and data, executives have more timely and accurate information that allows them to make better decisions.

Summary— All About the Process

Predictive analytics encompasses a variety of new statistical techniques including data mining, predictive modeling, and machine learning, that analyze current and historical facts to make predictions about future or otherwise unknown events. At the same time—as with everything new—the more things change, the more they stay the same. Whether you are using a traditional forecasting process or training a deep learning algorithm to help classify consumer behavior, there are standard processes and principles that both follow.

Whether it's simple or advanced, we always go back to the fundamentals of defining a question, collecting and cleansing data, and transforming and modeling data to discover insights to solve that question. The results are communicated, recommendations are made, and effective decision-making is facilitated. The process is a recursive one; arriving at the end will take a good planner back to the beginning again to refine each of the steps based on the information they uncovered.

Too many times we get caught up in new technology or advanced methods and we end up overlooking or overcomplicating the basics that make them work. When you start focusing your attention less on the results and techniques but on the processes involved, you will improve precision, reduce bias, and, most importantly, provide better insights.

When you focus only on complex models and the output numbers, you end up missing potentially better fitting techniques and potential data issues. Although predictive analytics and everything it entails is more advanced than traditional forecasting and planning, we must not overcomplicate it and stick to the basics wherever possible. It is easy in any journey to get ahead of ourselves and lose sight of what we are trying to accomplish.

No matter how advanced your methods or analysis get before you start, you should always ask why you are doing it and define your need. In every project, attention should be paid to collecting, transforming, wrangling, and cleansing your data to get it into the proper format before you start modeling.

Complex models and fancy techniques are nice, but attention should be given to choosing the right model to fit your business purpose and ensure it is doing what you need it to do. The most advanced predictive analytics accomplish little if nobody knows or understands its results. To complete the process, you must step back and see if you need to simplify things, then communicate the analysis effectively.

Section Review

Multiple Choice: Identify the choice that best completes the statement or answers the question.

1. What is NOT a process step in predictive analytics?

    a) Collecting and pruning data.
    b) Estimating and evaluating models.
    c) Constraining outputs to match targets.
    d) Managing the results.

2. If the data contain an outlier you can:

    a) Clip it or prune it.
    b) Just get rid of that data point.
    c) Just leave it in the data set.
    d) All of the above.

3. Which of the following is NOT a data cleansing process?

    a) Extracting only data you trust.
    b) Building dimensions.
    c) Formatting data.
    d) Filling in data that are missing.

4. What kind of modeling technique would you use for describing past behavior?

    a) Clustering analysis.
    b) Regression analysis.
    c) Time-series analysis.
    d) Descriptive analysis.

5. Training a model to fit the training data set may result in:

    a) Overfitting the data.
    b) Underfitting the data.
    c) Making a more accurate prediction.
    d) All of the above.

True or False

6. ☐ Data cleansing includes finding errors in completeness, correctness, and timeliness.

7. ☐ An algorithm is a mathematical model with an endless number of possible steps.

8. ☐ Time-series models need to be trained or rerun every time you get a new data point.

9. ☐ The training data set will contain the answer to the problem.

10. ☐ It is important to present just the facts and data so people can make their own decisions.

PART III
PREDICTIVE ANALYTICS AS DATA ANALYSIS

After reading this section, you should be able to:

- Explain what data mining is and how it enables predictive analytics.
- Understand what constitutes big data and how we manage it.
- Determine how much data to use.
- Distinguish the differences between classification, clustering, and prediction.
- Implement different methods of segmenting data or attributes and understand their pros and cons.

Data Analysis and Data Mining

Demand planners don't just tell someone they will sell 42 widgets in the next period. A great deal of their time is working with and understanding the data.[31] Besides forecasting, planners are often asked to find relationships between variables; to explain what and why something in the past occurred with the data; and to organize history and drivers so others can use them. All of this relies on mining and analyzing data.

Data Mining: *A process that includes the collection, exploration, pattern identification, and deployment of data to gain insights and extract useful information.* Data mining may also be explained as the logical processes of finding the kind of useful information that can reveal insights. Once you discover the information and patterns, you can use them to develop predictive and descriptive models, or visualize them to reveal business insights.

Often, the terms "data mining" and "predictive analytics" are used interchangeably. This is understandable because, in many ways, you cannot do predictive analytics without data mining and both work together to provide insights. Predictive analytics is focused on future outcomes. It requires data sets, detecting patterns, and capturing relationships. The methods and tools of data mining play an essential role in supporting this.

Data mining involves effective data collection and warehousing, as well as computer processing. It uses statistical methods or genetic algorithms for segmenting the data, pattern recognition in large data sets, and identification of relationships. With the right tools and algorithms, data files can be automatically searched for statistical anomalies, patterns, or rules, and then structured for use.

Predictive analytics processes these data using different statistical methods such as extrapolation, regression, neural networks, and machine learning to detect patterns in the data and derive a forecast. These algorithms are created and reviewed based on splitting the data sets you have retrieved and structured. That axiom again comes to mind: "Garbage in, garbage out." With the right focus and data upfront, it greatly improves the ability and efficiency of the predictive modeling.

What Is Data Mining Used For?

In the business world, data mining is used for examining raw data. These data can consist of sales history, prices, and customers. Planners and analysts will discover patterns among different data and, often, transform and cleanse it. Data mining can feed other models, develop better marketing strategies, and improve business performance. Data mining also serves to identify new patterns of behavior among consumers.[32,33]

Data Mining Is Used to Examine Large Amounts of Data

Anomaly detection identifies data points atypical of a given distribution and clusters them into useable data sets. In other words, it finds the outliers. Though simple data analysis techniques can identify outliers, data mining anomaly detection techniques identify much more subtle attribute patterns and the data points that fail to conform to those patterns.

Data Mining Tools Sweep Through Databases and Identify Previously Hidden Patterns

An example of pattern discovery is the analysis of retail sales data to identify seemingly unrelated products that are often purchased together. Other pattern discovery problems include detecting fraudulent credit card transactions and identifying anomalous data that could represent data entry errors.

Data Mining Is Used to Store and Extract Data from Internal and External Sources

Databases hold key data in a structured format, so algorithms built using their own language (such as SQL macros) to find hidden patterns within organized data are most useful. These algorithms are sometimes inbuilt into the data flows, e.g., tightly coupled with user-defined functions, and the findings presented in a ready-to-refer-to report with meaningful analysis.

Data Mining Helps Identify and Fix Issues in Data

Techniques such as Self-Organizing-Maps (SOMs) correct, replace, or segment data to help visualization of data. Multi-task learning for missing inputs (where an existing, valid data set is compared with another compatible but incomplete data set) is another way to seek out missing data.

Data Mining Is Used for Finding the Hidden Facts in Data

Through pattern evaluation, data mining helps a business better understand customer behavior, which leads to better decisions like targeting new customers or entering new markets.

Data Mining Can Integrate Separate Data Sets and Transform Data

Data can be evaluated and relationships identified so you can understand what features and variables to use in your models.

Data Mining Can Assist in Feature Extraction

It creates and finds new features based on attributes of your data. These new features describe a combination of significant attribute value patterns in your data.

Data Mining Can Be Used for the Data Visualization

It can present raw data in an informative presentation so your business partners can make better decisions. Data mining techniques are applied to give live insight and monitoring of data to stakeholders.

Data Mining Helps Structure Unstructured Data

It makes use of text, sentiment, video, and much of the information available on social media that is virtually untapped today. Text Analysis is one example and data mining can automatically find patterns within the text embedded in hordes of text files, word-processed files, PDFs, and presentation files.

Types of Data

In Supply Chain and Operations, raw materials are substances that are used in the manufacturing of goods. They are the commodities to be transformed into another state that will either be used or sold. For algorithms or predictive models, data are the raw materials with which every insight begins.

A piece of data, or collection of them, can help drive a predictive analytics process and uncover insights. Data are the building blocks and inputs, and without data, it is nearly impossible to find answers and make decisions. That said, data are not the destination. Data are not a decision. While data may take on many forms and be used for many things, data by themselves are not insight.

Data: *Information in raw form.*

Information: *A collection of data points that we can use to understand something about the thing being measured.*

Insight: *Valuable information gained by analyzing data and other inputs to understand what is going on with the particular situation or phenomena.* The insight can then be used to make better business decisions.

Data on their own are meaningless. Data are just raw material that needs to be transformed, analyzed, turned into understanding, and shared. And that needs to be done by people with the appropriate skills, training, and commitment. At the same time, predictive modeling (or any business insight) without data is equally meaningless. No matter how skilled you are, or how good your model is, predictive modeling without data is like trying to produce a finished product without the proper parts. That's where data mining comes in.

There's no arguing the power of data in today's business landscape. Businesses are analyzing a seemingly endless array of data sources to glean insights into just about every activity—both inside their businesses and out. Right now, it seems that enterprises cannot get their hands on enough data for analysis purposes. They are looking at multiple sources and types of data to learn more about customers and markets and predict how they will behave.

What are the different types of data sets? We can think about data sets in terms of how they are organized as well as the types of sources.

Data Set: *A collection of data organized as a stream of information in logical record and block structures.* Data sets are either structured or unstructured and the source can be internal or external.

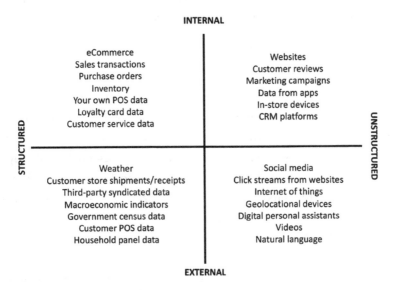

Fig e | Types of data and data sources

Internal Sources

Internal sources of data are those that are procured and consolidated from different branches within your organization. Examples include purchase orders, internal transactions, marketing information, loyalty card information, information collected by websites or transactional systems, and any other internal source that collects information about your customers.

Before you begin to look for external sources, it's critical to ensure that all of a business's internal data sources are mined, analyzed, and leveraged for the good of the company. While external data can offer a range of benefits (we'll get into that later), internal data sources are typically easier and quicker to collect and can be more relevant for the company's purposes and insights.

External Sources

External sources of data are those that are procured, collected, or originate outside of the organization. Examples include external POS or inventory data from a retail partner, paid third-party information, demographic and government data, web crawlers, macroeconomic data, and any other external source that collects information about your customers. The collection of external data may be difficult because the data have much greater variety and the sources are much more numerous.

Structured Data Sources

Structured data is both organized and easy to digest and generally refers to data that have a defined length and format. It is sometimes thought of as more traditional data that may include names, numbers, and information that is easily formatted in columns or rows. Structured data is largely managed with legacy analytics solutions given its already-organized nature. It may be collected, processed, manipulated, and analyzed using traditional relational databases. Before the era of big data and new data sources, structured data was what organizations used to make business decisions.

Unstructured Data Sources

Unstructured data does not have an easily definable structure, is unorganized and raw, and typically isn't a good fit for a mainstream relational database. It is the opposite of structured and includes all other data generated through a variety of human activities. Common examples are comments on web pages, word processing documents, videos, photos, audio files, presentations, and many other kinds of files that do not fit into the columns and rows of an excel spreadsheet.

These new data sources are made up largely of streaming data coming from social media platforms, mobile applications, location services, and Internet-of-Things technologies. Since unstructured data sources are so diverse, businesses have much more trouble managing their unstructured data than they do with traditional structured data. As a result, companies are being challenged in a way they weren't before and are having to get creative to pull relevant data for analytics.

You may believe that only super large companies with massive funding and advanced technology are implementing data analytics and pushing the limits of the types of data that are collected. While 90% or more of the data we use in our forecasting today is internal structured data, it is important to understand that 90% plus of external data is unstructured.[34]

With the increase in available data along with the expansion of data storage capabilities and data analytics tools, the playing field has leveled. While data are not insights, new types of data fuel newer insights and this focus on data has embedded itself into the culture of an increasing number of businesses.

What Is Big Data?

We can no longer ignore data. Now that we have begun to define it and find new ways of collecting it, we see it everywhere and in everything humans do. Our current output of data is roughly 2.5 quintillion bytes a day and as the world becomes ever more connected with an ever-increasing number of electronic devices, it will grow to numbers we haven't even conceived of yet.

We refer to this gigantic mass of data as "big data." First identified by Doug Laney, then an analyst at Meta Group Inc., in a report published in 2001, big data has commonly been defined as "information that is high-volume, high-velocity, and/or high-variety beyond normal processing and storage that enables enhanced insights, decision-making, and automation."[35]

The problem is that "high volume" and "normal" are relative to your company size and capabilities. For this reason, I prefer to look at big data as the continual growth in data beyond your company's ability to store, process, or use it.

The challenge with the sheer amount of data available is assessing it for relevance. The faster the data are generated, the faster you need to collect and process them. Not only that, data also can be structured in many different ways and comes from a wide variety of different sources that need to be tied together and sorted out. Finally, when we talk about big data, we think of it as raw information and overlook the strategies to deal with it and the tools to manage it.

PREDICTIVE ANALYTICS AS DATA ANALYSIS

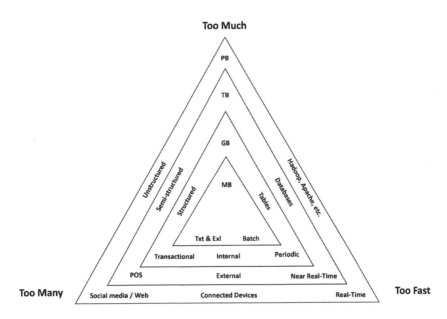

Fig f | Infographic demonstrating the complexity of data

Big data means something different for each company. As far as your company is concerned, it is all the data you cannot store, process, and interpret. We fail to do these things because the data are either too much to handle, are coming in from too many different sources, or are coming in too fast (or a combination of these). Understanding these three vectors is key to identifying big data in our organizations compared to traditional data sets.

Too Much Data

Big data is about size and refers to the large amount of data involved. The size of available data is growing at an increasing rate. If there was ever "small data," it was generated internally from enterprise transactional systems and stored on local servers. Today, businesses are constantly collecting data from many different outlets like social media, website lead captures, emails, e-commerce and more. This has begun to outgrow an organization's capabilities to manage these larger amounts of data—a major issue for those looking to put that new data to use instead of letting it go. If this sounds familiar, you are dealing with big data, and it's probably a big headache.

More data sources that create more data combine to increase the amount of data that have to be analyzed. The world holds an enormous amount of data, possibly an incomprehensible amount. With over 90% of today's data being generated in the past two years, that comes to about 2.5 quintillion data bytes daily. Perhaps 10 or 15 years ago, terabytes qualified as excessive data, but these days you're not really in the big data world unless you're dealing with petabytes (1,000 TB) or exabytes (1 million TB).

To deal with these larger amounts of data, companies are moving from desegregated data sources to data lakes and warehouses, and data management systems. Storage is transforming from local servers to the Cloud and external partners like Amazon and others. For processing, we are considering tools like Hadoop and Apache. Business intelligence software for data cleansing and data visualization is becoming more prevalent. In predictive analytics, we are considering new methods and approaches to analyze larger sets of data and capture greater insights.

Too Fast Data

Big data isn't just big; it's growing fast. It's also coming in at lightning speed and needs to be processed just as quickly. In the olden days (three to five years ago), companies would usually analyze data using a batch process. That approach works when the incoming data rate is slower than the batch processing rate and when the result is useful (considering there's a delay). With new sources of data and the need to be more agile in decision-making, the batch process breaks down. The data are now streaming into the server in real-time, in a continuous fashion and the result is only useful if the delay is very short.

Think about how many website clicks, consumer transactions and interactions, and credit card swipes are being completed every minute of every day. Consider the sheer number of SMS messages, the 300,000 social media status updates, the 140,000 photos uploaded, and the 500,000 comments made every minute. Add to this the Internet of Things with its constant real-time transmissions and you'll have a good appreciation of the speed at which data are being created.

We need real-time tools (or close to real-time) to collect, analyze, and manage all this data, then act on it. Demand sensing is the key to this. Demand sensing is sensing demand signals, then predicting demand, and producing an actionable response with little to no latency.

According to the Summer 2012 issue of *The Journal of Business Forecasting*, demand sensing sorts out the flood of data in a structured way to recognize complex patterns and to separate actionable demand signals from a sea of noise.[36] Besides this, speed also calls for building big data solutions that incorporate data caching, periodic extractions and better data orchestration, and deploying the right architecture and infrastructure.

Too Many Types of Data

Data is big, data is fast, but data also can be extremely diverse. Data diversity refers to all the different types of data available. Data was once collected from one place (more than likely internal) and delivered in one format. It would typically be in the form of database files such as Excel, CSV, or Access. Now there is an explosion of external data in multiple forms and unstructured data that don't fit neatly on a spreadsheet. This, more than any of the other data complexities, can quickly outpace an organization's ability to manage and process their data.

The assortment of different types of data is one of the most interesting developments as more information is digitized. A few decades ago, data would've been in a structured database in a simple text file. Nowadays, we no longer have control over the input data format. Consider the customer comments, SMS messages, or anything on social media that helps us to better understand consumer sentiment. How do we bring together all the transactional data, POS data from trading partners, and sensor data we collect in real-time? Where do you put it?

Although these data are extremely useful to us, it can create more work and requires more analytics to decipher it so it can provide insights. To help manage the variety of data, there are a several techniques we can use. We no longer just extract and load, we are now importing data into universally accepted and usable formats such as Extensible Markup Language (XML). To sort through the amount and all the different types of data, we use data profiling techniques to find interrelationships and abnormalities between data sources and data sets.

The bottom line is that data are much more than just a buzzword or simply lots of data. It is a way to describe new types of data and new potential for greater insights. Just using the word "big" may do well to describe the data, but we still need to remember that even big data is still the small building blocks when it comes to adding business value. For big data to be valuable, we need more data coming in faster from multiple sources—and we need the systems, analytics, techniques, and people to manage that process and derive value from it.

N=all
(How Much Data
Do You Use?)

If we can get some insights from a small amount of internal structured data, then think how much more we may glean from big data that is larger, external, and structured as well as unstructured. If too little data limits the ability to see correlations and more data opens up more possibilities (and may reduce overfitting), why not use as much data as you can get? If we can find some answers in the little data we know, how many more problems can we solve if we let the models look at all the data we can find? If a sample is okay, then "n = all" is exponentially better.

There is a debate about how much information is enough data and how much is too much. According to some, the rule of thumb is to think smaller and focus on quality over quantity. On the other side, Viktor Mayer-Schönberger and Kenneth Cukier explain in their book *Big Data: A Revolution That Will Transform How We Live, Work, and Think*, that "when data was sparse, every data point was critical, and thus great care was taken to avoid letting any point bias the analysis. However, in many new situations that are cropping up today, allowing for imprecision—for messiness—may be a positive feature, not a shortcoming."[37]

Of course, larger data sets are more likely to have errors, and analysts are less likely to have time to carefully clean every data point. Mayer-Schönberger has a response for this, saying that "moving into a world of big data will require us to change our thinking about the merits of exactitude. The obsession with exactness is an artifact of the information-deprived analog era." Corroborating this, some studies in data science have found that even massive error-prone data sets may be more reliable than simple and smaller samples. The question becomes this: are we willing to sacrifice some accuracy and control in return for learning more?

Like so many things in demand planning and predictive analytics for businesses, one size does not fit all. You need to understand your business problem, understand your resources, and understand the trade-offs. In this new era of big data comes big responsibilities. No one can tell you how much data you need for your predictive modeling problem. The amount of data you need ultimately depends on a variety of factors:

The Complexity of the Problem

Not necessarily the computational complexity (although that is an important consideration), but the complexity of the business problem you want to solve. How important is precision versus information? You should define this business problem and select the data most relevant to it. For example, if you want to forecast the future sales of a particular item, the historical sales of that item may be the most relevant. From there, other drivers that may contribute to future sales or understanding past sales may be selected. Attributes with no correlation to the problem are not wanted.

The Complexity of the Algorithm

How many samples are needed to demonstrate performance or to train or evaluate the model? For some linear algorithms, you may find you can achieve good performance with a hundred or a few dozen examples per class. For some machine learning algorithms, you may need hundreds. For a nonlinear algorithm like Random Forest or an artificial neural network, you may need thousands of examples per class. Some algorithms, like deep learning methods, continue to improve as you give them more data.

How Much Data Are Available?

Are the requirements beyond your company's ability to store, process, or use? A great starting point may be to consider what you have available and what is manageable. What kind of data do you already have? In Business-to-Business, most companies possess customer records or sales transactions. These data sets usually come from CRM and ERP systems or similar. A lot of companies are already collecting third-party data in the form of POS data. From here, consider other sources both internally and externally that may add value or insights.

This does not solve the debate and the right amount of data is still unknowable; it's an intractable problem that you must discover the answers to through empirical investigation. Your goal should be to continue to think big and act with what you have or, more importantly, think about what you *need* to solve the problem given the algorithm you are using. The best time to plant a tree was 10 years ago. Focus on the data available and the insights you have today while building the roadmap and capabilities to the data and insights you may be able to achieve in the future. Even though you may not use it now, don't wait until tomorrow to start collecting what you may rely on in future.

Data Mining Techniques

There is no question we are dealing with more data in a greater variety of formats, and it is coming at us faster than ever. With the onslaught of big data and the need to covert this data into insights, we require processes and techniques to manage not only the data we have now, but the data that is yet to come.

As explained previously, data mining is a process that includes the collection, exploration, pattern identification, and deployment of data to gain insights and extract useful information. It is also known as the knowledge discovery process.

For the most part, data mining is a logical process of finding useful information. Using a broad range of techniques, you can use this information to increase revenues, cut costs, improve customer relationships, reduce risk, and more. By understanding what is relevant in the data, companies can make good use of that information to assess likely outcomes. Data mining also helps with sifting through all the chaotic and repetitive noise in your data and accelerating the pace of informed decision-making. While data mining techniques are a means to drive efficiencies and predict customer behavior, predictive analytics is where a business can really set itself apart from its competition.

Most data mining falls in the broader range of clustering, descriptive, anomaly, and regression analysis. To select the best technique, you must choose according to the type of business and the type of problem your business is facing. A generalized approach has to be used to improve the accuracy and cost-effectiveness of using data mining techniques. While there are many data mining techniques, the following are the ones that are most widely used.

Clustering

Clustering: *An approach or combination of methods where the primary objective is to group related data points together.* It utilizes many machine learning models and is one of the oldest techniques used for data mining. It is often used to create clusters or segments that are used as inputs in other analyses. This process involves grouping chunks of data together based on their similarities, which helps you to understand the differences and similarities between the data. As an example, you may choose to cluster customers based on demographic characteristics like age or gender, or how often they shop at your store or website. These groups not only segment your data but allow you to better understand what is going on within the database.

Classification

Classification: *An approach or combination of methods where the primary objective is to predict the target class using observed values.* Similar to clustering, it is widely used as a data mining technique and uses machine learning models such as the decision tree or neural network system. Classification helps in deriving important information about data and metadata (data about data). Compared to clustering, it can become slightly more complex, forcing you to collect various attributes together into discernable categories that you can then use to draw further conclusions. As an example, if you're evaluating data on individual customers' age and purchase histories, you can classify them as "young," "medium," or "older" age groups. You could then use these classifications to learn even more about those customers' buying habits and sub-groupings.

Visualization

Visualization is one of the easier, more useful, and possibly overlooked data mining techniques to discover data patterns. Many do not even consider it a technique but rather a process. Either way, it can be used to see, group, and discover patterns. Visualization is the technique of extracting and visualizing the data in a very clear and understandable way, displaying the results in the form of pie charts, bar graphs, statistical representation, and graphical forms. There are a lot of data mining techniques that will produce useful or even hidden patterns such as Scatterplots, Bar-plots, and Heat-maps+.

Association

Association is a type of statistical technique that helps find an association between two or more variables in a database. It discovers hidden patterns in data sets that are used firstly to identify the variables, and then to identify the variables that appear most frequently. In this case, you will look for specific events or attributes that are highly correlated with another event or attribute. As an example, you might notice that when your customers buy a specific item, they also often buy a second, related item. This is usually what is used to populate "You may also consider purchasing" sections of online stores.

Pattern Recognition

Pattern recognition is similar to association and involves statistical techniques that relate to the collection and description of data. These can be some of the most basic techniques in data mining, but they give you the important ability to recognize patterns in your data sets. Examples include Histogram, Mean, Median, Mode, Variance, Probability Distribution, and Regression.

Whether you are structuring your data for further analysis, cleansing a large data set, or finding insights in the data set you have, data mining is the collection of techniques you have for making the most out of the data you've already gathered. This may include advanced machine learning methods, simple statistical approaches, or visualization and business intelligence—as long as you apply the correct logic and ask the right questions, you can end up with valuable insights and give you and your company an edge.

Reconciliation of Time, Space, and Item/Location

Clustering in Data Mining, as we have learned already, is an approach or combination of methods where the primary objective is to group data points together. Another way of looking at clustering is this: it is the grouping of a particular set of objects based on their characteristics and then aggregating them according to their similarities. You may not realize it, but much of the top-down versus bottom-up forecasting debate actually surrounds data mining and the clustering of data before you apply a predictive model.

It's very common in forecasting and planning to aggregate or cluster data to increase the signal/noise ratio. There are several papers available that are worth exploring regarding the effect of hierarchical and temporal aggregation on forecast accuracy. Transforming the data through aggregation or disaggregation allows you to gather additional information about the series at hand, resulting in better forecasts.

- Item, Location, and/or Consumer or End User; in general, the most unstable and prone to the highest error.
- Product Group, Region, and/or Segment; typically has moderate error.

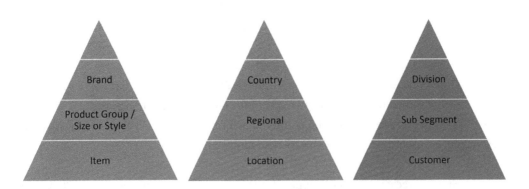

Fig g | Graphic showing the most common forecasting hierarchies

- Brand, Country, and/or Division; typically more stable due to aggregating all the variation from lower levels and consequently has the lowest error.

Each one is an attribute that may have many levels of aggregation. With today's data, you could easily add more attributes with even more levels. Think of price as an independent variable—you could use data at each price increment of a penny or bucket them by each dollar change or another aggregation of the data at some higher increment. Even time can be aggregated and reconciled, from months to weeks to days to hours.

Despite all the potential attributes, levels of aggregation, and combinations of them, historically the debate has been condensed to just two options: top-down and bottom-up. The top-down approach uses an aggregate of the data at the highest level to develop a summary forecast, which is then allocated to individual items based on their historical relativity to the aggregate. We can generate a forecast based on the ratio of their contribution to their sum of the aggregate, which is, in essence, a naïve forecast.

More aggregated data is inherently less noisy than low-level data because noise cancels itself out in the process of aggregation. But while forecasting only at higher levels may be easier and provide fewer errors, it can degrade forecast quality because patterns in low-level data may be lost. High level works best when the behavior of low-level items is highly correlated and the relationship between them is stable. Low level tends to work best when the behavior of the data series is very different from each other (i.e., independent) and the method you use is good at picking up these patterns.

The major challenge is that the required level of aggregation to get meaningful statistical information may not match the precision required by the business. You may also find that while some internal stakeholders do not want much granularity (i.e., customer level for production purposes), some inputs are at the lower item or customer level. More often than not, though, you'll need to provide multiple levels of aggregation, which all come with varying degrees of noise.

For anyone trying to forecast, it becomes apparent that one size (generally) does not fit all. The choice between top-down and bottom-up now has a third option: middle-out. With this approach, we start from somewhere in the middle of a hierarchy, for example, from a specific product line or category. Others prefer a hybrid approach, forecasting some items at lower levels and others aggregated. This is a good idea because forecasts can and should be done at multiple levels of aggregation to serve the various needs of the business.

The increase in the detail of data and systems capabilities allow us to perform dynamic hierarchy and multiple iteration forecasting. Just as with ensemble methods in machine learning that are composed of multiple weaker models that are independently trained and whose predictions are combined to make the overall prediction, we can do the same thing with reconciliation and hierarchies. Multiple weaker hierarchies can be combined using regression or other approaches to optimize the overall prediction at every level.

So, how should we approach reconciliation and aggregation of forecasts? Consider the following when deciding what level of aggregation to start and end at:

- The level of aggregation of the inputs into the process such as POS data, website clicks, or sales and marketing intelligence, etc.
- The level of aggregation needed as an output and the downstream decisions to be made using the outputs.
- Hierarchy and reconciliation procedures within software design.
- The planning process design or constraints and the planning team's resources.
- The aggregation of the optimal statistical algorithms and parameter settings.

After you have considered the ins and outs, you should always attempt to forecast at the highest level of aggregation compatible with the process and decision goals. This means we include only the levels needed for the purpose of the forecast. Too often we believe more detail always means better precision when, in fact, it could be making things measurably worse.

It is part of a Demand Planners' responsibility to understand the attributes, levels, inputs, outputs, and model limitations. We no longer have only a debate between top and bottom but need to look at things dynamically. Managing this effectively can maximize your resources while improving the forecast the business needs.

Clustering Analysis and Segmentation

Clustering, like regression, describes the class of problem and the class of methods. Clustering methods are typically organized with a modeling approach such as centroid-based or hierarchical. All methods are concerned with using the inherent structures in the data to best organize the data into groups with maximum shared commonalities.

These days, planning demand is getting increasingly complex. As a result, demand planning teams often take advantage of techniques like clustering or segmentation to divide up the supply chains, items, customers, and other attributes into smaller segments. Once the data is broken down into segments, it is easier to understand and use in a meaningful way. Breaking down the data into these segments makes specific issues in the data more obvious. It also helps in prioritizing the different segments.

Segmentation: *The process of defining and sub-dividing a large homogenous data set into clearly identifiable segments having similar or dissimilar characteristics.* The usage of this approach can be company-wide, and segmentation can mean something radically different depending on whom in the organization you are speaking with. The goal of the cluster analysis is to take a granular look at the different segments and apply optimal strategies for each.

The method of analysis that is most appropriate, of course, depends on your specific situation. Methods range from rule-based segmentation approaches to machine learning unsupervised clustering algorithms. Perhaps the simplest form of segmentation analysis today is a constraint (or rule-based) approach. This is where we select an *a priori* constraint. More advanced cluster analysis uses statistical models to discover groups of similar or dissimilar groups based on the smallest variations within an attribute.

Clustering algorithms are to segmentation what predictive analytics is to demand planning. Unlike predetermined constraint methods, clustering algorithms can use the data themselves to define the cluster sizes or even clusters themselves. Important types of cluster analysis are connectivity-based clustering (hierarchical clustering) and centroid-based clustering (such as K-Means). The five major types of clustering and segmentation algorithms are:

Constraint-Based

This is not commonly mentioned when discussing clustering algorithms but at the same time is the most widely used for segmentation in business planning. It is not mentioned because this is technically more of a classification than a clustering. It is a grouping method based on pre-defined rules or constraints of a division of an attribute. An example would be dividing a data set based on items with sales over $1 million and other similarities. Even though it is not a clustering algorithm, it is worth mentioning it here as its outputs are widely used to cluster or segment items or customers in planning and forecasting.

Connectivity-Based

This approach is predicated on the concept that every object is related to its neighbors and the notion that the data points closer to each other (when plotted on a graph, for example) exhibit more similarity to each other than the data points lying farther away. With this relationship between members, these clusters have hierarchical representations. These models can follow two approaches. In the first, we start with classifying all data points into separate clusters and then aggregating them as the distance decreases. In the second approach, all data points are classified as a single cluster and then partitioned as the distance increases. Examples of these models are hierarchical clustering algorithms.

Centroid-Based

This type of grouping method involves iterative clustering algorithms where each object is part of the cluster with a minimal value difference and is derived by the closeness of a data point to the centroid of the clusters. The number of clusters should be pre-defined. This methodology is primarily used for optimization problems. K-Means clustering is a popular algorithm that falls into this category.

Distribution-Based

These clustering models are based on the notion of how probable it is that all data points in the cluster belong to the same distribution (i.e., Normal, Gaussian). This process requires a well-defined and complex model to interact with the data, making this a challenging undertaking. However, these processes can achieve an optimal solution and calculate correlations and dependencies very effectively. A popular example of these models is the expectation-maximization algorithm that uses multivariate normal distributions.

Density-Based

This model type creates clusters according to the high density of members in a determined location within a data set. It isolates various density regions and assigns the data points within these regions to the same cluster. Popular examples of density models are DBSCAN and OPTICS. These kinds of processes may have lower performance in detecting the limit areas of the group.

Segmentation and clustering is not about just items and customers, but also a wide range of attributes. Besides item and customer, you can look at size, lead times, complexity in planning, revenue, inventory turns, COGS, market share, and channels, etc. A large number of segmentation methods are available. All identify similarities and differences in a data set—they differ in terms of how you get to the answer and how complex the process is.

Constraint-Based Clustering (Rule-Based Methods)

Constraint-Based Clustering: *A process for finding any classification scheme that makes use of IF-THEN rules and user-specified preferences or constraints to find and determine clusters.* It is the most common rule-based classification method.

As mentioned before, constraint-based methods—as we are describing them—are really a classification. That said, the outputs can be used to group data, and are widely used for segmentation like (ABC) type groupings. This approach first requires the defining of groups before you can segment like items or customers into them. It uses different means to divide a data set into parts, or segments, which are defined, meaningful, and ultimately reveal insight that is actionable.

Constraint-Based Clustering appears to be like clustering, but there is a difference between this and other clustering algorithms in the context of data mining. One difference between classification and clustering is that classification is used in supervised learning where predefined labels are assigned to instances according to their properties. Clustering, on the other hand, can be used in both supervised and unsupervised learning. In unsupervised learning, instances are grouped based on their features or properties.

For a constraint-based method, or what we can call a rule-based classifier, it separates observations into groups based on their characteristics and if/then logic where it splits data into separate groups if it meets a certain condition, i.e. IF (condition) = THEN (solution) . A rule-based system consists of two main components: a set of facts about a situation, and a set of rules for how to deal with those facts.

The set of facts are a combination of data, such as sales volume and a condition such as "is greater than **x**." The set of rules, also known as the rule's engine, describe the relationship between the IF condition and the THEN solution statements. For example, a rule might be "IF an item has volume above **x** THEN it is an '**a**' Item."

With these two basic concepts, it is possible to build a rule-based model to recommend the segmentation of products (or any other attribute in a data set) into two or more groups according to certain attributes. Machine learning algorithms or expert opinion can be used to determine the rules.

Most rule-based systems are typically built from the combined knowledge of humans who are experts in the given domain. The domain experts specify all the steps taken to make a decision and how to handle any special cases. This knowledge is then incorporated into the system.

Most common (ABC) type segmentations rely on this type of model along with expert opinion, and use a single dimension like annual sales volume or some other attribute. The items are then grouped in decreasing order based on the value of the attribute. The array can then be split into multiple segments based on rules and constraints. While this is usually three classifications (ABC), it can just as easily be two or four or ten if you would like that level of granularity.

Example: Consider a Pareto distribution of items based on their annual sales volume. For simplicity, you can segment by putting 80% of the value in the "**A**" items, 15% in the "**B**" items, and 5% in the "**C**" items.

As you can see in figure h, this works very well for a quick and easy Pareto analysis of any attribute, but what if you would like to add customer segmentation to an item or compare more than just one attribute? A common approach, still using rule-based segmentation, is to divide the attributes on an x- and y-axis and create constraints for each. Constraints may be binary, creating a 2x2 matrix or adding multiple combinations like 3x3 (9-box or ABC/XYZ).

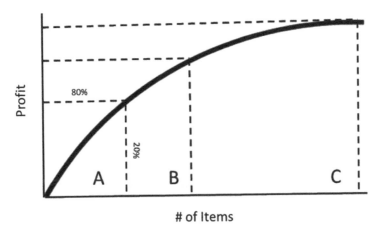

Fig h | Graph illustrating the Pareto Principle

Example: Identify the inherent variation of the item by checking its demand variation index (DVI) or the coefficient of variation (COV). Then, plot it along the x-axis. On the y-axis, classify forecast value added (FVA%) or a performance metric like MAPE. For our constraints, we could use whether it had a positive or negative FVA% on the x-axis and a constraint of greater or less than 68% demand variation on the y-axis.[38]

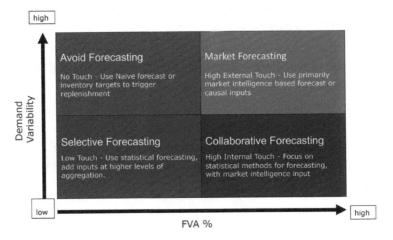

Fig i | Graph showing planning strategies based on defined parameters

More advanced learners can construct a classification model based on the training data received for classification. The model must first be committed to a single hypothesis or set of rules that covers the entire dataset before training occurs. Rule-based classification algorithms are an iterative process consisting of first generating a rule that covers a subset of the training examples and then removing all examples covered by the rule from the training set.

The data classification process involves learning first, then classifying. In learning, the training data are analyzed by a classification algorithm. In classification, test data are used to estimate the accuracy of the classification rules. If the accuracy is acceptable, the rules can be applied to the new data tuples. Due to the model construction, more advanced machine learners take a long time for training and less time to predict.

For any constraint-based model, descriptive modeling works to divide the data into groups that satisfy user-specified preferences; it does not predict a target value but focuses more on the intrinsic structure, relations, interconnectedness, etc., of the data. Many algorithms and data mining tools have been developed and implemented to extract information and discover knowledge patterns that prove to be advantageous for decision-making.

Pros and Cons of Constraint and Rule-Based

Pros: One of the key benefits of a rules system is that writing and implementing rules is quite easy and therefore easy to understand and explain as well. If we know about the area of interest, we can create rules based on simple IF-THEN statements.

Cons: Rule-based systems are deterministic. Not having the right rule in place can result in false positives and false negatives. Systems of rules can start off being quite simple but can become rather unwieldy over time as more and more exceptions and rule changes are added. Another challenge faced by rule-based systems is when the data and scenarios change faster than you can update the rules. You can reach a point when you lose track of what is going on and how many exceptions there are.

Types of Constraint and Rule-Based Methods

- Bayesian Classification
- Artificial Neural Networks
- Decision Tree
- Constrained K-Means
- Support Vector Machines (SVM)
- Classification Based on Association

Connectivity-Based Clustering (Hierarchical Clustering)

Connectivity-Based Clustering: *A statistical method for finding relatively homogeneous clusters of cases based on dissimilarities or distances between objects.* The most commonly used connectivity-based method is hierarchical clustering.

Connectivity-based clusters are based on the idea that objects are more related to nearby objects than those further away. It uses a statistical method for finding relatively homogeneous clusters of cases based on similarities and dissimilarities (or distances) between objects. Clusters are therefore developed based on the distance between objects in the data set.

This algorithm starts with all the data points being assigned to a cluster of their own. Then, the two nearest clusters are merged into the same cluster, continuing in this fashion until there is only a single cluster left. Another name for it is Hierarchical Clustering, which, as the name suggests, is an algorithm that builds a hierarchy of clusters. You can think of this, for example, as starting with 10,000 SKUs, each being its own individual cluster. It then will begin to combine the SKUs or clusters sequentially, reducing the number of clusters at each step until only the number of clusters you wish remains. Partitioning methods are very similar, but their starting point is one cluster and then splits cases into new clusters until a stopping criterion or the number of desired clusters is reached.

Hierarchical or connectivity-based clustering typically works by (1) identifying the two clusters that are closest together, and (2) sequentially merging the two most similar clusters. Then, it repeatedly executes those two steps; this continues until all the clusters are merged. This is known as agglomerative hierarchical clustering. Agglomerative clustering uses a bottom-up approach, wherein each data point starts in its own cluster.

In theory, it can also be done by initially grouping all the observations into one cluster, and then successively splitting these clusters. This is known as Divisive Hierarchical Clustering. Divisive Clustering uses a top-down approach, wherein all data points start in the same cluster. You can then use a parametric clustering algorithm like K-Means (which we will discuss shortly) to divide the cluster into two clusters. For each cluster, you further divide it down into two clusters until you hit the desired number of clusters.

The main output of Hierarchical Clustering is a visual snapshot known as a dendrogram, which shows the hierarchical relationship between the clusters.

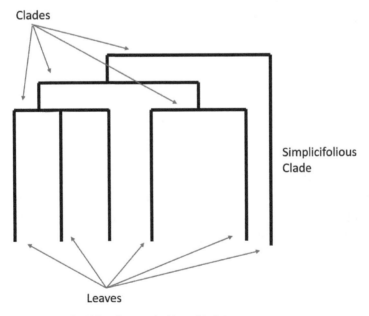

Fig j | Dendrogram for hierarchical clusters

Clades are the branches. Usually labeled with Greek letters from left to right (α β, δ, ...), each clade has one or more leaves. The leaves in the above image are:

- Single (simplicifolius): F
- Double (bifolius): D E
- Triple (trifolious): A B C

A clade can theoretically have an infinite amount of leaves. However, the more leaves you have, the harder the graph will be to read with the naked eye. The clades are arranged according to how similar (or dissimilar) they are. Clades that are close to the same height are like each other; clades with different heights are dissimilar—the greater the difference in height, the more dissimilarity.

To decide which objects/clusters should be combined or divided, we need methods for measuring the similarity between objects. You can measure similarity in many ways, including:

- Euclidean Distance: the "ordinary" straight-line distance between two points,
- Manhattan Distance: the distance between two points measured along axes at right angles,
- Pearson Correlation Distance: a number between -1 and 1 that indicates the extent to which two variables are linearly related,
- Spearman Distance: a ranking and number that shows how closely two sets of data are linked.

After selecting a distance metric, it is necessary to determine where distance is computed. For example, it can be computed between the two most similar parts of a cluster (single-linkage), the two least similar bits of a cluster (complete-linkage), the center of the clusters (mean or average-linkage), or some other criterion. Many linkage criteria have been developed.

Where there are no clear theoretical justifications for the choice of linkage criteria, Ward's method is the sensible default. This method works out which observations to group based on reducing the sum of squared distances of each observation from the average observation in a cluster. This concept of distance matches the standard assumptions of computing differences between groups in statistics (e.g., ANOVA, MANOVA).

Pros and Cons of Connectivity-Based Clustering

Pros: It is easy to use and works well on smaller data sets with which you are familiar. The dendrogram makes it easy to visualize and for others to follow. It also can be very helpful in creating smaller, manageable clusters and can produce an ordering of the objects, which can provide information in a visual way.

Cons: It does not work well with large data sets and data you are not familiar with. You can easily be misled by dendrograms and hierarchical clustering. Unless you know the data, you can be led astray if there are outliers. Also, as the data grow, so does the difficulty in managing and visualizing the clusters, and they quickly become unmanageable.

Types of Connectivity-Based Clustering

- Agglomerative Hierarchical Clustering (Agglomerative Nesting—AGNES)
- Divisive Hierarchical Clustering (DIANA)

Centroid-Based Clustering (K-Means)

Centroid-Based Clustering: *A statistical method for finding relatively homogeneous clusters of cases based on areas of higher density than the remainder of the data set. K-Means is the most common type.*

In contrast to hierarchical, centroid-based clustering organizes data into non-hierarchical clusters. Here, like with the K-Means method, it starts with the total number of clusters and calculates the mean of each cluster. It then goes through an iterative process to find out to which group a certain object really belongs.

K-Means

K-Means: *A common method used for centroid-based cluster and unsupervised learning algorithms that clusters n objects into k clusters, where each object belongs to a cluster with the nearest mean.*

In this method, we compute the distance of each point from each cluster by computing its distance from the corresponding cluster mean and assigning each point to the cluster nearest to it. The procedure repeats until the distance between cluster centers is maximized (when the sum of squared

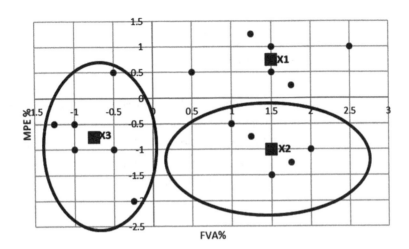

Fig k | Graph showing K-Means with 3 clusters and defined parameters

errors within the group cannot be lowered any more or another specified criterion is reached).

Example: Look at items using forecast value added (FVA%) and item bias using mean percentage error (MPE). Plotting them, "x" is the centroid of the clusters. The advantage here is, if we were to provide a rule that we needed a certain number of items in each segment or choose a constraint where the x- and y-axes separate, we get a very different result than we would if we allowed the statistical mean to calibrate the area of each cluster. After multiple iterations, it will group the like items based on various combinations of the two attributes in our example (FVA% and MPE) to find the optimal grouping of SKUs. You now have three groups of items based on two dimensions and similar planning attributes.

We can follow a simple procedure of classifying a given data set into several clusters, defined by "k," which is fixed beforehand. We first select several classes/groups to use and randomly initialize their respective center points. To figure out the number of classes to use, take a quick look at the data and try to identify any distinct groupings and place them as far away from each other as possible. The center points or vectors of each group or cluster are used to calculate the distance to each point and are the 'X's" in the graphic above (k=3).

The next step is to take every point belonging to the data set and associate it to the nearest vector or center. The clusters are then repositioned as points and all observations are associated with the nearest cluster. Each data point is classified by computing the distance between that point and each group center and then allocating the point to the group whose center is closest to it.

The K-Means clustering technique uses the mean (i.e., the centroid value) of a cluster, to represent that cluster. For example, if a cluster (X1) of data consisted of points (1.25, 1.25), (1.75, 0.25), (1.5, 1.5), (1.5, 1), (0.5, 0.5), and (2.5, 1), the sum of the values would be (9, 4.5). Divide the total by the number of members of the cluster, which in this example is 6. In the example above, 9 divided by 6 is 1.5, and 4.5 divided by 6 is 0.75, so the centroid (X1) of the cluster is (1.5, 0.75).

Based on these classified points, we re-compute the group center by taking the mean of all the vectors in the group. As a result of this loop, we may notice that the k centers change their location. Repeat these steps for a set number of iterations or until the group centroids have stabilized. The cluster is stabilized when the sum of the squared group errors has no change in its value. You can also opt to randomly initialize the group centers a few times, and then select the run that looks like it provided the best results.

The quality of the entire cluster can be measured by the cluster variation, which is the sum of squared error between all data points in a cluster and the centroid, defined as:

$$E = \sum_{i=1}^{k} \sum_{p \in C_i} dist(p, c_i)^2$$

where

E is the sum of the squared error for all data points in the data set,
p is the point in space representing a given data point, and
c_i is the mean of a cluster (both p and ci are multidimensional).

In other words, for each data point in each cluster, the distance from the data point to its cluster center is squared, and the distances are summed. This objective function tries to make the resulting k clusters as compact and as separate as possible from other clusters.

Pros and Cons of Centroid-Based Clustering

Pros: Centroid-based algorithms are efficient. K-Means, for example, has the advantage of being pretty fast to set up, as all we're really doing is computing the distances between points and group centers with very few computations. Another advantage of centroid-based methods is that it can scale to larger data sets relatively easily and easily adapts to new examples.

Cons: With K-Means you have to select how many groups/classes there are. This causes problems for clustering data when the number of clusters cannot be known beforehand. With any clustering algorithm, this too will be sensitive to outliers and centroids can be dragged by them and might end up with their own cluster if you are not careful. While this does scale with data, it does not scale as well with dimensions, and as the number of dimensions increases, a distance-based similarity measure converges to a constant value.

Types of Centroid-Based Clustering

- K-Means
- Clustering Large Application (CLARA)
- Generalized K-Harmonic Means
- Fuzzy C-Means

SPOTLIGHT

How Volvo Mobility Used Clustering to Improve Their Car Sharing Experience

We are in the heart of a tech boom that is upgrading every aspect of our lives. With our mobile smartphones, we now can stream music and movies, have anything delivered to our door without leaving our house, and even rent someone else's home for a weekend getaway. These services have permanently raised expectations in convenience, quality of experience, and the ability to feel and be productive.

Now you can even stream cars like you stream music. Today, over 50% of the world's population lives in cities. By 2050, that number will increase to over 70%. That's 2.5 billion more people than today. With that growth also comes increased demands on urban planning and public services—a lower need for privately owned vehicles but also a different way of thinking about and using space. Car-sharing services have bridged this gap and have eliminated the concerns of repairs and parking while adding the advantages of convenience, quality, and efficiency.

Rapidly changing technology, coupled with environmental concerns and urban space restrictions, is pressuring the traditional car-ownership model. Instead of forcing consumers to buy one vehicle for every driving need, car-sharing programs let customers select vehicles for specific occasions—an SUV when extended family is in town, a convertible for a weekend getaway or a compact for the downtown commute. Car-related services—much like music on demand or renting the designer dress just for a Friday night out—are changing to meet today's consumer needs.

One of the leaders in this emerging field is a new brand from Volvo Car Mobility they call "M," which is using predictive analytics and AI-related technologies to provide the best customer experience and revolutionize the car-sharing business. "Volvo Cars is becoming more than just a car company," CEO Håkan Samuelsson said in a statement. "We recognize that urban consumers are rethinking traditional car ownership. M is part of our answer."

Established in 2018, M is a wholly owned and standalone entity within Volvo Car Group that aspires to deliver a better alternative to car ownership for urban and metro consumers. M's mission is to enable more people to move freely, meaningfully, and sustainably. Its proprietary technology and analytics-led platform aim to advance a new generation of consumer mobility services that provide a more intuitive user experience.

Finding Connections

One of the biggest challenges for most car-sharing enterprises is matching the consumer needs to where the supply of vehicles may be. Doing this is about more than just balancing supply and demand—it's about clustering, classification, and the art of geospatial demand prediction. Nils Oppelstrup, COO of Volvo Car Mobility explains that they use proprietary machine learning technology to segment hubs, customer attributes, and needs to optimize utilization.

In their networks, they have consumers that can pick one of the thousands of vehicles from hundreds of different hubs at different times. M also takes into consideration customer preferences and external variables when allocating their supply of vehicles. To better understand and shuffle or relocate vehicles efficiently, they could not rely on biased assumptions. They found that, often, identifying clusters of activity was counterintuitive, and they could not predefine the number of segments. To overcome this, they utilized an affinity propagation matrix, which allows them to do cluster analysis without defining the number of clusters ahead of time (K). Also, it evaluated all the connections, with each data point sending messages to all other points informing its targets of each target's relative value.

Demand Sensing

Volvo also distinguishes its car-sharing service from competitors by focusing on how people use their cars. Their intuitive app is used to collect massive amounts of data and track users' specific needs and preferences. M then customizes the experience based on those data. The incoming demand gives them a real-time feed of desired location and time combinations.

Even though a lot of the journeys are spontaneous, Volvo experts can still use the intents to understand near-time demand and spot trends/behaviors. This means the app's data can predict where and when demand occurs and provide dependable access to cars. Using a data-informed approach and operational design to unlock the station-based model, it aims to deliver greater availability to more people, allowing a seamless service to customers.

Demand Shaping

In addition to segmenting supply and predictive analytics to enhance consumer experiences, Volvo also uses prescriptive analytics to optimize their ideal inventory. According to Nils Oppelstrup, "Looking at the utilization of our stations show that the hubs do their job in absorbing a lot of demand. Spokes get booked out first. However, this is a reactive measure. We want to get out in front of that."

K-Means clustering algorithms go a long way to doing this. It helps segment customers based on behaviors and other unclassified variables to find common denominators in the groups that have the best behaviors that may be micro-targeted. This helps them target users in specific areas, and batch invites based on response rate and supply capacity. By leading with analytics and using clustering algorithms like affinity propagation and K-Means, Volvo can reach close to 100% utilization, boost EBIT significantly, and allow for better service levels.

Summary— Finding Answers in Data

Finding answers in data is sometimes analogous to finding a needle in a haystack. The problem, though, may not be the size of the haystack or where the needle is buried, but in understanding the haystack itself. To truly find insights in data, we need processes, focus, and resources—and a culture to support these.

A 2014 study by McKinsey reported that a data-driven organization is 23 times more likely to outperform their competition. These findings showed marked improvements in customer acquisition, customer loyalty, and forecasting. As a result, according to the McKinsey study, data-driven organizations were 6.5 times as likely to retain the acquired customers, and finally 19 times as likely to be profitable as a result.[39]

Despite this, whether you call it data-driven or analytics-led, the truth is most companies continue to be data-starved and analytics-averse in their decision-making process. Less than 15% of businesses say their organization's culture supports data-driven decision-making—there is a clear disconnect.

We know that reliance on analytics to drive decisions has many benefits inside organizations:

- Decisions can be made based on evidence instead of gut feeling.
- Data analysis offers actionable insights into a variety of areas, both internally and externally.
- Data management provides a better signal for predictive analytics.
- Data-driven intelligence provides a competitive advantage.

Having a mound of data or even cutting-edge technology does not make a data-driven or analytics-led enterprise. To gain competitive advantage, we must harness the data to help generate insights and develop a culture that relies on and looks to data and predictive analytics to drive decisions. For executives, putting aside gut feelings and personal ideas of what the data is telling them is difficult, but one that will help their company make stronger decisions. Rather than competing against your instincts, good data and analytics is simply a better way to get more information and provide better insights.

Becoming more data- and analytics-driven needs to be a proactive exercise by you and the entire organization. To get there you should consider the five follow actions.

Start Collecting Data Today

Even if you may not be using the data today, consider what is available and what you can collect and store for later use. As you continue your journey, you may find new uses for data you currently hold or new technology can extract value from previously untapped data streams. If you want to use data to drive decision-making in future, you need to be collecting them now.

Focus on the Data You Can Use Now

Be careful when collecting data for data's sake. Find a way to highlight the important data of today. Wherever you're generating data—whether it's within internal databases or third-party cloud platforms—there are probably easy ways to organize your haystacks to find which ones you can look in today. You do not want your relevant data to be swimming in an ocean of irrelevant information that you do not need yet, rendering the task of analyzing it almost impossible. This means you have to tackle the root of the problem; collect data as they become available but work only with the data you need.

Automate Data Collection and Management Workloads

The return on investment is not in the data collection, storage, and retrieval but in the analysis and insights it can provide. Continual steps should be taken to automate the distillation of data-driven insights and the incorporation of those insights into business processes. Manual touchpoints throughout the data management life cycle impede many companies' ability to ingest, aggregate, store, process, analyze, consume, and otherwise make the most of their data resources. To fully optimize an analytics-led organization, you must automate as much as you can the pipeline of data so that it can focus on predictive analytics, strategic insights, and decision-making.

Don't Keep It to Yourself and Make Data Accessible

For data to make the journey to insights, it must be translated into a business process. To maximize its impact, data should not be restricted to only yourself and what you use. Rather, the goal should be to get good data out there where everyone can see, and into the hands of those on the front line. And to truly embed data into mainstream thinking and behavior, organizations need to look at how they can build data insights into business processes by default. If you have a good distribution system to manage and broadcast your data, the company can control what employees see and what information they have, without compromising the integrity or safety of the business intelligence.

Strive to Have A Data-Driven or Analytics-Led Culture

Once you start collecting data, sorting out what you can use now, finding the right people, and making data and information available to everyone, your organization can start to use analytics to drive decisions and validate strategies. I admit this is easier said than done, but the more a company allows data to influence their decisions (rather than gut feeling), the greater their competitive advantage. Not only will data analytics be increasingly validated by positive feedback on data-driven decisions, it will become a necessity to remain competitive.

Becoming data-driven involves more than technology and tools. It also requires a shift in the enterprise's mindset and culture. Culture plays a central role in setting expectations about the extent to which data are democratized, how data are viewed across the organization, and how they are positioned among the company's strategic assets. Companies who have incorporated data into their decision-making can step back from their personal feelings and understand what the data are telling them. They recognize that the insights and recommendations that the data hold can help them make stronger, more informed decisions that move the company in the right direction. As they get results, they can look back and see which strategies led to the best outcomes to improve decision making going forward.

Section Review

Multiple Choice: Identify the choice that best completes the statement or answers the question.

1. A data set is generally explained as:

    a) Only what is used to train machine learning algorithms.
    b) An organized stream of information.
    c) The final product or label.
    d) A collection of features.

2. The number of people that clicked on a product on your website is an example of:

    a) Internal structured data.
    b) External structured data.
    c) Internal unstructured data.
    d) External unstructured data.

3. To be big data, it must:

    a) Be greater than a terabyte of data.
    b) Have a latency closer to real-time.
    c) Be unstructured and external.
    d) None of the above.

4. Which of these are NOT data mining techniques?

    a) Classification and predicting the target class using observed values.
    b) Visualizing data into graphs and charts.
    c) Predictive analytics.
    d) Finding associations between two or more variables.

5. A clustering technique where you sort objects into a pre-determined set of clusters based on a mean is an example of:

    a) Centroid-Based.
    b) Distribution-Based.
    c) Rule-Based.
    d) Constraint-Based.

True or False

6. ☐ To do predictive analytics, you must first do some type of data mining.

7. ☐ Unstructured data are data that are external to the planning system.

8. ☐ Big data is relative to a company and its ability to store and process it.

9. ☐ Having more data is always better for predictive analytics so models can learn.

10. ☐ A dendrogram can be used to visualize Connectivity-Based Clustering.

PART IV
PREDICTIVE ANALYTICS AS AN APPROACH

After reading this section, you should be able to:

- Explain the differences and advantages of different classes of business forecasting methods.
- Understand the concepts and uses of Bayes' Theorem.
- Describe how Logistic Regression is used and how it may enable Artificial Neural Networks.
- List the main components of decision trees and why and how to prune models.
- Give insights into deep learning and the future of AI in business forecasting.

Consumer-Driven Forecasting

Over the last few years, for many organizations, analytics has become the top priority and area for investment due to recognition of its growing importance. Business executives, as well as Forecast Analysts and Demand Planners, are tasked with leading these improvements and the next generation of analytics that can support the current and future needs of their organization. This includes building processes and methods that utilize descriptive and diagnostic analytics such as end-to-end visibility, reporting, and dashboards. The competency must also span predictive capabilities, such as anticipating and even influencing future demand. The sheer amount and complexity of today's data are challenging enough, but we must turn this data into useful insights quicker for better decision-making.

Predictive analytics is gaining importance day-by-day as it helps to identify opportunities and threats and gives early warning signals. It is a proactive approach to managing a business in this dynamic and complex environment. Predictive analytics comes with new ways to view group data, new approaches to understand demand drivers, and new methods to model and predict outcomes and probabilities. In today's environment of big data, it is very important to embed predictive analysis as an integral part of business processing and decision-making.

Recent improvements in data storage and technology have reached an inflection point, addressing key challenges of implementing consumer-driven forecasting. The amount and diversity of information (structured and unstructured) are exploding. Turning data into information and then into action is difficult but it is becoming more important as each day passes. Companies need to evolve and integrate into their businesses a new breed of talent to deploy new models and technologies—they cannot just cobble together existing pieces. They need a revolution in how they use predictive analytics approaches and methods.

The Predictive Analytics Toolbox

Abraham Maslow said, "If all you have is a hammer, everything looks like a nail." The meaning is simple—if we have only one way to do things (hammer), then we might think all problems (nails) have the same tool (hammer). Therefore, we always choose the hammer even if the problem needs a totally different kind of solution. The lesson learned from this is to understand that different problems require different techniques—not just one way, not just one tool.

Broadly speaking, there are two approaches to demand forecasting. One is to obtain information or make assumptions about the likely purchase behavior of the buyer; the other is to obtain information or make assumptions about patterns of past purchases. This is not to imply that there are only two tools the Demand Planner can use. There is a wide variety of models that come from an assortment of techniques and that fall under a mixture of different comprehensive classes of methods. All these techniques are available to Demand Planners, all of which rely to varying degrees on judgment and statistics.

Unfortunately, many people see every data point as another nail and limit what tools they use when developing a new forecast. For some executives and salespeople, their approach is simply based on

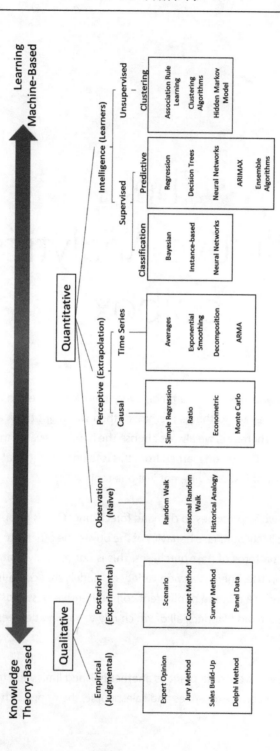

Fig 1 | Infographic of classes of methods and types of models

what they did last year. For others, it is looking at averages or smoothing techniques and only looking at the past. Others neglect the past and only look at the data's relationship with other variables, therefore neglecting the independence of what they are forecasting. Still others even try to teach or train the models to no longer depend on judgment at all, assuming more sophisticated techniques must be better.

The truth is that data come in all types and volumes—and the applications of data insight are just as vast. Data may be cross-sectional or time-series, and stationary or non-stationary. Insights may be for classification, clustering, or prediction and can be used for different time horizons. One size does not fit all, nor is one method the right tool for every demand planning and predictive analytics problem. We need to understand all the tools we have at our disposal and how each one can be used.

Classifying Business Forecasting Methods

There are many different criteria we could have used to classify the different types of methods, but the use of knowledge and how the algorithms gain information provide the best visualization of what is available. Below are the broad categories of methods arranged according to how they use data, how much knowledge they rely on internally or externally, and what they do with the information they have. As you can see in Fig I, the far left comprises pure qualitative and human opinion and progresses right to almost pure quantitative and machine-based methods. Keep in mind that every method serves a purpose.

Knowledge (Theory-Based) Methods

A theory is a supposition, or a system of ideas intended to explain something. This includes most qualitative approaches including judgmental and experimental models. Knowledge-based forecasts use qualitative or subjective inputs to generate a prediction of the future. They rely on the opinions of experts, people's experiences, judgment, intuition, or just plain guesses. These techniques are often used when no other data are available, or information is unknown to statistical data sets.

While there are concerns that judgmental approaches and methods in forecasting can be less accurate, add bias, and are a poor method for developing a robust demand plan, they still have merit and a place in our toolbox. Not only do we need to understand them because they are already being widely used, they also can add value with the right input from the right people in the right method. Often, Sales and Marketing people have valuable information about sales promotions, new products, competitor activity, and so forth, which should be incorporated into the forecast.

Knowledge methods:

- Take less (or no) data, less skill, but come with less accuracy.
- Can be used when little or no historical data are available, like with new product forecasting.
- Can be good if lots of tribal knowledge or seasoned experience is available.
- Involve lots of potential bias.

Deductive Logic (Numerical-Based) Methods

While qualitative forecasting methods rely on the judgment of experts, quantitative techniques like causal and time-series methods rely on mathematical models and data. As opposed to opinion and gut feelings, these methods use correlation and objective logic. These techniques rely on predefined models and data sets to replicate patterns or relationships that the model uses to predict a future point or relationship. Adding quantitative forecasting tools helps temper enthusiasm or flat-out "wishcasts" or guestimates. It also statistically provides more insights into the inherent expected variability and a truer picture of consumer influences as well as historic trend, seasonality, and impact of external events.

Time Series Models: *A collection of values observed sequentially over time and used to perform time-based predictions.* Here, one needs only the data of a series to be forecasted. Forecasts are generated by extrapolating the data from the past into the future. Data may have different amounts of level (or stationarity), trend, seasonality or cycles, and noise. For business forecasting, time-series models are the most commonly used of all models. For this reason, and for their ability to forecast off the companies own historical data, they are a staple for anyone in demand planning or business forecasting. These are great techniques to learn for anyone new to the field.

A Causal Model: *A collection of values observed cross-functionally and based on cause-and-effect relationships.* The assumption behind a causal or relational model is that, simply put, there is a reason why people buy our product or why **x** moves similarly when **y** occurs. If we can understand what that reason (or set of reasons) is, we can use that understanding to develop a demand forecast. With forecasting and predictive analytics being used increasingly for decision-making purposes inside organizations, understanding casual models and the relationship of variables has become much more important. With this type of analysis and the right data, we can uncover consumer sentiment, plan eCommerce business more efficiently, and provide insights to others on drivers and variables that impact the business.

Deductive logic methods:

- Require only a moderate amount of data, moderate skills, or some statistical knowledge, and can provide good results with the right variables and modeling.
- Work best when strong relationships between variables are stable or known.
- Can show a large degree of variability over longer forecast horizons.
- Do not perform well with new products or items with little historical data.

Inductive Learner (Machine-Based) Methods

Up until this point, we would forecast based either on what we thought (qualitative) or what the data thought (quantitative). Either way, the forecast would be generated on its own merits each time from the data set or using judgement without past iterations. Whether we're forecasting qualitatively or quantitively, we are solving the problem for the first time every time we forecast.

Machine Learning: *An algorithm or technique that enables systems to be "trained" and to learn patterns from inputs and subsequently recalibrate from experience without being explicitly programed.* A machine learning algorithm differs in that it will take information from the previous iteration or training data set and apply it to help build the current or future model. Another way to think about the difference is to consider learning algorithms as employing inductive logic where it starts with observations and arrives at general conclusions.

Many of these models use labels and features or input variables. We have used the term "feature" a few times and it comes up a lot in machine learning. **Feature:** *An individual measurable property of a characteristic that is being observed.* This can be any predictor variable or attribute data. Feature engineering, which means building and filtering features, is what powers most machine learning algorithms.

The training data always contain the answer or target. In machine learning a **label** is: *The target or final* *output in a machine learning model.* You can also consider the output classes to be the labels. When data scientists speak of labeled data, they mean groups of samples that have been tagged with one or more labels.

Once the model gets trained, it can start making a prediction or decision when new data is given to it. This can be used for clustering, classification problems, or predictive analytics. These models are opening up new opportunities and insights and Demand Planners are starting to add them to their toolbox. By using these techniques and algorithms, the models can teach us new things and provide more precise forecasts once it learns patterns in data.

Inductive learner methods:

- Require a lot of data and more advanced skills, and can produce good results,
- Handle multi-dimensional and multi-variety data in dynamic environments,
- May not have the ability to derive confidence intervals prior to being put into production, and
- Will help us keep pace with the planning of tomorrow as data get bigger and problems become more complex.

Advanced Statistical Methods and Data Models

The objective of advanced statistical techniques such as those in Inductive Learner Methods (machine learning) is similar to many of the traditional approaches we use today. Our primary goal in forecasting, no matter how we do it, should be to create the most accurate forecast with the lowest error and bias. The difference comes in how much and what kind of data we may have, and what kind of algorithms and systems we are using. Hopefully, these will assist us to generate better results more efficiently.

As interest in AI has risen, machine learning and more advanced methods have gained prominence. These methods are now being used to predict financial series, the direction of the stock market, and macroeconomic variables. Some of them are even applicable to playing and winning at AlphaGo (the Chinese abstract strategy board game won by Google's AI technology in 2016).[40] In the fields of demand planning and business forecasting, planners are adopting many advanced methods with the goals of identifying less obvious interactions between variables and building more accurate models with a greater number of features.

These models are not always the panacea for automatically improving forecasting accuracy. Typically, they are computationally more demanding than traditional models. As such, they require greater dependence on technical skillsets to be implemented, placing them at the intersection of statistics and computer science. Without any base knowledge or being completely dependent on a system, these models can easily generate implausible solutions, leading to exaggerated claims of their potential. Finally, for some businesses, there may be a security risk that needs to be taken into consideration. Security is less of a risk now, but it will become a concern because more and more information is being put into the Cloud and processes are becoming increasingly automated, making data more vulnerable to hacking.

This simply means you should be careful, understand the basics that go into these models, and investigate further before jumping in too far and accepting a more advanced model as the solution to your forecasting problems. On the other end of the spectrum, in a business environment marked by rapid change and economic uncertainty, maintaining the status quo regarding forecasting is not a viable option if you are to remain competitive.

For Demand Planners seeking to stay ahead and improve their forecast accuracy and process, machine learning and other advanced techniques present an opportunity. First and foremost, if implemented well, these methods can significantly improve the accuracy of forecasts. These tools can also be leveraged to automate forecasting models and perform computations on large data sets at high speeds. By automating the labor-intensive components of forecasting and improving predictions, planners can focus on activities that yield a higher return and bring more value to the process.

As the next generation of Demand Planners, we have a responsibility to better understand what tools we have available. This requires a stronger grasp of the basic concepts underlining common machine learning and advanced forecasting techniques. While we will not go into great technical detail or attempt to make you an expert data scientist, we will try to aid your understanding and provide an overview of some of the most-utilized methods. This will help you grasp the purpose and potential of each and, hopefully, develop your thirst to learn more deeply about some of these methods on your own.

Machine learning tools and advanced statistical methods greatly enhance the volume and types of data that can be used because they can hold more data and compute those data faster than humans. Frequently used models and techniques in business forecasting include:

- Bayesian networks,
- Logistic and non-linear regression,
- Artificial neural networks,
- Decision trees,
- Radiant boosting, and
- ARIMA and ARIMAX.

Many of these methods can be configured to collect and reconcile very large data sets in an automated fashion. Moreover, they can help to determine business drivers and greatly reduce forecast error. Using these techniques to produce at least a baseline forecast can help planners move away from mundane tasks and focus on understanding forecast drivers, key business events, and microeconomic indicators and macroeconomic factors that may impact the business. Ultimately, understanding and leveraging these and other models can produce more insights and better support business decision-making.

As companies are relying more and more on the data they collect, it is no surprise that data-powered, automated systems are replacing traditional methods. Using advanced modeling in demand prediction is enabling a wide range of companies to leverage machine learning models in data exploration and extrapolation.

Machine learning algorithms are designed to learn from the data and predict which drivers have the greatest impact on financial performance. Over time, the model becomes more accurate and produces forecasts more quickly. If there is enough data to train a model, it is almost certain to outperform human data analysts and researchers.

The variety of algorithms provides a range of options for solving problems, and each algorithm will have different requirements and tradeoffs in terms of data input requirements, speed of performance, and accuracy of results. We will review just a few, providing a high-level overview of what goes into them, how they work, and how they may be used.

Naïve Bayes

Bayesian (Generative Learning Model): *A class of supervised learning methods that explicitly apply Bayes' Theorem for problems such as classification and regression. It is a classification technique with an assumption of independence among predictors.*

When it comes to machine learning and supervised learning techniques, we can achieve excellent results using simple methods and models. Much like a random walk method or naïve time-series forecast, the Naïve Bayes is overlooked and underestimated. A Naïve Bayesian model is easy to build and doesn't require complicated iterative parameter estimation that makes it computationally more efficient and, therefore, suitable for very large data sets if there are resource constraints. Despite its simplicity, the Naïve Bayes often does surprisingly well and often outperforms more sophisticated methods.

What is Naïve Bayes?

Naïve Bayes is a family of probabilistic algorithms that take advantage of probability theory and Bayes' Theorem. It predicts the class or value for problems such as classification and, with some modifications, regression. They are probabilistic, which means that they calculate the probability of each class for a given set of features, and then output the class with the highest observed probability in the data set. In simple terms, Naïve Bayes assumes that the presence of a particular feature in a class is unrelated to the presence of any other feature. Even if these features depend on each other or upon the existence of the other features, the assumption is that all of these properties contribute independently to the probability.

For example, a person may be considered a potential customer **(c)** if they are female **(x1)** between 25 and 44-years old **(x2)** and live within a 40-mile radius of your store **(x3)**. Even if these features depend on each other or upon the existence of the other features, these properties independently contribute to the probability that these people may be customers and that is why it is known as "Naïve." These probabilities are calculated using Bayes' Theorem, which describes the probability of a feature, based on prior knowledge of conditions that might be related to that feature.

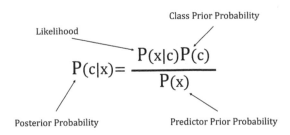

$$P(c|x) = P(x_1|c) \times P(x_2|c) \ldots P(xn|c) \times P(c)$$

Above,[41]

> **P(c|x)** is the probability of hypothesis target **(c)** given the attribute **(x)**, known as the posterior probability.
> **P(c)** is the probability of hypothesis **x** being true (regardless of the data), known as the class prior probability of the posterior.
> **P(x|c)** is the probability of **x** given that the hypothesis **c** was true, known as the likelihood or the probability of predictor given class.
> **P(x)** is the probability of **(x)** (regardless of the hypothesis), known as the predictor prior probability.

Let's explore this by using the following hypothetical example. The "gender" attribute has the values "female" and "male" and the target is whether or not they make a purchase, i.e., "yes" and "no." The conditional probabilities of each gender value for each class value can be calculated using the following steps.

Gender	Purchase
male	no
female	yes
female	no
male	no
female	yes
male	yes
female	no
female	yes
male	no
female	no

Fig m | Table data set of frequency

Start by converting the data set into a frequency table.

These frequencies can be converted into a likelihood table by determining the probabilities of each class and predictor. For example, "female" probability is 6/10 or 0.60 and probability of purchasing "yes" is 4/10 or 0.40.

Now, we use the Naïve Bayesian equation to calculate the posterior probability for each class. The class with the highest posterior probability is the outcome of prediction.

We can then address specific problems or hypotheses, such as: Females have a higher probability of purchasing than males. Is this statement correct?

We can solve this using the method of posterior probability described above.

	yes	no	Likelihood
male	1	3	0.4
female	3	3	0.6
Likelihood	0.4	0.6	

Fig n | Table data set converted into likelihood

P(yes|female) = (**P**(female|yes) * **P**(yes)) / **P** (female)
We know that **P**(female|yes) = 3/4 = 0.75, P(yes) = 4/10 = 0.40, and **P**(female) = 6/10 = 0.60.
Therefore, **P**(yes|female) = (0.75* 0.40) / 0.60 = 0.5 or 1/2.

And we can compare this with the probability of males purchasing:

P(yes|male) = (**P**(male|yes) * **P**(yes)) / **P**(male)
= (0/25*0.4)/0.4
= 0.25 or 1/4.

Therefore, we can conclude that, at least in this data set, females are more likely to purchase than males.

With a Naïve Bayes model, we can now start to make predictions for new data. By adding more data and features, we may get a more accurate probability of a female living within 40 miles from the store and who is between 25 and 44 years old purchasing something within the next year.

Pros and Cons of Naïve Bayes

Pros: Naïve Bayes is easy to build, quick to deploy, and performs well as a classifier. As a matter of fact, when assumption of independence holds, a Naïve Bayes classifier performs better compared to other models such as logistic regression with less training data. Finally, it performs very well in the case of categorical input variables compared to numerical variable(s).

Cons: It can be oversimplified, can produce bad estimations of true probability, and it requires you to understand the independent predictors. But more to the point, Naïve Bayes is based on these independent predictors and in practical applications it is almost impossible to get a set of predictors that are completely independent, especially in large data sets with many features.

Applications of Naïve Bayes Algorithms

- Classification: It is widely used to determine if an incoming email is spam or not spam. In addition, it may be used to classify a news article about technology, politics, or sports.

- Association: This can be like sentiment or customer analysis. Returning to our example of female purchasing, association may also be used to check for positive or negative interactions in text or responses.
- Factor analysis and probabilities: It builds a recommendation system that uses probabilities and information to predict whether someone will click on a link or buy something.
- Prediction: As a classifier, it can learn fast and be used for making near real-time predictions.
- Multi-Class Prediction: This algorithm is well-known as a multi-class prediction feature and can predict the probability of multiple classes of a target variable.

Types of Bayes Models

- Naïve Bayes
- Gaussian Naïve Bayes
- Multinomial Naïve Bayes
- Averaged One-Dependence Estimators (AODE)
- Bayesian Belief Network (BBN)
- Bayesian Network (BN)

Regression

Regression: *A class of cause-and-effect models, where the first relationship between cause (independent variable) and effect (dependent variable) is determined, which then is used to prepare a forecast.*

Regressions are the workhorse of predictive analytics and demand planning and have been co-opted into machine learning. Regression modeling is a powerful and remarkably simple method that is very useful for displaying relationships between variables or predicting outputs that are continuous in nature. This is usually the first type of method mastered by Demand Planners and can even be done quite easily in Excel. For Demand Planners who not only want to predict demand but better understand its drivers, regression is an important tool and a dependable performer in your machine learning toolbox.

What is Regression?

Regression is a simple cause-and-effect modeling that also can be a machine learning technique that investigates the relationship between dependent (target) and independent variables (predictor). Regression can be used to build or train models (mathematical structure or equation) for solving both supervised learning problems related to predicting numerical (regression) or categorical (classification) values, as seen in logistic regression. It is concerned with modeling the relationship between variables that are iteratively refined using a measure of error in the predictions made by the model.

Because regression is a key model in advanced business forecasting, it is highly recommended that you go beyond what is explained here to understand more of how it works. Along with the other models, this is a high-level overview. Regression is comprised of many details not covered here that you should be familiar with such as F-statistics, Durbin-Watson, T-test, and other important statistics measures.

Linear Regression

Regression models come in all types and applications. One of the most common is a simple Ordinary Least Squares (OLS) method. **Ordinary Least Squares (OLS):** *An estimation method that minimizes the sum of squared residuals to arrive at the best model.* It is most often used in regression because of its statistical properties. The first step in finding a linear regression equation is to determine if there is a relationship between the two variables. This is often a judgment call for the Demand Planner.

Let us look at an example using the following data set where the attribute **x** is the input variable or the temperatures on different days and **y** is the output variable or the amount of cold soft drinks that were sold.

Be careful. Just because two variables are related, it does not mean that one causes the other. This is the classic correlation does not equal causation discussion and should always be at the back of your

	X (temp)	Y (sales)
day 1	72	295
day 2	75	308
day 3	80	314
day 4	78	317
day 5	82	324
day 6	84	329
day 7	85	335
day 8	88	339
day 9	90	346
day 10	92	352

Table 0 | Sample data set

mind. Second, if you attempt to find a linear regression equation for a set of data (especially through an automated program like Excel), chances are you will find one even if one does not exist. Simply finding a regression equation does not necessarily mean the equation is a good fit for your data. One useful technique is to make a scatter plot first to see if the data roughly fit a line before you try to find a linear regression equation.

Let's go back to our example where our table represents selling cold soft drinks and you would like to see the correlation of one degree of temperature increase to the sales of your product. Linear Regression establishes a relationship between a dependent variable (temperature) and one or more independent variables (sales) using a best fit straight line (also known as regression line).

As we can observe, there is a very strong correlation and you discover that there are constant sales of about 104 units, and for every 1-degree increase of temperature there is a 2.68 unit increase in sales.

This can be represented by the following equation:

Y=a+bX

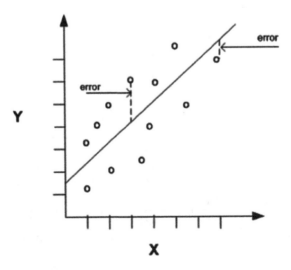

Table p | Graph depicting regression

(**Y**) is the variable you wish to predict
(**a**) is intercept or constant
(**b**) is slope of the line or regression coefficient
(**X**) is the predictor or independent variable

To compute the values of **a** or **b**, the formulas are:

$$a = \frac{(\Sigma y)(\Sigma x^2) - (\Sigma x)(\Sigma xy)}{n(\Sigma x^2) - (\Sigma x)^2}$$

$$b = \frac{n(\Sigma xy) - (\Sigma x)(\Sigma y)}{n(\Sigma x^2) - (\Sigma x)^2}$$

There is another way to look at this. For starters, we could make a chart of your data, filling in the columns with **X*Y, X^2**, and **Y^2** values for each observation and then sum your columns.[42]

From the above table, $\Sigma(X) = 826$, $\Sigma(Y) = 3,260$, $\Sigma(XY) = 270,289$, $\Sigma(X^2) = 68,606$, $\Sigma(Y^2) = 1,065,476$, and n is the sample size (10, in our case).

	X (temp)	Y (sales)	XY	X^2	Y^2
day 1	72	295	21,240	5,184	87,025
day 2	75	308	23,111	5,625	94,956
day 3	80	314	25,158	6,400	98,898
day 4	78	317	24,697	6,084	100,255
day 5	82	324	26,594	6,724	105,183
day 6	84	329	27,619	7,056	108,109
day 7	85	335	28,434	7,225	111,904
day 8	88	339	29,845	7,744	115,023
day 9	90	346	31,169	8,100	119,938
day 10	92	352	32,421	8,464	124,186
	826	3,260	270,289	68,606	1,065,476
	Σ(X)	Σ(Y)	Σ(XY)	Σ(X^2)	Σ(Y^2)

Fig q | Table of sample data set with sum of squares

The next step is using the formula equation to find your **a** and **b** values

Find **a**:

((3260 × 68606) − ((826 × 270289)) / 10 (68606) − 826^2) = 396846 / 3784

=104.8747

This is our constant or intercept and is the expected mean value or height of the regression line when **X**=0

Find **b**:

(10(270289) − (826 × 3260)) / (10 (68606) − 826^2) = 10130/3784

= 2.677

This is the slope of our regression line and it demonstrates that for every 1-unit change in temperature, we will increase sales by 2.677 units.

Now going back to our regression formula, we now have a regression predictive model which is:

Y=intercept+slope(**X**)
Y=104.8747+2.677(**X**)

Using this, we can estimate that for the next observation, which will theoretically have a temperature of 87 degrees, we can then predict that sales will be approximately 338 units.

337.77=104.8747+2.677(87)

Pros and Cons of Regression

Pros: It is easy to build a model (or process) and easy to interpret the results. Regression modeling can work with almost any size data set and is useful if you want it to be quickly incorporated into the model. The method can help determine which factors matter the most, which it can ignore, and how those factors interact with each other. Regression works best for cases where features are expected to be roughly linear, and the problem to be linearly separable.

Cons: Much like Naïve Bayes, regression assumes that data are independent, which may not always be the case. If observations are related to one another, then the model will tend to overweight the significance of those observations. Another con is that these methods may be highly sensitive to outliers in the data set. Finally, with these methods it is assumed that the cause-and-effect relationship between the variables remains unchanged and is linear, which may not always be the case. To achieve this, you may have to transform your feature set with logarithmic or other mathematical functions.

Applications of Regression Algorithms

- Factor Analysis: This is widely used to determine if two or more variables are related and to better understand what happened and potential influencers.
- Regression: Finds and tests relations and correlations between variables and then simulates outcomes based on adjustments to the variables to create what-if scenarios.
- Association: Analyzes risk and some models can be used to interpret probabilities of outcomes.
- Classification: Logistic regression can be used to solve problems of classification.
- Prediction: Can go far beyond forecasting impact on sales. For example, we can forecast the number of shoppers who will click a link or better understand demand drivers.
- Descriptive Analysis: It may be used to understand error and relationships for ensemble modeling and, when there are one or more inputs, you can use a process of optimizing the values of the coefficients by iteratively minimizing the error of the model.

Types of Regression Models

- Ordinary Least Squares Regression (OLSR)
- Logistic and Probit Regression
- Polynomial Regression
- Stepwise Regression
- Lasso Regression
- Multivariate Adaptive Regression Splines (MARS)
- Locally Estimated Scatterplot Smoothing (LOESS)

Logistic Regression

Logistic Regression: *A statistical method used to model a binary dependent variable that may determine the probability of a certain class or event existing.*

Simple linear regression is important, but there are many other types of regression that we must understand as well. In fact, there are a dozen or more types of regression algorithms designed for various types of analysis. Each type has its own applications and it is important to choose the best technique based on the type of independent and dependent variables, dimensionality and other characteristics of the data, and the purpose of the analysis.

The most basic variation of what we already reviewed with the linear regression is adding additional independent variables. Multiple linear regression shows the relationship between one dependent variable and one or more independent variables. Basically, everything you know about the simple linear regression modeling extends (with a slight modification) to the multiple linear regression models. The major difference between simple linear regression and multiple linear regression is that multiple linear regression has more than one independent variable, whereas simple linear regression has only one independent variable.

There are other regression models as well. If you need a non-linear model there is Polynomial Regression; to help minimize overfitting, there are models such as Ridge and LASSO Regression; and if you need to model multiple independent variables, you can use Stepwise Regression. If, for example, you want to predict if an image is of a cat or where the dependent variable is categorical (only specific values or categories are allowed), you can use Logistic Regression.

Logistic Regression is a foundational model that is used frequently in machine learning algorithms to help answer probability types of questions. While it is listed as a type of regression model, it is less a calculation and more an iterative process. This can be used for anything from predicting failures to identifying if the object in a picture is a cat or not. It works by modeling the probability of a certain class or event such as sale or no sale, win or lose, working or failure, etc.

Just as in simple linear regression, with logistic regression we look at the relationship between an independent variable and a dependent variable. Much like other regression models, the input values (**x**) are combined linearly using weights or coefficient values to predict an output value (**y**). A big difference with Binary Logistic Regression is that the dependent variable is a binary value (0/1) rather than a numeric value.

Below are sample example logistic regression equations:[43]

$$\ln[p/(1-p)] = a + bX$$

or

$$[p/(1-p)] = \exp(a + bX)$$

where

(**ln**) is the natural logarithm
(**p**) is the probability that the event occurs (0-1)
p/(1-**p**) is the "odds ratio"
ln[**p**/(1-**p**)] is the log odds ratio, or "logit"

All other components of the model are the same as we had in our simple linear regression model.

The logistic regression model is simply a non-linear transformation of the linear regression. The "logistic" distribution is an S-shaped distribution function (called a sigmoid curve), which is similar to the standard-normal distribution that results in a probit regression model.

The estimated coefficients must be interpreted with care. Instead of the slope coefficients (**b**) being the rate of change in **y** (the dependent variables) as **x** changes, as in our simple linear regression model, now the slope coefficient is interpreted as the rate of change in the "log odds" as **x** changes. Another way of possibly looking at logistic regression is as linear regression when the outcome variable is categorical and where we are using log odds as a dependent variable. In simple words, it predicts the probability of occurrence of an event by fitting data to a logit function.

Probability of occurrence is just another way of saying, "the odds of it occurring." Consider that the odds ratio, as the name suggests, is the ratio of two odds. For example, let's say we want to measure the difference between men and women when clicking on a website link. Let's say that 75% of the women and 60% of the men click the link.

>Odds=**P**(event)/[1-**P**(event)]

or

>women clicking = .75 / (1-.75) =3
>men clicking = .6 / (1 - .6) = 1.5

Using the probability of occurrence, we learn that the odds are two to one that women will click the link as compared with men. The odds ratio would be 3/1.5 = 2, meaning that the odds are 2 to 1 that a woman will click the link compared to men.

Another term that may need some explaining is log odds, also known as logit. Log odds are the natural logarithm of the odds. The coefficients in the output of the logistic regression are given in units of log odds. Therefore, the coefficients indicate the amount of change expected in the log odds when there is a one-unit change in the predictor variable with all other variables in the model held constant.

Finally, the coefficients (Beta values **b**) of a logistic regression algorithm can be estimated from your training data using maximum-likelihood estimation.[44] **Maximum Likelihood Estimation:** *A method that determines values for the parameters of a model.* The maximum-likelihood estimation is a "likelihood" maximization method, whereas ordinary least squares are a distance-minimizing approximation method. Maximizing the likelihood function determines the parameters that are most likely to produce the observed data in such a way that it maximizes the Probability of **y** given **x** (likelihood). With this estimation, the algorithm uses different "iterations" in which it tries different solutions until it gets the maximum likelihood estimates.

The Logistic Regression model is most commonly used as a classifier and is the go-to method for binary classification problems. It may also be used as a predictor by simply using the probabilities of an event as your outcome. As an example, with categorical data of time spent on your website and if the person clicks a link or does not click, we can use the same formula to estimate the probability of a person who spends less than 20 seconds on the site clicking: **y**=0.045. The closer to zero, the lower the likelihood, and conversely the closer to 1 the greater the likelihood.

In practice we can use the probabilities directly. Because this is classification and we want a crisp answer, we can snap the probabilities to a binary class value or discrimination threshold; for example, less than .5 is 'will not click' and greater than .5 is 'may click'. Obviously 0.045 is much less than .5. We can predict that people 'will not click' and will not make a purchase if that is the maximum time they are spending on your site.

Pros and Cons of Logistic Regression

Pros: It's a widely used technique because it's very efficient and doesn't require too many computational resources. It doesn't require input features to be scaled or normalized and it does not require any tuning. Finally, it can be implemented easily and quickly. Because of its simplicity and the fact that it can be implemented relatively easily and quickly, logistic regression is a good baseline that can be used to measure the performance of other more complex algorithms.

Cons: Logistic Regression is not one of the most powerful algorithms available. Many times, more complex algorithms can easily outperform these models. Logistic regression will not perform well with independent variables that are not correlated to the target variable or are very similar, or correlated, to each other. Last of all, non-linear problems can't be solved because its decision surface is linear.

Applications of Logistic Regression Algorithms

- Classifier: The Logistic Regression model is most commonly used as a classifier. It is the go-to method for binary classification problems.
- Association: It works to help remove attributes that are unrelated to the output variable as well as attributes that are very similar (or correlated) to each other.
- Factor Analysis: It uses the probability of occurrences to predict whether someone may click on a link or buy something.
- Prediction: It may also be used as a predictor by simply using the probabilities of an event as your outcome. As an example, it can be used with categorical data to identify relationships between the amount of time spent on a website and the frequency of somebody clicking or not clicking a link. We can then make predictions about somebody clicking the link based on how much time is spent on the site.

Artificial Neural Networks

Artificial Neural Network (ANN): *A class of supervised learning and pattern matching methods and a computational model based on the structure and functions of biological neural networks.* Information that flows through the network consists of units (neurons), arranged in layers, that convert an input vector into some output.

An artificial neural network is loosely modeled on the neuronal structure of the mammalian cerebral cortex. It is patterned off the way scientists believe we as humans learn, and simulates the network of neurons that make up the brain but on a much smaller scale—hence its name.

In a typical artificial neural network, the information flows in only one direction and even with increased computer processing power, consists of just a few hundred neurons. Compare this to the human brain, which has billions and billions of neurons. Despite the smaller scale, these models can be very powerful when it comes to processing nonlinear relationships between inputs. Just like a human brain, the outputs are generated in just seconds with the right system.[45]

What Is an Artificial Neural Network?

Artificial Neural Networks (ANN) are a class of pattern matching techniques inspired by the structure of biological neural networks. The models comprise basic elements, called neurons, that can make simple mathematical decisions. By putting the neurons together in layers, they can analyze inputs and problems and provide outputs and answers.

The outputs are generally a number within a range like 0 to 1 similar to that of our logistic regression. In some ways a logistic regression is a neuron, and when we combine them, what we are creating is a neural network. Developing the final prediction is generally done by training the model and calibrating all of the "weights" for each neuron and repeating two key steps: forward propagation and back propagation.

In forward propagation, we apply a set of weights to the input data and calculate an output. For the first forward propagation, the set of weights is selected randomly.

In back propagation, similar to the way the brain "learns," we measure the margin of error of the output and adjust the weights accordingly to decrease the error.

Training neural networks generally involves first feeding the model a large amount of data. In a supervised learning system, the data are already programmed with what the output should be, or an example set. After the initial data output, the network analyzes how close it was able to get to the example set. The network then changes the weights applied to different neurons throughout the network in order to get closer to the original example set.

These calculations and reweighting can occur thousands of times, and only stop when the network cannot improve the accuracy any further given the data provided and its programmed parameters. Finally, once the network has been trained with enough learning examples, it reaches a point where you can present it with an entirely new set of inputs that it's never seen before and see how it responds.

For example, to build a network that identifies potential customers, the initial training data set might be a series of customers and non-customers with various attributes and features, including demographics and geographic information. Each input is accompanied by the matching identification or class, such as "customer" or "not customer" and the answers allow the model to adjust its internal weightings to "learn" what a customer is. After it has been trained, when it's fed data about a 27-year-old female that lives in a certain area code, it will tell us whether she will likely become a customer or not.

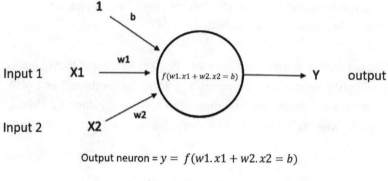

Output neuron = $y = f(w1.x1 + w2.x2 = b)$

Fig r | Graph of sample ANN

The basic components in the neural network are the neurons, often called nodes, and their weights. Each node receives input from some other nodes, or from an external source, and computes an output. Each input has an associated weight (**w**), which is assigned based on its relative importance to other inputs. The node applies a function **f** (defined below) to the weighted sum of its inputs.[46]

Where

> **Y** is a dependent variable (output)
> **X** is a set of explanatory variables (input)
> **f** is the Activation Function
> **w** is weights of the inputs
> **b** is the model error term or bias (The main function of Bias is to provide every node with a trainable constant value in addition to the normal inputs that the node receives).

Artificial neural networks are typically organized in layers made up of many interconnected nodes that contain an activation function. A shallow neural network has three layers of neurons: an input layer, one or more hidden layers, and the output layer.

Input Layer

The input layer should represent the condition for which we are training the neural network. All the

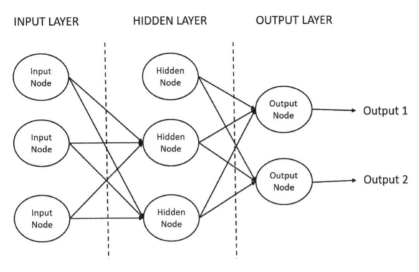

Fig s | Graph showing sample ANN layers

inputs are fed into the model through this layer and it deals with all the inputs only from the external environment. No computation is performed in any of the Input nodes, it just transfers the inputs to the hidden layer.

Hidden Layer

The hidden layer is the collection of neurons that have the activation function applied; it is an intermediate layer found between the input layer and the output layer. The hidden nodes have no direct connection with the outside world (hence the name). There can be more than one hidden layer, which are used for processing and performing computations on the inputs received from the input layers. They then transfer information from the input nodes to the output layer.

Output Layer

The output layer is responsible for collecting, computations, and transferring information from the network externally in accordance with the way it has been designed to give. The pattern presented by the output layer can be directly traced back to the input layer.

Activation Function

An activation function takes in the weighted sum of all the inputs from the previous layer and then generates an output value (typically nonlinear) and passes it to the next layer. It is like the extra force or effort applied over the input to obtain an exact output. In neural networks, these can be used at nodes in a hidden layer to squash the input. This introduces the valuable non-linearity to the neural network. Popular examples are the linear (or identity) activation function that performs no input editing, and the sigmoid activation function, which you may remember from logistic regression.

Weight

A coefficient for a feature in a linear model. The weight is the parameter within a neural network that transforms input data within the network's hidden layers. Weighting places more focus on different nodes or different functions on the same group of nodes. This is the heart of a neural network and represents the influence (negative or positive) of each input on the output as identified by the neuron.

I want to emphasize that artificial neural networks are complex and have many different components and variations—far too many for us to go into here. Like other models, I recommend you find additional resources and learning materials on this type of model.

Pros and Cons of Artificial Neural Networks

Pros: They can generalize and infer complex relationships within data that are not immediately apparent using traditional methods. Because of this, there are no restrictions placed on the input variables, such as how they should be distributed, and they can produce an output with incomplete knowledge with the loss of performance based on how important the missing information is. Lastly, they can be more efficient than some other models; parallel processing abilities mean the network can perform more than one job at a time.

Cons: To process any significant model in parallel without latency makes neural network hardware system dependent. Next, the lack of rules for determining the proper network structure means the appropriate artificial neural network architecture can only be found through trial and error or by comparing the predictive performance of multiple models, all of which must be developed. Finally, the lack of explanation behind probing solutions may be one of the biggest disadvantages. To some, this is still a black box and the inability to explain the "why" or "how" behind the solution can generate a lack of trust in the outputs.

Applications of Artificial Neural Network Algorithms

- Classification: They are widely used for a variety of tasks from image recognition to natural language recognition. Neural networks are also used in self-driving cars, character recognition, image compression, stock market prediction, and more.
- Factor analysis: The network can be fed a steady stream of data with a steady number of changing example sets or guidelines. The artificial neural network can then change weighting in order to achieve the desired outcomes.
- Associations: ANNs can find and test relationships between variables and then simulate outcomes based on adjustments to the variables to create what-if scenarios.
- Pattern analysis: ANNs can figure out patterns and can analyze different strains of a data set using an existing machine learning algorithm or a new example.
- Prediction: With both supervised and unsupervised learning, an artificial neural network can be fine-tuned to make an accurate prediction or accurately weight and process data.

As a relatively new phenomenon, artificial neural network algorithms still have room to improve and grow. As computation power increases and the architecture behind these structures is being improved, neural networks continue to open up possibilities. As we are exposed to more algorithms and data sets going forward, it is easy to see these models transforming predictive analytics and the demand planning field.

Types of Artificial Neural Network

- Feed-forward neural networks
- Recurrent neural networks (RNN)
- Convolutional neural networks (CNN)
- Back-propagation
- Modular neural networks
- Radial basis function network (RBFN)

Decision Trees

Decision Trees: *A type of classification and regression method that constructs a model of decisions based on actual values of attributes in the data.*

Decision trees are one of the simpler algorithms but they can easily become overwhelming and complex. Just as we compared a neural network to our brains, a decision tree has many analogies in real life. As the name indicates, it uses a tree-like model of decisions, complete with roots, branches, and leaves.

The decision tree process begins with a single event and root. From this root, multiple outcomes develop that form its branches. The branches are at the tree's heart and reflect the different decisions that can be made. Its branches fan out to create more outcomes and branches and, ultimately, multiple leaves. Eventually, this very simple decision tree process can become a massive set of jumbled numbers and outcomes that need pruning. Analogies aside, these models are widely used, easy to train, easy to visualize, and have influenced a wide area of machine learning covering both classification and regression.

What are Decision Trees?

Decision trees are a "must know" machine learning technique. Decision tree is a family of supervised learning algorithms that are frequently utilized; plus, they are very versatile and work well. Unlike some of the other models we have reviewed, trees easily can be used for solving regression and classification problems. They can map non-linear relationships very well and they can help predictive ensemble models with high accuracy, stability, and ease of interpretation. The general purpose of using decision trees is to create a training model that can be used to predict the class or value of target variables by learning decision rules inferred from prior data (training data).

Decision trees build classification or regression models in the form of an upside-down tree structure. It breaks down a data set into smaller and smaller subsets while, at the same time, an associated decision tree is incrementally developed. The concept and algorithm are relatively simple compared to other models.

The decision tree algorithm tries to solve the problem at hand by using a flow chart or tree type representation. Each internal node of the tree corresponds to an attribute, and each leaf node corresponds to a class label. You start with the best attribute of the data set, which is the root node at the top of the tree. You then split the entire data set into smaller data sets forming branches down from the root to internal nodes. Subsets should be made in such a way that each subset contains data with the same value for an attribute. You continue to repeat this for each new subset creating more subsets until you find the leaf node or the end of all the branches in the tree.

This sometime leads to poor performance while predicting the test values, which is why we prune the tree (sub-nodes that don't really affect the accuracy of the model are trimmed from the decision tree.) This reduces the depth of the tree and increases the prediction accuracy.

When building the model, one must first identify the most important input variables and then split records at the root node and at subsequent internal nodes based on the status of these variables. The purity of the nodes is defined using calculations like the Gini index, information gain, classification error, and entropy, among others.[47]

The most common method is entropy, which is the measure of how disordered your data are. **Entropy:** *As it relates to machine learning, is a measure of the randomness in the information being processed.*

The higher the entropy, the harder it is to draw any conclusions from that information. Entropy is often used to determine how the direction of travel and split values are chosen. At each step, or each branching, the data are split in such a way as to maximize the information gain/minimize the entropy of each node.

If it decreases, the split is validated and we can proceed to the next step. If it's not validated, we must try to split with another feature or, alternatively, stop this branch altogether. Ultimately our objective is to keep going until we either cannot split anymore or we've reached a pre-defined stopping criterion that gives us outputs or groupings that we can use.

A Random Forest model works in the same way we just described but with this method we grow multiple trees as opposed to a single decision tree. To classify a new object based on attributes, each tree gives a classification and the tree "votes" for that class. The forest chooses the classification that has the most votes or overall trees in the forest, if you will. And, in the case of regression, it takes the average of outputs by the different trees.

Back to our more basic single decision tree. A simple example is where we are predicting values for a continuous variable. Let's say we have a sample of customers with multiple attributes. We start by splitting them into two homogeneous sets based on gender. From there we continue to split based on other attributes. This creates additional subsets and ultimately, we discover that a female under 30 years of age lives in the northern section of town, has two children and a dog, has a loyalty card for our store, and is a customer.

Now, of course, we need to be careful about overfitting and autocorrelating variables, because this is easily done with these types of models. When you have so many variables, they will fit on the most effective variable they encounter, leaving other plausible variables out. With new customers fitting into the model, we must be wary of becoming so granular that, while the training data fits, it will not fit new, unseen data sets. The possibility of a new person fitting all of the labels is highly unlikely. In the case of multicollinearity, this will likely mean that there is a material probability that the algorithm fits not on the "right" variable, but on a strong variable correlated with the right variable.

The basic components of this model are the nodes (root, internal, leaf) and branches, and the most important steps in building the model are splitting and pruning.[48]

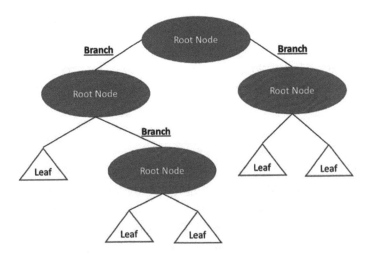

Fig 1 | Graph showing a sample decision tree structure

Root Node

It represents the entire population or data set, and this further gets divided into two or more homogeneous sets and branches leading to other internal nodes.

Internal Node

This is when a sub-node splits into further sub-nodes. Internal nodes, also called chance nodes, represent one of the possible choices available at that point in the tree structure. The top edge of the node is connected to its parent node and the bottom edge is connected to its child nodes or leaf nodes.

Leaf Node

When the nodes are unable to split from the final node, we arrive at the leaf, or terminal, node. This is the end of the nodes or that branch of the tree and represents the result of a combination of decisions or events.

Branches

This is a subsection of the tree that represents chance outcomes or occurrences that emanate from root nodes and internal nodes. A decision tree model is formed using a hierarchy of branches.

Splitting

This is a process of dividing a node into two or more sub-nodes. Only input variables related to the target variable are used to split parent nodes into purer child nodes of the target variable. Both discrete input variables and continuous input variables (which are collapsed into two or more categories) can be used. You might ask when to stop growing a tree? One way of doing this is to set a minimum number of training inputs to use on each leaf. Another common way is to set a maximum depth for your model. Maximum depth refers to the length of the longest path from a root to a leaf.

Pruning

This is almost the opposite process of splitting and is the removal of internal or sub-nodes and branches. This way, we reduce the complexity of a tree, and thus increase its predictive power by reducing overfitting. There are two types of pruning: pre-pruning which uses Chi-square tests or multiple-comparison adjustment methods to prevent the generation of non-significant branches, and post-pruning which is used after generating a full decision tree to remove branches.

Pros and Cons of Decision Trees

Pros: The main advantage is that it is less black box and more of a white box solution. It is simple to understand and to interpret, not only for the person building the model but for the end user as well. It is versatile with the ability to handle both numerical and categorical data as well as multi-output problems. Other techniques are usually specialized in analyzing data sets that have only one type of variable. It also takes little data preparation.

Cons: Error propagation or a wrong decision (item split) can lead to all following decisions being wrong as well. With that, small changes in the data can have an enormous impact on the results. Another fundamental flaw of decision trees is that they are very prone to overfitting and thus need to be pruned. A final disadvantage that comes up a lot is that despite starting off simple, they can grow to be complex. Large decision trees with many branches are complex and time-consuming affairs.

Applications of Decision Trees Algorithms

- Classification: They are widely used for a variety of tasks from building knowledge management platforms for customer service that improve first call resolution, to general business decisions.
- Factor analysis: Assessing the relative importance of variables. Identifying factors leading to better gross margins at a retail chain, for example. It is one of the fastest ways to identify the most significant variables, and relationships between two or more variables.
- Descriptive analytics: Can identify skewed data or outliers that may indicate issues that need addressing. Fraudulent statement detection is one example.
- Clustering: Decision trees can help in deciding how to best collapse categorical variables into a more manageable number of categories or how to subdivide heavily skewed variables into ranges.
- Prediction: They can be fine-tuned to make an accurate prediction using the tree model derived from historical data.

Types of Decision Trees Models

- Random Forest
- Classification and Regression Tree (CART)
- Conditional Decision Trees
- Gradient Boosting Machines (GBM)

ARIMA and ARIMAX

ARIMA Model: *Part of the group of time-series models that assume that future sales depend on previous values of the same series. ARIMA or ARIMAX are acronyms that stand for (AR) AutoRegressive (I) Integrated (MA) Moving Average (the X is an explanatory variable).*

ARIMA models, sometimes called Box-Jenkins modeling, are widely used statistical methods for time-series forecasting. They are versatile models that can perform moving average, exponential smoothing, random walk, and seasonality functions, with different weights and lags to better reproduce history and make predictions. With variations such as ARIMAX, they can bring in explanatory variables like a combination model and are extremely powerful for bringing time-series and causal variables into a single process and output.

It's a forecasting method that projects the future values of a series based entirely on its own inertia at different time lags. In other words, it assumes that sales of the current period depend on the sales of one period before. One period before means a lag of one period, and two periods before means a lag of two periods, and so on. Each model assigns different weights and uses different combinations of variables, depending on the nature of the data set being forecasted. All of this is to create explanatory variables from its own historical data by using autocorrelations to identify the historical values that best predict future demand.

This, like regression, is a standard model now for advanced business forecasting. While we hit the key concepts and components here, there is no way we can give it the full attention it needs in these pages. ARIMA and ARIMAX are being used more and more in time-series modeling and systems increasingly offer this capability. It is highly recommended you better understand concepts of autocorrelations coefficients, stationary data, and things like chi-square statistics.

What is ARIMA?

ARIMA was first introduced by Box and Jenkins (1970), who detailed ARIMA's estimation and prediction procedures. It is a class of model that captures a suite of different standard temporal structures in time-series data. It may be viewed best as a "filter" that tries to separate the signal from the noise, and the signal is then extrapolated into the future to obtain forecasts.

Breaking down the acronym **ARIMA** and understanding the aspects of the model we can see:[49]

- **AR**: Autoregression. A model that uses the dependent relationship between an observation and some number of lagged observations. An **AR** model looks like a linear regression model except that in a regression model, the dependent variable and its independent variables are different; whereas, in an **AR** model the independent variables are simply the time-lagged values of the dependent variable, so it is autoregressive.
- **I**: Integrated. The use of differencing of raw observations (e.g., subtracting an observation from an observation at the previous time step) to make the time-series stationary.
- **MA**: Moving Average. A model that uses the dependency between an observation and a residual error from a moving average model applied to lagged observations. An **MA** model is a weighted moving average of a fixed number of forecast errors produced in the past, so it is called moving average. Unlike the traditional moving average, the weights in a **MA** are not equal and do not sum up to 1.

A nonseasonal ARIMA model can be expressed as

ARIMA (**p,d,q**)

where

> **p** is the number of autoregressive terms and is the number of lag observations included in the model, also called the lag order.
> **d** is the number of nonseasonal differences needed for stationarity, also called the degree of differencing.
> **q** is the size of the moving average window and number of lagged forecast errors in the prediction equation and is also called the order of moving average.

Determining the number of differences and lags needed for traditional ARIMA models can be more of an art than a science. ARIMA is more of a process to identify a weighted moving-average model than it is a method. It is an iterative process involving assessing the data set, identifying the model, estimating the parameters, checking model adequacy, and forecasting.

Asses Your Data Set

ARIMA models works best when your data exhibit a stable or consistent pattern over time with a minimum number of outliers. This is why the first step when using the ARIMA model (and many other time-series models) is to check for stationarity. **Stationary Data:** *Time-series data are stationary if their mean, variance, and co-variance do not change over time.* It is worth noting that most time-series data are not stationary; if a time-series has a trend or seasonality component, it is not stationary and it must be made so before we can use ARIMA to forecast. Ultimately, we need the data to show constant variance over time. Plotting the data is sometimes enough to see if the data are stationary.

Without these stationarity conditions being met, many of the calculations associated with the process cannot be computed. If your data are not stationary at this step, you need to prepare your data by using transformations (i.e., square roots or logarithms) to stabilize the variance and differencing to remove the remaining seasonality or other trends.

Differencing is an excellent way of transforming a nonstationary series to a stationary one. This is done by subtracting the observation in the current period from the previous one. Thus, instead of working with the final dollar amount or count, you are now working with the delta. This process essentially eliminates the trend if your series is growing at a fairly constant rate.

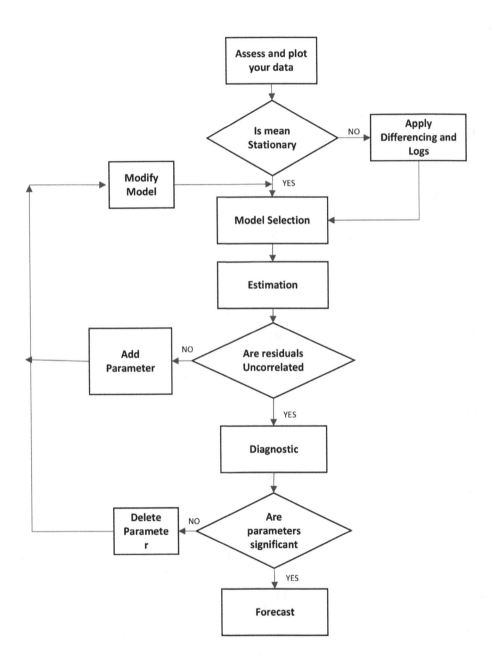

Fig u | Graph showing sample ARIMA process

If it is growing at an increasing rate, you can apply the same procedure and difference the data again. You can continue this process as many times as needed to create a stationary data set. This should be done the same way with different lags to adjust for seasonality and other circular events as well.

Identify the Initial Model

Another important concept in ARIMA modeling is autocorrelation because it influences how many previous observation values are considered in the final model. **Autocorrelation:** *In time-series forecasting, this refers to the correlation an observation has between itself and another observation.* These different observations in time-series are called lags and autocorrelation can occur between the current lag and the previous lag, and even lags several months and years prior to the current lag.

For a time-series to be stationary, we can specify an appropriate ARMA (**p,q**) model based on the patterns of its autocorrelation and partial autocorrelation functions. We can plot these using correlograms to show the patterns of the Autocorrelation Function (ACF) and Partial Autocorrelation Function (PACF) to decide whether to include an **AR** term (**p**), **MA** term (**q**), or both.

Autocorrelation Function (ACF): The plot summarizes the correlation of an observation with lag values. The x-axis shows the lag and the y-axis shows the correlation coefficient between -1 and 1 for negative and positive correlation, respectively. The ACF values fall between -1 and +1 calculated from the time-series at different lags to measure the significance of correlations between the present observation and the past observations, and to determine how far back in time (i.e., how many time-lags) they are correlated.

Partial Autocorrelation Function (PACF): The plot summarizes the correlations for an observation with lag values that are not accounted for by prior lagged observations. PACF values are the coefficients of a linear regression of the time-series using its lagged values as independent variables. When the regression includes only one independent variable of one-period lag, the coefficient of the independent variable is called First Order Partial Autocorrelation Function; when a second term of two periods lag is added to the regression, the coefficient of the second term is called the Second Order Partial Autocorrelation Function, and so on. The values of PACF will also fall between -1 and +1 if the time-series is stationary.

- If autocorrelation coefficients trail off exponentially to zero, an autoregressive (**AR**) model is indicated. This lag is taken as the value for **p**.
- If the partial autocorrelation coefficients trail off to zero, a moving average (**MA**) model is indicated. This lag value is taken as the value for **q**.
- If both values trail off to zero, a mixed ARMA model is most likely needed.

Estimation and Diagnostics

After the model is properly identified, our next step is estimation. At this step it is recommended to look at a few versions of the model and validate the best fit. To validate, you are comparing the predicted values to the actuals in the validation sample for an estimation of the model coefficients and to diagnostically check the goodness of fit.

- Estimation: Estimation involves using numerical methods to minimize a loss or error term. In fact, most ARMA models are nonlinear requiring a nonlinear estimation procedure. Only some simple AR models are linear, which can be estimated with the Ordinary Least Squares (OLS) procedure. For either procedure, the criterion for getting the best estimates of coefficients is the same, that is, to minimize the sum of the squared errors.
- Diagnostic Checking: The idea of diagnostic checking is to look for evidence that the model is not a good fit for the data. Regardless of what estimation procedure is used in modeling, the criteria for testing the goodness of fit are the same. We use familiar tests such as R-squared to measure the degree of correlation between the dependent variable and the independent variables, and we use the t-statistics to test the significance of the coefficients and the standard error to measure how closely the model fits the data.

Forecasting

The final step is generating the forecast. If the model does not forecast accurately, the model is not an efficient model. It is important to remember that all of this is an iterative process so, as new information is gained during estimation and diagnostics, you can circle back to previous steps and incorporate them into new models. You can continue this process until an acceptable model is obtained.

Pros and Cons of ARIMA

Pros: ARIMA models generally outperform other time-series models. These models can be very accurate and efficient, especially for short-term forecasts (one to four periods). And while these models do need to be recalibrated and rerun when new data is introduced, they react to fluctuations in demand better than a simple moving average.

Cons: Unfortunately, it does have drawbacks. It is perceived to be complex, which discourages use and application. Also, compared to many other time-series methods, they require large amounts of data to accurately determine the best model. Finally, if we are comparing this to the other models we review in this book, ARIMA on its own does not include naturally independent variables (this can be accomplished with ARIMAX model, for example) and they need to be re-evaluated when new data are collected.

Applications of ARIMA Process

- Recommendation and probabilities: Predicting the expected number of incoming or churning customers.
- Descriptive analytics: Explaining seasonal patterns in sales.
- Data mining: Detecting unusual events and estimating the magnitude of their effect.
- Prediction: Most commonly used as a more advanced process and model for short-term time-series forecasting.

Other forecasting techniques such as exponential smoothing can make the ARIMA model more accurate by applying a weighted combination of seasonality, trend, and historical values to make predictions. In addition, we can include explanatory variables such as causal inputs and drivers. You can try a combination of models that allow for inclusion of other predictors using methods such as ARMAX or dynamic regression. These more complex models allow for control of other factors in predicting the time-series.[50]

Types of ARIMA Models

- First-order autoregressive model ARIMA(1,0,0)
- Random walk ARIMA(0,1,0)
- Differenced first-order autoregressive model ARIMA(1,1,0)
- Without constant = simple exponential smoothing ARIMA(0,1,1)
- With constant = simple exponential smoothing with growth ARIMA(0,1,1)
- Seasonal ARIMA (SARIMA)
- Fractional ARIMA (FARIMA or ARFIMA) Model with explanatory variables (ARIMAX)

AI and Deep Learning

Many of the revolutionary approaches being used today in demand planning may just be scratching the surface of what's possible. With the vast amount and variety of data available, along with new computational capabilities, the sky is the limit for this field. AI and deep learning can open new doors, new possibilities, and new insights.

We are already seeing machine learning methods that can analyze features, relationships, and complex interactions in a training data set and build a model, which can be used for demand forecasting. Deep learning has the potential to go even further and allow machines to solve more complex problems even when the data sets are very diverse, unstructured, and inter-connected.

Deep Learning: *A subset of machine learning based on algorithms that attempt to emulate human thought and behavior to solve complex problems.* We call it "deep learning" because the neural networks have numerous layers, each providing a different interpretation to the data that enables learning.

Deep learning is a rapidly changing technology that is revolutionizing many business processes, including forecasting models. There are certain advantages with deep learning models that make them particularly valuable:

- They recognize complex and less obvious interacting patterns,
- They produce more accurate forecasting models than traditional methods,
- They produce different layers of related forecasts from the same data set,
- They find forecastable clusters previously unseen, and
- They enable rapid, less expensive prototyping on Cloud platforms.

As business cycles continue to get shorter and product introductions become more frequent, more frequent and granular forecasts are needed. In traditional forecasting, a separate model must be built for each product or business unit (each of these is called a "series" as in "time-series forecasting"). Deep learning takes a slightly different approach to the data and model. With deep learning, we can use a single model that is capable of generating many related forecasts at various levels. This approach is even able to forecast from previously unseen data. For new items, this means it can produce a new product forecast from only a few data points. For mature items, you can generate item-level forecasts from multiple data points at the same time.

Armed with deep learning, companies are increasingly moving to more granular and faster forecasts, such as forecasting demand for individual SKUs or profit centers, rather than divisions or business units. Deep learning also may minimize the need for domain expertise as it self-learns feature similarity without much supervision. Since the primary reason for including overrides in demand forecasting is to add information about customer purchase behavior or external factors, a deep learning-based approach can capture the same with much higher accuracy. What's more, techniques like Recurrent Neural Network (RNN) can be employed to make the models better at adaptive learning, hence making the system self-reliant with negligible manual interventions.

Finally, most forecasting approaches are based on the idea that a forecast can be improved if the underlying factors of a data set can be identified and forecasted separately. Therefore, by using traditional approaches that extract information from historical observations we may gain insights by isolating components (e.g., seasonality) and modeling them separately.

With ensemble modeling and deep learning, we may be able to transform historical data through Multi-Cluster Time-Series Analysis (MCTSA), which allows us to gather additional information about seasonality and the series at hand, resulting in better forecasts. This modeling approach uses unsupervised clustering analysis along with a multi-layered artificial neural network to model time-series data. It combines information from many different clusters of attributes and levels of aggregation, augmenting various features of the series in the process into improved seasonal profiles and providing a robust and accurate forecast.

Consider an item that is sold not only in retail brick-and-mortal stores (that purchase the stock a month or more in advance of their selling season) but is also sold direct to the consumer to ship the next day during the middle of the selling season. When looking at sales at the store level, the seasonality of the product itself is typically entangled with the seasonality of the store. Ensemble models that utilize unsupervised clustering techniques with deep learning predictive models can help find the forecastable clusters, as well as related forecasts.[51]

Over the years, we have seen business forecasting and demand planning change and continue to adapt. As we move into the fourth industrial revolution and digital age, we will continue to embrace new technology and new techniques. Systems and methods will never be able to replace good processes and great people, but combining systems, processes, and people will become part of our daily jobs going forward. As methods like deep learning and AI become more advanced and accessible, we can find ways to integrate them into our processes to become more efficient, produce even better forecasts, and provide the business with even more insights.

SPOTLIGHT

How Walmart Uses Kaggle to Find the Best Method

Not only does Walmart have over 11,000 brick and mortar stores, it is the second largest online retailer as well. Walmart is one of the leaders in using big data, the Internet of Things, and machine learning to improve their shoppers' experience. In 2017, Lauren Desegur, VP of Customer Experience Engineering at WalmartLabs, said machine learning is the key to enhancing the customer experience.

Walmart already uses machine learning to optimize the delivery routes of their home deliveries. You also can see it used in the forecasting and demand planning process. Walmart uses machine learning to classify the different types of trips that people take to their stores. They continually look at new methods and new ways to plan seasonality and promotions using new models and approaches as well.

One of the ways they are making these discoveries, as well as finding new talent they can recruit, is through sponsored Kaggle forecasting competitions. Over the years, Kaggle has become the premier data science and predictive analytics competition where the best and the brightest turn out to compete. Now owned by Google, Kaggle has created a platform for organizations to sponsor and host competitions that have fueled new methodologies and techniques in data science, and have given organizations new insights.

In 2017 Walmart challenged the Kaggle community of over 1 million users to recreate their classification system and forecasting using only limited transactional data. This would help Walmart innovate and improve upon their planning and machine learning processes.

Walmart provided over 600,000 rows of training data (data already labeled with the corresponding classification). The data contained 143 weeks of previous sales at 45 stores and their 99 departments, noting if the week contained a holiday and what the status of the following were: temperature, fuel prices, markdown (discounts), consumer price index, unemployment rate, store type, and store size. Using this information, sales of the next 39 weeks would be forecasted and checked for accuracy. The challenge would be to train models to predict sales as accurately as possible, and Walmart graded participants on their accuracy.[52]

Walmart was interested in using this competition to find new talent and identify the best new methods and approaches. They were interested in forecasting future sales in individual departments within different stores and were particularly interested in sales on four major holidays: Super Bowl day, Labor Day, Thanksgiving, and Christmas. Given these events are all major selling opportunities and happen only once a year, they were keen to make optimal strategic decisions to ensure maximum profitability.

The Kaggle competition had close to a thousand teams compete in a kind of a crowdsourced project, and several people were hired into Walmart's analytics team. This crowdsourced approach led to some interesting appointments of people who would not have been considered for an interview based on their resumes alone. One, for example, had a background in physics but no formal analytics or planning background.

In terms of the methods and approaches used, we also saw a very diverse field. Models ranged from Auto-Regressive Integrated Moving Average (ARIMA), Unobserved Components Model (UCM), different types of Regression and Random Forest, to Artificial Neural Networks, just to name a few. Many descriptive methods were employed to help understand and cluster the data before predictions were even made.

The teams all used different ways to solve the problem. However, one clear trend rose to the top. The winner of that year's Walmart Kaggle competition was a simple and traditional unweighted average of six component models. All the winners' models were variations of time-series methods using weekly historical data adjusted to shift the week Christmas landed onto a common seasonal profile. Other models that were very competitive were ARIMA types of models that also used time-series data to find historic patterns.

The big lesson came not from that event but another Walmart Kaggle competition two years earlier. The winning method was a regression class model using decision trees and predictive variables. In an interview, Kaggle CEO and Founder, Anthony Goldbloom, said two kinds of machine-learning approaches win competitions: those that are handcrafted using ensembles or decision trees, and Neural Networks. So, after thousands of competitions by thousands of competitors, the absolute clear winner and best predictive model is still potentially an all-of-the-above strategy.

The Kaggle competitions are an excellent way for companies to sponsor data and predictive analytics projects that aim to solve real-life problems. The solutions that win are dependent on what the data structure is, what the defined problem is, what resources are available to use, and the process that is employed. While each solution had subtle differences and results, for most competitions, there was not a lot of difference between first and sixteenth place. The top performers were those that had a wide range of methods and models at their disposal and understood how they work, and were not tied to a single solution.

Summary— Strategies Using All of the Above

You may think that a more complex model or algorithm means a better forecast, and a simpler statistical method means it is inferior. That is not at all true. There are many simple forecasting methods in our toolbox that have specific purposes and provide even better insights and results than more complex methods. At the same time, more complex methods or approaches can be very useful in other cases.

Fancy techniques are great, but our overriding goal is to select the model that fits our business purposes and the resources available to us. We need to evaluate the model properly to ensure that it can do what we need it to. The most sophisticated techniques and most advanced technologies accomplish little if nobody understands the results. To complete the process we must step back, sometimes simplify, and communicate our analysis effectively.

The issue of complexity versus accuracy versus resources and effort is particularly important and should be evaluated in every situation. Complex methods may do well under conditions for which they were designed but tend to suffer when applied to new conditions. Conversely, human judgment can be hampered by bias—something which machines can eliminate. Further, machines can uncover insights that we as humans cannot imagine on our own.

All methods help you better understand data and make predictions, but each may take a very different approach. By understanding the differences—the strengths and trade-offs of each—we see that they are complementary and can use best parts of each one. Ultimately, the best result may be to combine different methods, algorithms, and models in a way that plays to the strengths of each, and together provide the best result.

You may just find you use a K-Means unsupervised algorithm to gain insights on promotions and other data that can be used in an ARIMAX supervised learning model, along with a Judgmental Expert Opinion added in to finalize your prediction, which of course is compared to a Naïve Random Seasonal Walk after actuals are ascertained for Forecast Value Added (FVA%). In other words, everything may not be a nail and you may find you need a hammer, screwdriver, pliers, and a mechanical auto-calibrated impact wrench to complete the job.

Section Review

Multiple Choice:

1. A forecasting method that relies on quantitative predefined models may be best categorized as:

    a) Deductive Logic (Numerical-Based) methods.
    b) Knowledge (Theory-Based) methods.
    c) Inductive Learner (Machine-Based) methods.
    d) Additive Logic (Historic-Based) methods.

2. A multiple regression is called "multiple" because it has several:

    a) Data points.
    b) Dependent variables.
    c) Independent variables.
    d) All of the above.

3. What is a decision tree commonly used for?

    a) To show probability relationships.
    b) To classify and group like attributes.
    c) To present the flow of data.
    d) To reveal the true level of a problem's complexity.

4. In ARIMA modeling, data series are stationary, if:

   a) There is no growth or decline in the data series.
   b) The data fluctuates around a constant mean.
   c) The variance of the data series remains essentially constant over time.
   d) All of the above.

5. A _____ model is usually the gold standard for most forecasts.

   a) Descriptive
   b) Causal
   c) Machine learning
   d) None of the above

True or False

6. ☐ Traditional time-series and causal modeling are examples of Deductive Logic (Numerical-Based) methods.

7. ☐ Logistic and linear regression work very similarly where the dependent variable is a binary value.

8. ☐ Regression can be used to predict numerical or categorical values.

9. ☐ Maximum Likelihood Estimation will tell you the likelihood that your model will perform well.

10. ☐ ANN can be used for deep learning and to enable AI.

PART V
PREDICTIVE ANALYTICS AS A FUNCTION

After reading this section, you should be able to:

- Understand what a predictive analytics and analytics-driven culture may look like.
- Know the characteristics that make a good Demand Planner.
- Identify the core competencies that help in different types of roles.
- Structure the predictive analytics function effectively inside your company.
- Win support for a predictive analytics and planning function in your organization.

A Predictive Analytics Culture

It's no secret that business owners are struggling to tackle the widening disparity between staffing needs and qualified applicants. According to a report released in January 2017 by the National Federation of Independent Business (NFIB), 80% of businesses that were hiring said they had few or no qualified applicants for their open positions.[53] Thirteen percent of respondents named the low quality of available labor as the most pressing challenge to their businesses.

This trend is even more prevalent in demand planning and related fields. Every company beginning its journey in predictive analytics is hiring for these roles to help improve business decisions, forecasting, pricing, finance, and operations. Data Scientist roles were the toughest to fill in 2017 according to CareerCast.com's Jobs Rated report, based on analyzed data from the Bureau of Labor Statistics, industry publications, and trade statistics.[54] Within supply chains, Demand Planners, with their unique skill sets and requirements, consistently top the list as the most difficult to find and retain. The problem may not be that there aren't enough qualified candidates—it's that employers may not be defining the role or requirements correctly.

A predictive analytics organization starts with data and an analytics-driven culture. For business intelligence, predictive analytics is the mature organization that finds competitive advantage from forward-looking insights and a better understanding of their consumers and business drivers. To maximize these benefits, we need to build a culture of predictive analytics and data-driven decision-making throughout the entire organization. When you start that journey, using data effectively will more than likely change the culture on all fronts. So be prepared.

To fully capitalize on this, we need to understand the role and function of predictive analytics inside your organization and where the function should reside and why. We need to consider how this function may impact other departments and what role it plays in decision-making. And crucially, if we are building a predictive analytics function that drives the business, what kind of people do we need?

These people are known by many different titles inside an organization: Demand Planner, Data Analyst, Forecast Analyst, Demand Insights, Business Forecaster, or Predictive Analytics Manager, just to name a few. No matter what they are called, they play a critical role inside an organization. They are often the person behind the curtain that helps provide insights to all parts of the organization and yet is not fully understood by anyone.

A Good Planner

Business forecasting and planning is about people, process, and technology. Unfortunately, when one reads most articles on the topic today, this isn't evident. Practitioners speak only about process and software providers speak only about technology. Little to no attention is paid to one of the most important variables in planning: people.

As companies evolve to become more analytics-driven, the planning role also needs to evolve. Companies must focus on creating and maintaining a revolutionary talent strategy to drive the evolutionary processes and systems within the demand planning area. Sadly, most companies are driven by the bias of what they read or just a lack of understanding about demand planning. The result is that talent management is neglected. Since demand management processes depend on talented and dedicated people, businesses that do not evolve their demand planning talent management process are at great risk.

My goal is to revive a focus on the people part of the equation and show how to achieve effective demand planning by instituting a best-in-class talent management strategy. For the demand planning function to succeed, organizations must have in place:

- Strong talent based on core competencies,
- Career-path culture and visibility within the organization,

- Proper training and development, and
- True performance-based management.

These four pillars will enable demand planning organizations to keep up with the processes and technology they try to employ. Without a focus on developing and sustaining forecasting and demand planning talent, organizations may find it difficult to mature their overall supply chain effectiveness.

Finding the Right People

Demand planning and forecasting roles are not created equal. A good Demand Planner will have strong analytical and critical thinking skills and a broad understanding of multiple business functions while excelling in a core competency, or holding subject matter expertise in a specific functional topic.

Historically, organizations have looked for an individual who is analytically minded yet can still deal with ambiguity and relate to people. They seek the magical unicorn or person who has the contradictory ability to make sense of the data, then sit in front of Sales and Marketing and speak their language too. That is not an easy combination to find. What they end up with is the Jack of All Trades but Master of None. An organization may be better off building a team of focused individual skill sets that complement each other.

Understanding the needs of the department and the skills of its people allows one to structure roles to maximize the expertise of each individual and, therefore, increase the performance and value of the overall department. It goes back to the basic ingredients of a good Demand Planner—forward-thinking, analytical, business acumen, and communication skills, but with the understanding that he/she may not be an expert in each discipline. Realistically, a good Demand Planner will have all of these skills while excelling in an individual skillset or subject matter.

Seven Habits of Highly Effective Demand Planners

Ever wondered why some Demand Planners are rock stars while others struggle? The difference between success and failure does not necessarily depend on intellect or analytical abilities but more on behavior, core competencies, and leadership skills.

Let me take you through the seven habits of highly effective demand planning leaders that are necessary to succeed in this new world order.

Problem Solvers

They can look at an issue using objective analysis and evaluation to form a judgment and develop new strategies. They are not afraid to voice their opinions and lead from the front. And they bring solutions, not problems. Highly effective Demand Planners make well-informed, effective, and timely decisions (and don't hesitate to do so), even when data are limited, or solutions produce unpleasant consequences. They can visualize the total process, aid in locating problems, use information and gathering techniques, analyze situations, and identify implications of different courses of action.

Social Intelligence

Socially intelligent people tend to be effective communicators—at all levels of the organization. Even Stephen Covey, author of *7 Habits of Highly Effective People,* had a version of this habit: "Seeking to understand requires consideration; seeking to be understood takes courage."[55] A good Demand Planner will try to be an effective listener first and foremost and ask questions to better understand assumptions and needs. This person will work on being able to express ideas or information clearly, and in the context of a deep understanding of the other person's needs and concerns, we significantly increase the credibility of our ideas.

Critical Thinking

They actively and continually look for connections and wonder why. They visualize links between seemly disparate things or events. They look at how things are impacted or effected or even correlate to other things. They apply logic to break down ideas into their strengths and weaknesses to solve problems and get the job done. Rather than going by their gut feelings, they favor having a quantitative basis for their decisions forming a logical opinion about something based on the information available.

Learning Agility

Learning agility is a mindset and collection of practices that allow leaders to continually develop, grow, and utilize new strategies that will equip them for the increasingly complex world of demand planning. Agile learners demonstrate an interest in personal development, seek feedback from multiple sources about how to improve, and modify behavior based on feedback and analysis of past mistakes. This person is the one who attends conferences regularly to keep up on what is new and expand their horizons. This person is the one reading this right now!

Ambiguity

Not only are they okay with ambiguity, but they expect the unexpected and succeed in a world where they are expected to be wrong. In some ways, their superpower is being able to communicate risk and uncertainty and try to tame the beast. Being comfortable with ambiguity means leaning into uncertainty, not running away from it. Good Demand Planners know that ambiguity is a fact of life when it comes to business. Ambiguity cannot be ignored. Ambiguity is embraced as an educator and mentor for the highly successful Demand Planner.

Entrepreneurial

The ever-changing nature of business means that success depends not just on adapting but innovating. They are creative in their approaches and are not afraid to try something new. They are not locked into the way we used to do things and look for new solutions. They do not work in a silo but collaborate with others. People with strong entrepreneurial skills know how to identify—and pull together—the key individuals to get things done. Finally, they are very customer-centric, being focused on adding value internally and externally.

Self-Awareness

They possess an inner compass that gives them the confidence that their decisions are right. Highly successful Demand Planners possess the ability to stand strong and be wrong with confidence. They know that in the boardroom or S&OP meeting others smell fear and will attack uncertainty. Demand Planners instill confidence in others regarding their forecasts and the demand planning process. They take pride in doing the right thing instead of having the right outcomes. With this, they are not afraid to take chances and learn from their setbacks and failed attempts. They make practice and experimentation part of their daily lives.

Talent Management

Most of the time when we look at trying to improve forecast accuracy, people's attention naturally turns to the methods and technology we use. There is another—even more—contributing factor that will not only improve our demand plans but also demand planning. The people part of demand planning is often more important and, with proper focus, helps achieve effective demand planning by instituting a best-in-class talent management strategy. Here are the four key pillars of effective talent management, how they relate to demand planning, and how they can be utilized.

Finding the Right Model

One simple way to look at it is to compare the "art" and "science" of forecasting. While the skills may be there for both, and the task of forecast generation can be completed by either, different people have different core competencies and are either a master of art or a master of science.

Which person is best suited to data mining or more advanced predictive and prescriptive analytics? Which one is best suited to the Collaborative Planning, Forecasting and Replenishment (CPFR) process with a customer who is more about relationships than data? These may be polar extremes, but consider the different soft skills and core competencies needed for centralized vs. decentralized roles, different time horizons, and even segmented data that may be model-driven vs. marketing-driven.

As companies and their demand planning functions evolve, specialized roles may be introduced. For example, companies in higher stages of maturity may create a more senior role tasked with representing demand planning in broader supply chain transformation initiatives. The advancement of an S&OP process may require the leadership and support of an S&OP coordinator. PLM could require either deep analytics to support other areas in the organization or a Launch Leader or Product Innovation Planner role that is highly collaborative.

Collaboration and Communication

Once demand planning organizations have categorized their roles, they can begin to communicate the value of the roles within an organization. Job descriptions often focus on an outline for HR to grade positions, properly align them in the hierarchy, and then advertise them internally and externally. In many cases, these job descriptions do not focus on clarifying the role the position plays in the organization or the challenges and nuances involved. Clarifying this information beyond a job description is important in helping practitioners understand expectations and for the broader supply chain organization to know how positions interrelate and serve planning processes. It also helps to demonstrate that the role is on a par with other senior roles to build respect for the position.

It is not enough to define the role. It must also be communicated, or sold, within the organization. Similarly, it is not only about building a demand planning organization, but also creating and selling the business case for the function to key stakeholders within the company. Take some time to educate the Supply Chain, Sales and Marketing, HR, and executive leaders about demand planning terminology and vocabulary, as well as what demand planning means for the business. Be the cheerleader for what demand planning is and can do. Companies want the ability to better understand what the customer wants (in essence, they want to have the ability to better respond to demand).

From Desiderius Erasmus (ca. 1500) we get one of the best quotes ever: "In the land of the blind, the one-eyed man is king." In an organization that needs to plan for tomorrow and can't see what the demand is going to be, the department that can see is the key. While humility is honorable, being invaluable is indispensable.

Invest in Upgrades to the System

As demand planning leaders envision and design their demand planning organizations, they can use certifications as a way to identify strong candidates to lead demand planning processes and functions. Certifications have long been recognized as a mark of passion and professionalism. Obtaining certification is a true validation of experience and knowledge. It ensures that employees have the knowledge and skills necessary to be successful in senior management roles. IBF's Advanced Certified Professional Forecaster (ACPF) certification is recognized as the industry-leading demand planning and forecasting certification, and can be a win-win for the company as well as the certified individual.

Surveys show that IBF certified professionals demonstrate that they are passionate about the field and often receive greater compensation and recognition. Based on a 2013 Lifework Search study and a 2014 salary report (comparing 380 people who gave detailed interviews), certified professionals at Manager and Director level have salaries 5.4% higher than similar-level professionals without certification.[56] Other surveys show that employees with professional certifications outside of formal education are more likely to foster change, encourage collaboration and consensus, build critical relationships, and improve overall company performance.

Measure and Monitor Accuracy

We all know that forecasting can be a brutal job. And from my own experience, demand planning can be the punching bag of the S&OP process. How often have we heard that Demand Planners are never right?! And, in reality, the closer we are to being right, the more likely it is that somebody else will take credit for it.

To drive the behavior of planners to support demand planning processes and goals, demand planning leaders should expand the scope of criteria that planners are evaluated against. This should really go back to the core competencies of the planner and the value they add to the forecasting process.

One way many leading organizations are measuring this is with Forecast Value Add % (FVA%). The FVA% concept is designed to determine which, if any, steps in the forecasting process—particularly those steps conducted by practitioners—improve forecast accuracy, and which do not. This can be used to evaluate an analyst-generated statistical baseline model against a naïve forecast, or the effectiveness of a planner's overrides to that baseline. This helps the individual practitioner to better understand their impact on the collaborative process and provides feedback on their contributions so they can improve. This helps the company to better identify the drivers to forecast accuracy and measure the inputs and process rather than just the variability.

Leading companies have been able to improve demand planning and forecasting not by adding new systems or drastically changing processes but by going back to the foundation. They have focused on talent based on core competencies, developed the right culture for success inside the company, invested in people, and measured the right performance indicators.

To make this work, a company must understand that it is about more than a new system or new forecasting process. The key requirement is that a company understands talent management. They understand that when done properly, with talent based on core competencies, the right culture, proper training, and performance-based management, the result is a "recruiting factory" that is constantly producing top talent and improved forecasting ability and accuracy.

Core Competencies of Success

I am not discounting the knowledge or skills that already exist in demand planning. It is great if someone understands statistical techniques or has used relevant software, but this experience is not always available when resources are scarce. Plus, I have found that ability does not always equal aptitude. The truth is that a local, entry-level, or internal candidate does not always have those skills, and even some with those skills do not always exemplify them.

According to a study by Leadership IQ, 46% of newly hired employees will fail within 18 months, while only 19% will achieve unequivocal success.[57] In addition, focusing solely on the technical aspects not only increases the risk of a failed hire but can also lead to paying more than you would like for the same proficiency. Technically qualified applicants know their value, and in today's candidate-driven market, they often can demand top dollar. That means you could end up paying more than you can afford for a candidate who may not work out.

With the training and resources available today, it is relatively easy to acquire knowledge—however, in sharp contrast, natural talents are more stable over time. The key is to leverage talents as a multiplier. Organizations with great competency programs not only allow each person to find his or her own route to reaching a desired role—they encourage employees to start with their natural talents. This makes the journey more enjoyable for the individual and opens the door for exponential progress.

If skills can be taught, we need to find the right people who will thrive in this key role. To get truly successful Demand Planners, we need to look at the core competencies.

What are Core Competencies?

Let us look at the difference between a core competency and a skill. A core competency is an essential attribute or special natural ability to do something. Many often refer to this as a strength or talent and is like your personal differentiator. People can develop or be taught a skill, but a natural inclination towards the subject is a core competency.

A skill is slightly different in that it comes from someone's knowledge, practice, and training. This is a more specific learned activity that a person needs to perform an activity or job. Anyone with a little time can learn algebra as a skill through education, practice, and a few exams. But the person with the foundational core competency in this area will enjoy it more and become proficient at it (see fig v).

Job performance is a function of core competency, skill, and proficiency. A person's core competency determines the suitability and potential success of an individual for a role. Skill allows somebody to perform an activity to a required standard. Proficiency defines their level of competence.

Why focus on core competency? In a *Wall Street Journal* survey of over 900 executives, 92% reported that soft skills—including communication, curiosity, and critical thinking—are as important as technical skills.[58] It is the most important raw material for developing functional proficiency. Functional

Fig v | Formula for Proficiency

skills are easier to teach to those who have natural aptitudes in specific areas. Employees are proven to be more engaged and enjoy their work more when they are working in areas that tie into their natural instincts or core competencies.

Google seems to agree as well. They conducted a study that found that among the eight most important qualities of Google's top employees, STEM (Science, Technology, Engineering, Math) expertise came in last.[59] What came in at the top? All top seven characteristics of success at Google turned out to be soft skills like communicating, critical thinking, empathy, making connections, and similar core competencies. As employers seek to improve the culture fit and success of their new hires, we are seeing a shift away from an emphasis on hard skills in favor of core competencies.

What Should We Look for in a Demand Planner?

No matter what industry you are in or what position you're hiring for, skills such as listening and getting along with others are vital to success. Some of these competencies can either be translated differently depending on your position or be more or less important based on your specific fields. This list is not necessarily exhaustive, but for demand planning, forecasting, and related fields here are what I see as the top 15 core competencies clustered into three key areas.

The first group of competencies is Personal (or Behavior) and relates to how someone acts, reacts, and thinks. The second group is Functional (or Technical)—the natural abilities that are necessary for a specific function. The final group is Enterprise (or Professional) and allows for success in an organization at higher levels (see fig w).

Hiring is difficult; hiring a Demand Planner or related position is sometimes impossible. However, if we start redefining "qualified" and start giving core competencies the respect they deserve, the hiring process and the workplace will be transformed positively.

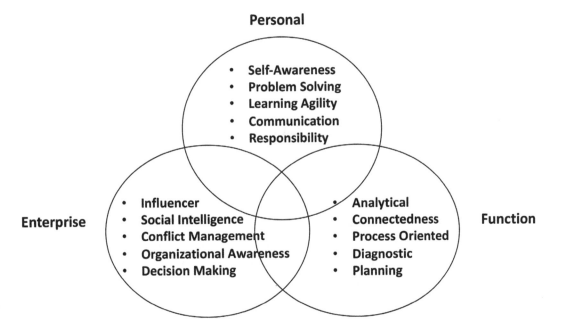

Fig w | 3 Key Areas of Core Competencies

Behavior/Personal Competencies

These are basic competencies relating to how someone acts, reacts, and thinks. These behaviors are natural instincts and are used in the management of personal relationships. These can be developed into skills and talents that are applicable to most disciplines and functions. They are part of the character of the person and are key to base performance. Examples are communication, integrity, problem solving, initiative, etc.

While there are many benefits to having high intelligence, many managers, supervisors, and other workers—particularly those who work in businesses where interpersonal relationships are key—have become keenly aware that workplace success depends on Behavior and Personal core competencies. Higher competencies in this area help us to be stronger internal motivators, which can reduce procrastination, increase self-confidence, and improve our ability to focus on a goal.

Good Demand Planners demonstrate a strong focus on getting things done along with a capacity for introspection. They set goals, establish personal standards, and have a continual desire to learn and grow. They also find it easier to communicate, creating better internal networks. Finally, they use those same competencies to self-reflect, which translates into an ability to objectively look at external things and people, as well as solve problems more efficiently.

Below is a list of five Behavior and Personal core competencies and descriptions of them as they apply to demand planning.

Self-Awareness

The first of our five competencies is self-awareness, which is key to realizing one's strengths and weaknesses, and gives us confidence when we know our decisions are right. According to a 1982 study by Boyatzis[60] of several hundred managers from 12 different organizations, accurate self-assessment is the hallmark of superior performance for analytical and data-focused positions such as Data Analysts and Data Scientists.

Problem Solving

Problem solvers can look at an issue objectively and evaluate it to form a judgment and develop new strategies. Problem-solving is a universal skill that applies to almost any position and any industry. However, while everyone does it, not all people are naturals at it. This is key for analytical roles such as Data Analysts and Demand Planners, as well as people in multi-tasking roles like CPFR Analysts.

Learning Agility

Agile learners demonstrate an interest in personal learning and development; seek feedback from multiple sources about how to improve and develop; and modify behavior based on feedback or self-analysis of past mistakes. According to a 2000 study by Lombardo and Eichinger, learning agility correlates significantly with long-term potential for promotion and success in a role.[61] It is universal and cuts across all positions and levels of seniority.

Communication

Good Demand Planners are able to express ideas or information to individuals or groups considering the audience and the nature of the information. The term communicative competence refers to both the tacit knowledge of a language and the ability to use it effectively. It's also the key to social acceptance. This is critical to collaborative roles such as Demand Planner and S&OP positions.

Responsibility

They generally take psychological ownership of what they say they will do. Having responsibility is the duty or obligation to act. Taking responsibility is acknowledging and accepting the choices you have made, the actions you have taken, and the results they have led to. True autonomy leads to both having responsibility and taking responsibility (more process and end-result focused roles such as Product Analyst, Launch Leaders, and CPFR Analyst type positions).

Functional/Technical Competencies

Functional Competencies relate to specific functions, processes, and roles within the organization. These are natural abilities or aptitudes that lean toward the development of skills that are necessary for that function. Examples for demand planning are Analytical, Process Orientation, Focus, and Technical competencies. Below is a list of Functional/Technical Competencies and descriptions of them as they apply to demand planning.

Analytical

Analytical people can apply logic to scrutinize and break down facts and thoughts into their strengths and weaknesses to solve problems and get the job done. They are adept at Synthesizing Information and demonstrate the ability to scrutinize and break down facts and thoughts into their strengths and weaknesses (analytical positions such as Data or Forecast Analyst or Data Scientist or Demand Managers).

Diagnostic

They have the ability to identify the information needed to clarify a situation, seek that information from appropriate sources, and use skillful questioning to draw out the information when others are reluctant to disclose it. Identifies the specific information needed to clarify a situation or to make a decision. People with this competency probe skillfully to get at the facts, ask questions, and seek the perspective of others to clarify a situation. Example roles include data or information driven roles such as Data Analyst or Scientist and Product Analyst and S&OP related positions.

Planning

Good Demand Planners demonstrate effective use of information-gathering techniques, analyzing situations, and identifying implications to make correct decisions. People who are especially talented in this theme have a craving to know more. Often, they like to collect and archive all kinds of information. They are comfortable with ambiguity: they know all the information needed to do well will not always be available. They are at ease to fill in the blanks based on their experience and intuition. Example roles include planning and forecasting roles such as Forecast Analyst and demand Manager as well as Product Analyst and Launch Leader.

Connectedness

Such people have faith in the links between all things. They believe there are few coincidences and that almost every event has a reason. They enjoy thinking about the past. They understand the present by researching history. This is a universal competency for most analytical and planning positions such as Data Analyst or Scientist, and Forecast or Demand Analyst.

Process Oriented

They demonstrate the ability to visualize the total process and aid in locating the problem. Especially skilled people of this kind can organize, but they also have a flexibility that complements this ability. They like to figure out how all of the pieces and resources can be arranged for maximum productivity. The particularly talented among this type are focused and can take a direction, follow-through, and make the corrections necessary to stay on track. They prioritize, then act. Example roles include Product Analyst, Launch Leaders, CPFR Analyst, and S&OP positions.

Enterprise/Professional Competencies

The following are universal professional competencies that anyone at manager level and above need to succeed. Professional competencies are competencies that allow for success in an organizational context. They are the accelerators of performance and, when lacking, are the reason people fail to move up through the ranks. Some examples are: Business Environment, Organizational Awareness, Negotiation, People Management, etc.

They have a gift for figuring out how people who are different can work together productively. They demonstrate a commitment to the mission and a motivation to combine the team's energy and expertise to achieve a common objective. They persuade others, build consensus through compromise, and cooperate with others to obtain information and accomplish goals. They have an enthusiasm that is contagious. They are upbeat and can get others excited about what they are going to do.

Below is a list of five Enterprise/Professional Competencies and descriptions of them as they apply to demand planning.

Influencer

An influencer persuades others to engage with them in a way that allows them to do their job effectively and to meet the goals of the organization. Influencers have the ability to implement and deal with change and create an environment that helps people change.

Social Intelligence

Socially intelligent people tend to be effective communicators—at all levels of the organization. They are effective listeners, leaving others feeling like they had a good connection.

Conflict Management

When Sales, Marketing, Finance, R&D, Supply Chain, and others are involved in the same discussion, it's common for there to be disagreement. These people can effectively leverage social intelligence to manage conflict and achieve resolution and consensus.

Organizational Awareness

People with this skill understand who's who inside an organization, their level of influence, and the interconnectedness of their network. People with strong organizational awareness know how to identify—and pull together—the key individuals to get things done.

Advanced Decision-Making

People with this competency understand the balance between risk and opportunity; are able to identify challenges and develop strategies to overcome them; and then create priorities once objectives are determined. These people make well-informed, effective, and timely decisions, even when data are limited.

Imagination and Storytelling

*"Imagination is more important than knowledge.
Knowledge is limited. Imagination encircles the world."*
– Albert Einstein

In many ways, imagination is an important asset in demand planning. Much of what we do is managing and communicating assumptions and ambiguity, i.e., being storytellers.

Imagination plays a critical role in what we do and can help us grow and improve our forecasts going forward. The truth is domain knowledge can be picked up quite quickly by most people. Industrial knowledge is a myth and skills and tasks are easily transferable between companies and industries. Even many technical skills can be learned with the right training. Creativity and objectivity, however, are more innate, and they are crucial in demand planning. They help us solve problems and find new solutions. Imagination can also spark passion, which is infectious and fosters collaboration and consensus.

You may not consider demand planning to be a creative role. Most people think of Demand Planners as analytical, number-crunching nerds. Some claim it is an art as well as a science. That is a view I wholeheartedly agree with—algorithms are our canvas and data is our paint. There are people who will discount this statement saying that people who consider demand planning to be an art do not understand the science well enough. But creativity and imagination lie at the core of this field. Creativity is the ability to make something out of nothing. Taking raw data and transforming them into insights requires an incredible amount of imagination. Most successful Demand Planners I know are innovative thinkers and creative in their approach to forecasting. Just as Van Gogh found inspiration in everything around him, Demand Planners have hidden creative juices that can inspire them to find elegant solutions to challenging problems.

Imagination Helps with Data Cleansing and Feature Selection

Much of our job consists of wrangling large amounts of data to find a signal that is usable. In machine learning, we spend time feature engineering and trying to understand which variables contribute the most. It's not just that the answers aren't cut and dry; the data and process are not the same every time either. We need to think outside the box and get creative in how we collect data, how we decide what data to use, and how we sort through the noise to develop a signal. It may not always be the obvious indicator or variable that provides the best answers. Imagination is needed to look at things in new ways, especially when using new data.

Imagination Allows You to Think Outside the Black Box

Imagination does not stop at data. It can guide us to new insights and new applications of our predictions. The kinds of analysis we can do are limited—literally—only by our imagination. I think the real magic comes from realizing that a problem can be solved with data you have lying around, or data that you can easily get. With creativity, you can present what you have discovered in new ways to different audiences. I encourage you to not just generate a number but tell a story that resonates with the people hearing it. The human brain is hardwired to crave narratives with plots and storylines. We need more than judgment and facts to help people make decisions. When we use our imagination, we paint a vivid picture of the future, complete with exciting opportunities, and get people to really understand what your data can do for the business.

Imagination Expands Your Horizons and Life

Beyond your process and modeling, imagination improves your learning process and also makes your life easier and more creative. Young children often learn best when they are playing—a principle that applies to adults as well. You'll learn a new task better when it's fun and you're in a relaxed and playful mood. Creativity can also stimulate your imagination, helping you adapt and retain information better. Plus, studies have shown that people who dream and play are less stressed and live longer—and every Demand Planner could use a little stress relief.

Imagination Ignites Passion in You and Those Around You

Creativity doesn't have to include a specific activity; it can also be a state of mind. Developing a creative nature can help you loosen up in stressful situations, break the ice with strangers, improve your presentation skills, and form new business relationships. A healthy imagination can also mean freedom and not limiting your thinking. Like a two-year-old who believes anything is possible, with the right mindset, you can achieve more. Even what others may perceive as impossible.

Imagination Provides a More Powerful View

Sometimes reality just sucks and your imagination is just a better view. Face it, in demand planning and business forecasting we get paid to be wrong. With all the noise, uncertainty, and life that occurs, the role of creativity and imagination cannot be underestimated. As we go from traditional forecasting to predictive analytics, advanced machine learning and AI, there will come a point where a system's reality will come face-to-face with human creativity. As one thing becomes a commodity (processing and technology) something else becomes a premium (creativity and imagination). Artificial intelligence might be able to do a good job of interpreting the data in a fraction of the time it takes a human, but it will never do an outstanding job. Creativity is the missing piece of the puzzle.

Why Should I Send My Team to That Conference?

When it comes to the Institute of Business Forecasting's (IBF) conferences, training, and professional certifications, there are countless benefits and advantages for both practitioners and employers. A business is constantly innovating and evolving so training your Demand Planners should be a continual process. Your people are your greatest asset and only they can propel your business forward, so why not give them the skills and knowledge to do so?

Hiring the right people and onboarding them effectively with proper foundational training is a great first step. Your process for your team's professional development is key to adapting to changes in the field and building and maintaining a competitive advantage. It should involve external training and professional conferences. Regular training will improve your company's bottom line. Mature organizations understand these benefits and make it part of their annual budgets and, often, part of employees' goals and objectives.

When deciding whether to send somebody on an IBF training course or to a conference, you should consider both hard and soft benefits.

Learning

The most obvious return on your investment when you attend IBF conferences or training is what you learn. No matter how experienced you are in your business, everyone can learn. The educational aspect can expose you to new ways of doing your job and help you be more productive. It allows you to keep up with changes in the field, making sure your team's skills and knowledge are up to date. Finally, it also helps you maintain knowledge and skills. To retain knowledge, skills need to be practiced and refreshed regularly, so elements are not forgotten.

Networking

Networking is one of the most common reasons for attending a conference. This is invaluable as there is much to be learned from your industry peers. They face many of the same challenges you do on a day-to-day basis and may have solved some of the problems you are dealing with now. Often, Demand Planners from other organizations, industries, and regions of the country become valuable resources you can call upon for help. Networking with peers can help us uncover ideas and spark inspiration, especially when we get to know each other on a professional and personal level.

Encountering New Technology

Too often, people shy away from software vendors at conferences. They fear that they will have to talk to salespeople, but these software providers and consultants are some of the best people to know if you want to learn more about planning and forecasting. New technology is being developed all the time and conferences are an excellent opportunity for discovering innovative products and services that can help you stay competitive. Plus, these vendors fully grasp what is happening inside your industry and what other companies are doing as best practices. Invest time with the sponsors/exhibitors at conferences and turn them into your friends and allies.

Sharing

There are a couple of ways that sharing provides benefits. If you send someone to a conference and they learn, network, and see emerging trends in our field, then that's great. It doesn't end there. That person will bring all that back and share it with all the folks who didn't get to go to the conference. Second, I encourage you to write, speak, and share your insights with your peers at a future event. As much as you benefit from the knowledge of others, it is equally rewarding to share your lessons learned or case studies with them. As an individual, it validates your professional experience, knowledge, and skillsets in the field. For the company, it helps promote your organization and others see you as an innovator in the field, which helps with recruiting and your company's reputation.

Advancement

Standing still can kill your business. By making sure your team is constantly advancing, you will remain competitive. With IBF's training, conferences, and certification programs, you can stay ahead of competitors by improving your company's planning and analytical skills and knowledge. You will be able to identify and fill skills gaps. Demand Planners that know more bring more to the table, and your business will reap the rewards.

Finally, through continued investment in training and conferences, your team will have a much higher sense of job satisfaction, which can improve their motivation towards their work. This reduces employee turnover and increases productivity, which directly improves profitability. It also prevents competitors from poaching your best employees.

The Future of the Predictive Analytics Function

Seth Godin, the bestselling author of the books *Tribes* and *Linchpin*, said in an interview that if you can only do what someone else tells you to do and nothing more, then they can find someone (or something) cheaper than you to do it.[62] If you can think creatively through problems, present solutions, and make decisions, then you're a resource that can't be replaced.

The Institute of Business Forecasting (IBF) asked hundreds of demand planning professionals a few simple questions to gauge where they see demand planning and forecasting in the year 2025. A summary of the report came out in the Winter 2017/2018 issue of the *Journal of Business Forecasting*.[63]

While we did not ask directly if the demand planning role will be fully automated in the future, we did ask what the core competencies for the role will be in the year 2025. This, along with other questions, painted a picture of a changing and elevated demand planning role, taking it from technical, individual contributor to business leader and provider of insights.

According to many industry observers, we are today on the cusp of a Fourth Industrial Revolution. Developments in previously disjointed fields such as AI and machine learning, robotics, advanced analytics, 3D printing, cognitive technology, and deep learning are all building on and amplifying each other. Smart systems—the Internet of Things—will help tackle problems ranging from supply chain management to operations. Concurrent to this, the digital revolution threatens to not only give us more data but do our jobs faster, better, and cheaper than you.

What does this mean to us? Will we be replaced? Your view of a demand planning robot of the future depends on how you view your role today. If you are only doing what someone else tells you and aggregating data or relaying what the forecasting system is generating, then they can find somebody (or something) cheaper. If we just need a number, technology can do this faster and more efficiently with a greater number of inputs and more accurate outputs.

If you view demand planning as a means to estimate demand and answer questions for various business needs, then you are the next generation and ahead of the curve. For the last few decades or more, a forecaster's role has been primarily to provide an accurate single point estimate to a supply chain based on sales history and inputs from salespeople. The fact is the entire business, not just the Supply Chain, needs insights into what will happen. Focus is turning to the profitability of the entire enterprise that requires timely and detailed analysis. What we are seeing today and into the future is that the demand planning role is changing, and we need to migrate from big data to big answers.

So, what does this say about the role of demand planning in the future?

Demand planning can help provide insight to many other functions and is uniquely qualified to help a company paint a fuller picture of what is to come. We are storytellers who use numbers as our language, and all departments in the business will benefit from what we have to say.

The Demand Planner of the Future Will Not Report to Supply Chain

It may not—and I believe *will not*—be a Supply Chain role; rather, it will be elevated to a more unbiased centralized function with specialties that support multiple purposes and enables decision-making across the organization. The focus of demand planning will be more on sales enablement as well as a general business enabler. When you have more than a dozen people acting as decision makers and influencers with lots of competing priorities for their time, attention, and money, having the right information at the right time is a big priority.

The Demand Planner of the Future Will Focus More on Pre- and Post-Analytics

The other thing the Demand Planner of the future may not be is the statistician and programmer you may think we need in the digital world of tomorrow. The truth is that as technology continues to advance it will not be the creators of the algorithms who are in high demand, but rather those who can interpret the outputs. We see this in our survey findings as well, with skills like software engineering making up only 1% of people's first choices and mathematics and statistics making up just a third of what the top choices received.

This is not to say that skills like R and Python and advanced analytical programming are not needed today. However, it does provide a possible glimpse of the Demand Planner of the future. Pre- and post-analytics that provide insights into what questions to ask and how to communicate the impact of the results for the business will be more in demand. These are two soft skills that may never be replaced by machines.

While these soft skills/core competencies are important, judging from the survey data and what we are seeing directionally, the Demand Planner of 2025 will be an elevated role that will creatively think through problems, present solutions, and make decisions. If this is you, you will be a resource that can't be replaced.

Transforming Your Predictive Analytics Function

As analytics and planning functions go through the process of establishing their organizational structure, they should start with a basic blueprint. This helps ensure that all of the different roles, skills, and responsibilities are addressed at the beginning. This structure offers a guide for both employers and employees to match talent and capabilities with the most appropriate positions and responsibilities.

For new analytics and planning departments, I recommend you centralize this function and these roles under one umbrella as much as possible from the outset. For leaders with current demand planning, forecasting, collaborative planning, and analytics capabilities in place, these organizational design principles can be leveraged to address any gaps that you may be trying to address. Ultimately, it is this structure that will get the right people in the right roles.

Where in the World are Analytics and Planning?

Demand planning, analytics, and related roles are gaining crucial importance in all organizations today. And the way a function is set up and run has a decisive impact on its success. People have gone round and round as to where demand planning should fall inside an organization with no clear consensus on where it should reside. I have reported to Sales, Operations, and even directly to the CFO. Wherever I have been, or wherever people place demand planning roles, nobody disputes the need for demand planning or the value of cross-functional collaboration.

One of the most common homes for demand planning is the Supply Chain with recent IBF surveys revealing that over 52% of companies house it there. The demand plan drives the supply chain in many companies, so it made sense in many organizations to place the function inside the Supply Chain department. But with the increase in data, the advent of advanced analytics, and the need for company-wide, data-driven decisions, companies are increasingly looking for other options.

Much like predictive analytics driving Sales or Supply Chain, equal importance is being placed on Product Life Cycle Management, Marketing, and Financial Planning. And that requires an independent, centralized function to support all departments. Data, insights, and knowing what will happen next are a universal need, not just a Supply Chain need. For predictive analytics to drive a business it needs to be a business function.

The benefits are clear: companies need to be more agile and efficient. Sharing the right resources makes sense. Leveraging predictive analytics inside your organization gives every business function greater visibility and better planning. Reducing latency in your processes, demand sensing, collaborative planning, and effective decision making are what every department can expect from a centralized demand planning and analytics function.

Getting Organized

How do you determine which organizational structure is best for you? That answer depends on the maturity of your company's demand planning and analytical capabilities. There are three potential scenarios that impact how you structure your demand planning and analytics.

Firstly, there are organizations where analytics is less understood, where there are only a handful of Demand Planners/Analysts, and where there is no executive sponsorship. In organizations that are just starting their voyage into predictive analytics, it's important to recognize that most companies don't need to use them in every area of operations. Nor will such organizations have enough analysts to justify centralizing resources. In this case, the best recommendation is to place the function wherever it has a willing sponsor or champion.

The second scenario is where the importance of demand planning has grown and the company has hired more analysts. As analysts increase in number, so do skill sets and company-wide adoption of processes and analytics. There may be a desire from senior management to embrace the digital transformation, meaning the need is quickly outpacing the supply of people or capabilities. In such cases, you may consider a hybrid approach. Many companies on their path to centralization begin with a Center of Excellence (COE) for analytics and demand planning. In this case, a decentralized team of analysts is complemented by a centralized COE who work on more advanced analysis and best practices.

The final option is a mature organization that fully embraces the possibilities that demand planning, predictive analytics, and data science can offer. Once an organization gets a critical mass of experts and qualified Demand Planners, one of the more centralized models is the right choice. A centralized enterprise-level organization makes it easier to meet strategic business initiatives efficiently and effectively. An analytics and planning department can (and should) be elevated to an independent, unbiased centralized function with a variety of specialized roles and teams that support multiple purposes and enables decision making across the organization.

Structuring Predictive Analytics Departments and Roles

We found that organizations with a centralized function collaborate with many parts of a company to bring key business intelligence into the demand plan. A group that is well-organized and well-positioned accesses more data, which improves the accuracy of forecasts and value of demand plans. This instills trust in the demand plan and engagement of key stakeholders in the planning process. We also found that centralized departments are also better at communicating the value of predictive analytics in an organization.

There are massive advantages for talent management too. Grouping analysts together helps to maximize the fit between analysts and the organization. According to what I have found, nearly half of all analysts working in centralized groups report a high degree of fit with their organization. By contrast, talent deployed as consultants or dispersed in other functional areas often feel like misfits—isolated from their core business and other analysts.

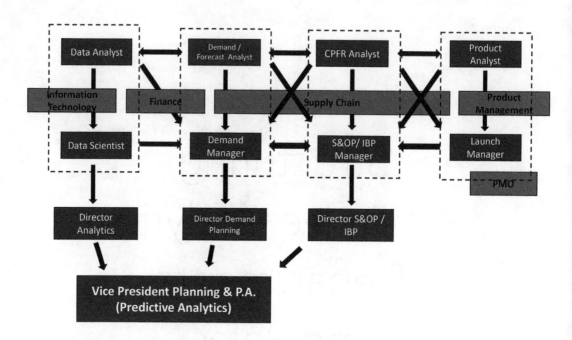

Fig x | Organizational structure for a planning and predictive analytics function

The organizational chart for an Analytics and Planning function can differ widely across organizations and industries. The exact naming and scope of responsibility of the team may vary slightly from organization to organization. These variations depend on the breadth and complexity of the analytics and planning capabilities being delivered, but the fundamental work and organizational structure should be about the same. The analytics and planning function has a range of objectives for the organization: from prediction and analytics to planning collaboration. The following illustrates a typical organizational structure for a centralized function, not focused on any specific industry.

There are countless roles today in data, analytics, and demand planning and many different ways you can climb the ladder. However, we see four primary analytics and planning career paths.

Analytics Development (Data Analyst, Data Scientist)

Analytics Development oversees the technical aspect of analytics environments and is responsible for producing analytical models for a company's major business processes. The main roles here are Data

Analyst or Data Scientist and the core competencies are problem-solving, diagnostics, and the ability to visualize links between seemingly disparate things.

These roles provide support to all lines of business and corporate functions. In the case of an organization with a decentralized analytics function, each corporate function may have a Data Scientist or Data Analyst dedicated to producing analysis specific to their business processes. However, those resources (typically) are ultimately under the control of the centralized Analytics and Planning function.

Business Analysis (Demand/Forecast Analyst, Demand Manager)

If Predictive Analytics is both an art and a science, the Business Analyst is the person who brings these two disciplines together. This role oversees the process of using analytics, data, insights, and experience to make predictions and respond to various business needs. The insight gained by business forecasting enables companies to automate and optimize their business processes. These are more traditional planning type roles such as Forecast Analyst, Demand Analyst, and Demand Manager. While they may be analytical problem solvers, they also demonstrate effective gathering and interpretation of information, having to analyze situations and identify implications to make decisions.

In some companies, these roles reside in Finance, Sales, or Supply Chain, but they really need to be elevated to a more unbiased, centralized function. With specialties that support multiple purposes and enable decision-making across the organization, an independent demand planning department provides enterprise-wide improvements. Centralizing the function means going from simply providing numbers to providing answers—it responds to business challenges and exploits commercial opportunities.

Collaborative Planning (CPFR Analyst, S&OP/IBP Manager, Analytics Translator)

These roles and resources are devoted to not only the inputs but also the impacts of the planning process. Both internal and external collaborative planning roles help develop the required synergies with customers and suppliers (and every function in between). These roles vary depending on the organization, but they include Collaborative Forecast and Replenishment (CPFR) Analysts and

S&OP Mangers or Champions. These roles share a common theme of being both data-driven and process-orientated; indeed, they must combine these two elements to ensure continuous alignment between planning roles and other functions, and between tactical and strategic plans. These roles are usually collaborative and end-result focused. The core competencies of professionals in these positions are process-oriented, ability to assume responsibility, and strong communication skills.

Even more recently, we have seen newer non-traditional roles creep up under collaborative planning as well. While these roles are not managing processes, they are managing the inputs and outputs and interpretation of processes. These are roles like Data Interpreters or Analytical Translators that bridge the gap between information and insights. They are highly collaborative and communicate the impact of data to multiple functions.

In a collaborative environment, everybody comes together. But given that people and processes are dispersed across the organization in multiple functions, there should be a centralized coordinator from the planning or analytics department who oversees everything. These collaborative roles serve to align all functional areas under a unified set of assumptions to enable and coordinate decision-making and bridge any gaps between data, forecast, product, and other areas both inside and outside the company.

Product and Market Management (Product Analyst, New Product Launch Leaders)

Whereas collaborative roles focus on outcomes, these roles deal more with execution. Positions include Product or Market Analyst and Launch Leader, the latter overseeing the final leg of new product introductions. These roles may deal with a specific product, merchandising, the market, or marketing campaigns. They deal both with the predictive and descriptive analysis and the execution of the plan. People in these positions are process- and project-oriented and have the unique competency to visualize the total process, identifying problems along the way.

Mature organizations tend towards a centralized position that leads these introductions from a final execution point of view and coordinates the analytics, planning, and deployment processes. These project-oriented roles may work closely with Commercial and Operations but report to the Analytics and Planning department.

Analytics and Planning Departments Work with the Overall Picture

This perspective is grounded in a Vice President or even Chief Predictive Analytics or Planning Officer having a seat at the executive table and direct accountability to the Chief Executive Officer. Let's look back to the 1990s when the IT function was buried under Operations or Finance with no chief-level officer governing its activities. Fast forward to the early 2000s and it became a recognized and respected function in its own right, with its own C-level leadership. Demand planning is in the same position IT was in the 1990s, waiting to get the recognition it needs to deliver its full potential.

As far as the overall function goes, the department will be data-driven and work collaboratively to provide a picture of what is to come or how to get there. As a centralized department, it helps a company see, interpret, and act on data and insights faster and more efficiently. Having specialized roles helps manage assumptions and processes from multiple inputs such as financial plans, market plans, sales plans, and industry information more effectively.

To meet the needs of both the employee and employer, companies should look at structuring around these key roles and developing a robust Analytics and Planning Department. Companies must also provide career paths to meet the challenges of today and the objectives of tomorrow.

SPOTLIGHT

Lowe's Data Interpreter/ Analytics Translator

In the early 1990s, a book came out titled Men are from Mars, Women are from Venus. Relating this to our world today, it may be more appropriate to say predictive analytics professionals are from Mars, Supply Chain is from Jupiter, Sales are from who knows where, and executives are from another solar system. Even though communication is critical, speaking a common language is difficult and, when it comes to communicating and interpreting data to other functions, it is almost impossible.

This is where a new role is emerging that helps bridge this gap. The Analytics Translator is a conduit between data scientists and other analytical roles and executive decision makers. They are multilingual in the sense that they can speak to multiple functions at their level and in their language. They are specifically skilled at understanding the business needs of an organization and are data savvy enough to be able to talk tech and distill it to others in the organization in an easy-to-understand manner.

One company that is at the forefront of using analytics to help drive the organization is Lowe's. Operating over 2,000 retail stores, they are the second-largest hardware chain in the world.

Lowe's mission is: "Together, deliver the right home improvement products, with the best service and value, across every channel and community we serve." Imagine doing this with hundreds of thousands of SKUs across multiple markets and stores. This becomes a serious data and analytics problem, one that requires a data interpreter to solve.

Lowe's has embraced analytics and data and has made it a competitive advantage. Think about the next potential hurricane. Lowe's uses weather forecasts and predictive analytics to help prepare stores so customers have what they need for major weather events. They have a retail analytics team that helps integrate analytics into the user experience. Another team carefully builds machine learning tools to help Lowe's pull apart historical sales at a very granular level to see just what shoppers are looking for in any given category. All of this needs to be brought together and translated so everyone in the organization can benefit from the data and insights.

"Executives like to believe that 99 percent of your time is spent on building the algorithms involved—but actually that's the smallest part," said Doug Jennings, VP of Data and Analytics at Lowe's.

To serve as middlemen between the data science team and other departments, ensuring that everyone involved understands both what is happening and what is possible, Lowe's created a team of "analytics translators." As organizations turn to analytics, modeling, AI, machine learning, and similar technologies, there is a growing danger that project goals or insights gleaned from data could somehow get lost in translation. Lowe's understood this and saw the need for an analytics translator or data interpreter to go beyond building models and start building insights.

These analysts or data translators are not necessarily solely analytical specialists or trained Data Scientists. Analytical translator professionals who work at Lowe's are doing the larger part of analytics and partnering with the business to create a roadmap of analytic solutions to solve strategic, tactical, and/or operational business problems. Part planner, part techy nerd, part peacemaker, part presenter, and part visionary, the translator's job is a new role that has emerged from the intersection of business processing and predictive analytics. For Lowe's, it helps smooth out the disconnects in business relationships. They operate as advisors, liaisons, project managers, and subject matter experts in presenting both data insights and business goals to the appropriate teams.

It seems like every company is or will be talking about data lakes, big data, and analytics. As more and more devices become connected via the IoT, companies everywhere will be scrambling to collect, structure, and organize all the data they can about their customers' habits and desires. For this new era, the continuing question will be if they will need a data translator to help explain the data insights that will be created.

For organizations that can afford a predictive analytics team, arriving at actual analytic insights can be challenging enough. Add in trying to decipher those analytics so everyone in the company can understand them, and it may seem impossible. Systems on their own may not fully understand the primary business motivators and traditional Demand Planners may not have enough technical expertise to know what questions to ask. Executives do not always comprehend the data and are looking for concise insights that the data or systems on their own can never provide. A data interpreter can do that one role, even for small organizations, to facilitate and be the intersection between data and insights.

The emerging role of Analytics or Data Translator adds resources to a team that may already include Predictive Analytics Professionals, Demand Planners, Data Scientists, Data Architects, S&OP Coordinators, and others. As a predictive analytics function becomes more independent and centralized, organizations start to make data and analytics available to more people and predictive analytics becomes a more shared service for everyone

Winning Support and Executive Buy-In

There is a distinction between the snake oil salesmen peddling a questionable forecast and a partner presenting a solution. Even though you know intuitively why demand planning and predictive analytics are important and why absolutely everyone should embrace it, others may not understand that yet. Here are five steps to convince your company they need to expand your predictive analytics capabilities.

Learn Their Language

One of the first steps in any forecasting cycle is defining the need. This should also be the first step in getting executive support for predictive analytics and advanced demand planning. You must understand not just what you think you can provide them but what they are looking for. The last step in any forecasting cycle is managing and communicating the output. In between is where you collect data and model them.

Think of garnering support from executives in a similar context where you understand the need, figure out how predictive analytics can fulfill that need, and then translate that to executives in a language they understand. An example of speaking their language is doing away with details and providing high-level summaries. Executives most often deal in numbers but also sometimes impacts on EBITA or cash flow. They may not want to know the probabilities or what models you used, but they may want to know what broader risks and opportunities analytics can reveal. Before you sell the idea of advanced analytics, you have to understand what it is they want and how much they can afford.

Educate

Educating people about the value of predictive analytics and demand planning is not limited to executives. In addition, educate everyone who is impacted by them (which is everyone). Whether others realize it or not, forecasts are essential because every business decision relies on predictions. Another way to look at educating people about the value of the function is to consider it your responsibility to build the brand of the department. This can also serve as a foundation to align the team's capabilities with the goals and aspirations of the broader company. Moreover, a strong brand can enable demand planning to be proactive about its role in the company. A good brand is all about who you are and what you want to be known for in the organization. It may seem unconventional to brand an internal department in the spirit of an Apple or Amazon, but it can have tremendous benefits in one's ability to compete for attention, budget, and relevance within an organization.

Find a Champion and Sponsor

This may or may not be the same person. A sponsor is someone who has some authority and ability to speak on behalf of the executives and helps with resourcing or sustainability. A champion can be anyone with influence and acts like a cheerleader for your process and department; someone who believes in what you are doing and helps others see its value.

There are many companies where having "a" forecast is not the problem; rather, the problem is that every department has their own forecast. Find out where your strongest ally or grassroots support exists. Here is where you can start building a champion for your process. Do not assume this person must be from Supply Chain either. I have found support for advanced analytics from a CFO, VP of Sales, Director of Online Marketing, and even HR.

Reveal the Value of What You're Proposing

The number one reason most people lose a sale is because they don't adequately reveal the value to the customer. Executives are rarely going to come to you with a pile of money and resources and tell you to build a planning department. You need to build the case and ask for it. This means a few things like understanding and developing a return on investment (ROI). This is one of the biggest questions I get from people trying to build departments and I admit it is a tough one. But if you cannot tell the executive team how they'll benefit, how do you expect them to buy what you are selling?

Do your research both internally and externally. Then, with confidence, explain what hard and soft benefits the company will gain through your proposal. Be willing to provide the hard truth that some may not want to hear. Identify what is being missed currently and what the advantages and limitations of changing things will be. Be honest, once again be confident, and, whenever possible, have rigorous, deductive proof. And don't oversell; know when to stop talking and start listening but not before you ask for what you and the company need to be successful.

You May Not Get What You Want

"You can't always get what you want but, if you try, you might find you get what you need"—a song written by Mick Jagger and Keith Richards—is an appropriate quote regarding the endeavor of getting executive buy-in. Finally, to be considered a part of the executive team, and not an outsider, you must appreciate executives' perspectives. You must be sensitive to the organization's structure, limitations, and priorities. At times, executives may be sympathetic to the need for a formal predictive analytics and planning function but may let other priorities take precedence. So be patient—winning the confidence or support of top management can take time. Management may not be ready to give you all that you're asking. Get what you can and make the best of it. Over time, they will recognize the need for this function and be ready to provide more support.

Summary— Data Science or Demand Planning

In the past decade, data scientists have become essential assets and are present in many top organizations. These professionals are well-rounded, data-driven individuals, with high-level technical skills, who are capable of building complex quantitative algorithms to organize and synthesize large amounts of information to answer questions and drive strategy in their organization. But, put these same professionals into the situation of driving a weekly sales forecast or a collaborative process, and most data scientists would perform terribly.

Data science projects usually come in stages and while they may manage a regular or on-going output, they thrive in a project-based environment. When a business has a unique question or problem, raw data is sourced and cleansed, an algorithm or models is trained and tested, and then it is put into production to make useful for the business. Compare this to a recurring business demand planning need whereby you are answering the same question every week or month and your data sources are updated daily. Data sources may also include many qualitative assumptions from Sales, Marketing, and customers, and you need to select models on the fly while in production and retrain your models every time you want to generate a new forecast.

In the past 30 years, forecast analysts have become an important part of most companies. These professionals are well-rounded, process-driven individuals with high-level business skills who are capable of managing complex planning processes to organize and synthesize large amounts of information used to answer questions and drive business processes. When it comes to understanding the drivers behind the forecast, using the scientific method, and using data analytics to solve other problems, these people struggle.

A common demand planning challenge is failing to consider the factors outside of their own four walls and not knowing what data to keep or discard, or how to interpret them. In this new world, this can include website clicks, dynamic pricing, or consumer information and sentiment. While most traditional demand planning only creates an estimate of demand, we need to look at the future and predict what will happen "if." To do this, we need data science and analytics. We need to go beyond knowing what has happened. This way, we can provide the best assessment of why something will happen or what drivers will impact something occurring in the future.

The problem is that much of forecasting, data science, and demand planning has not changed much over the years. Way too many Demand Planners are stuck in old technology (often Excel), looking only at historical sales data and churning out a forecast every week or month based more on art than science. Meanwhile, Data Scientists struggle with the ambiguity of forecast imprecision and making the transition to the demand planning world.

Both are a multidisciplinary blend of using data inference, critical thinking, processes, and technology to solve problems. Over the last few years, both demand planning and data science professionals are in strong demand and both careers have promising futures. And in many companies, they are not that different, and we are seeing these disciplines being centralized, combined, and overlapped.

The line between data science and demand planning roles is becoming more and more blurred. Both roles bring unique skills to a company. You need, in your role, to better understand what your strengths are, what you may need to improve, and what it takes to be a demand-planning-data-science-rock star.

The organizations that understand this are building predictive analytics functions and, consequently, building a competitive advantage. Instead of focusing on one size fits all, they are focusing on the core competencies and skills each person brings and exploiting them. They are working on building a diverse function that can handle data science, the planning process, and everything in between.

Section Review

Multiple Choice: Identify the choice that best completes the statement or answers the question.

1. The following is NOT a pillar that enables a demand planning organization:

    a) Strong talent base.
    b) Proper training.
    c) Benchmarking MAPE to industry or competitors.
    d) Analytics-driven culture.

2. Which are the competencies of a good Demand Planner?

    a) Handle ambiguity.
    b) High social intelligence.
    c) Learning agility.
    d) All of the above.

3. Which of the following are the most common technical core competencies?

    a) Knowing how to code.
    b) Seeing connections in things.
    c) Demonstrating effective use of information.
    d) All of the above.

4. The advantages of attending or sending your team to a conference are:

    a) To give you a competitive advantage.
    b) To retrain or refresh skills.
    c) To improve job satisfaction and engagement, reducing employee turnover.
    d) All of the above.

5. Centralized demand planning and predictive analytics functions can:

    a) Improve the accuracy of forecasts.
    b) Allow one person to do multiple roles.
    c) Minimize the need for collaboration with other functions.
    d) All of the above.

True or False

6. ☐ When hiring for demand planning roles it is always better to find someone in a similar industry and to prioritize analytical skills over other skills.

7. ☐ A core competency is what you teach if the employee already has basic technical skills.

8. ☐ Demand planning works best if it is a Supply Chain role.

9. ☐ Data interpreters, data scientists, product analysts, and launch leaders are all variations of the demand planning role.

10. ☐ Part of selling the idea of a predictive analytics function inside your organization is being able to accept and understand why they might say no.

PART VI

PREDICTIVE ANALYTICS AS A SYSTEM

After reading this section, you should be able to:

- Understand the differences between open-source and other software.
- Explain how to choose the right software and what it may cost.
- Have a good idea of what benefits may come with new technology.
- Know what it takes to be successful at a transformation project.
- Identify what a predictive analytics system is and why all the components are important.

Rise of the Machine

Undoubtedly one of the biggest areas of growth over the next few years will be in demand planning and business forecasting technology. Right now, demand applications account for just about a third of a $2 billion-plus market. By 2025, global revenue from demand planning applications alone is estimated to generate over $8 billion.[64] These applications are often (and will continue to be) a wedge purchase; a solution that is implemented as the first step in a broader analytics-driven digital transformation.

Part of this expansion will be due to the expanding role of predictive analytics and the diversity of vendors offering products. Before, you were married to a legacy ERP system or supply chain suite for your forecasting tools. This is quickly becoming outdated and new technology is enabling better and broader services. Now predictive analytics and forecasting can be available as a forecasting package or standalone system in the Cloud, as part of a Business Intelligence (BI) software, or as open-source technologies.

Along with the people and processes, the technology of demand planning is undergoing an enormous transformation. While it has historically been about capturing sales history and feeding a replenishment or manufacturing signal, companies are becoming more proactive and data-driven across the entire organization. With major advances being made in AI, machine learning and predictive analytics, businesses are investing heavily to get ahead of the competition and increase their bottom line. The advent of technology is allowing—and at the same time forcing—demand planning to become much more strategic and feeding Marketing, Finance, Product Management, and other areas of an organization.

Digitalized demand planning and predictive analytics processes are becoming imperative for organizations that want to stay ahead of competitors, target customers, and drive company profits. Making sales is no longer a matter of simply reacting—instead, it requires continuous proactivity to successfully predict and target demand. As AI capabilities offered by forward-thinking vendors continue to improve, they will become an increasingly intrinsic part of the demand planning function, further improving performance and efficiency.

Open-Source Tools Available for Forecasting

At the time of this book's release, the majority of advanced predictive analytics and machine learning projects are still being done by data scientists in programming languages such as Hadoop, Apache Spark, Python, SAS, and R. At the same time, it is estimated that 60% of forecasts created by Demand Planners still use Excel. This demonstrates not only the wide gap in technology but an opportunity in both what we do and how we do it.

I am not discounting these platforms and there is an underlying reason why people use them. For most, it is what they know and what they have access to, and there are some great features in all of them.

Let's start with the system that currently runs most businesses and the one you are likely most familiar with—Microsoft Excel. Yes, Excel will continue to be an analyst tool way into the AI revolution. Like author Nicolas Vandeput said in his book *Data Science for Supply Chain*, Excel is like the Swiss Army knife for an analyst. It is less of a black box than other platforms and allows you to see your data and how it is transformed.[65] Although you may not be able to do complex neural networks, it performs many time-series calculations more easily, which is sometimes all you need.

Of course, Excel has its limitations. Most of the more advanced modeling such as machine learning algorithms you will struggle with or not be able to do in Excel. There is also a data limitation, which makes using it for large data sets clunky and problematic. Also, when you start feeding it multiple SKUs or a whole lot of different variables, running all the different simulations and computations can weigh even the best machine down.

This is where open source comes in for analysts who want a little more. **Open-Source Software:** *A type of software where the source code is publicly accessible (open) and grants users the right to change, modify, or share it.* To help with big data, people have turned to open-source platforms like Hadoop and Apache Spark. For a lot of people in the data science world, they used software like SAS at college and learned to code in languages like R and Python. For larger data sets or more complex modeling, these have become the go-to software. All of these, as well as some others not mentioned, do an excellent job on the platforms they have set out. They are all relatively user-friendly and in many respects are simpler than an Excel macro.

What is Hadoop? It is used frequently with big volumes of otherwise unmanageable data. An open-source software framework for storing data and running applications on clusters of commodity hardware, it provides massive storage for any kind of data, has enormous processing power, and the ability to handle virtually limitless concurrent tasks or jobs. Hadoop is used by companies with big data like Airbnb, Uber, and Netflix.

What is Apache Spark? This is another platform used to manage data and actually can work with Hadoop. It is an open-source engine developed specifically for handling large-scale data processing and analytics. Spark offers the ability to access data in a variety of sources, including Hadoop Distributed File System (HDFS), OpenStack Swift, Amazon S3, and Cassandra.

What is Python? With origins as an open-source scripting language, Python usage has grown over time. It is an interactive and interpreted high-level object-oriented programming language. Easy to learn and understand, it is largely used as an open-source scripting language that supports many libraries used for data analysis (pandas), scientific computation (NumPy, SciPy), and machine learning (scikit-learn). Python is used by many of the larger tech giants such as Google, Quora, and Reddit.

What is R? R is a free open-source platform. As it is open source, it is highly extensible and there are quick releases of the software with the latest techniques. R is strong in visualizations and graphics and able to do multiple different functions. It is not hard to learn to code in R, and once you learn the fundamentals, the logic gives you endless possibilities. You can find multiple information sources for R on the web. Companies that use R include Facebook, Google, and Microsoft.

These are what we refer to as open-source software, which makes them unique compared to a demand planning tool you may purchase or modules you may install. In general, an open-source program is one whose source code is made available for use or modification as users or developers see fit. Additionally, they are available for free with a user community made up of fellow practitioners creating packages and codes anyone can use.

For big data and advanced analytics, the fact that these platforms are open-source and at minimal or no cost makes them attractive. Additionally, with open source, someone may have already tried to solve your problem and developed the model you need. Basic neural networks, decision trees, logistic regression, and even time-series models have been developed, tested, and are available for copying and pasting. Users do not find themselves limited to the methods and configurations of their off-the-shelf package that is part of a legacy system and can instead design and develop what they need.

People who work with open-source machine learning tools also find they have thriving online communities at their disposal that allow them to tap into collective thinking when they run into unexpected difficulties. R and Python are both open-source programming languages with large communities. New libraries or tools are added continuously to their respective catalogs. Those forums have hundreds of answers to common problems and, as machine learning tools become ever more popular, the knowledge base will expand even more.

Being open source also gives you the capability to code and create something new. Open source tools give developers the ability to tinker with them, thereby increasing the chances of rapid improvements or experimentation that can expand the features of tools.

But all of this does not come without risk. While college kids may cut their teeth on the surface of data analytics tools, not many people are experienced enough to code or create models. While coding is not as scary as it sounds, it still comes at the cost of time, effort, experience, and potential bugs. Not having the required resources may make specialized demand planning software more advisable.

Even open-source platforms come with limitations. A good planning system can do a lot more than just model, which justifies its cost. Besides being more user-friendly, most software offers the advantages of stability, easier deployment, better support, and governance. Even better, with advancements in software today, you can get advanced modeling and many now even offer interfaces that allow integration with open source platforms like R. This allows the benefits of advanced planning systems while providing modeling extension capabilities with R and Python.

How to Choose a System That's Right for You

Despite the importance of forecasting, demand planning software continues to be misunderstood by many businesses. Our research has revealed many are left unsatisfied with their software, even though demand planning tools can bring major improvements in business performance.

Unfortunately, many companies continue to labor under the illusion that an "almost" match is a good enough option. They either fixate on the most expensive products with all the bells and whistles or they over-simplify and assume any product will provide a decent forecast. The real focus should be on tracking demand streams and processes and finding the right technology that provides the right kind of support for your operations.

Systems that perform and support predictive analytics and demand planning include:

- Data Management systems with SQL databases, data warehouses, and data storage repositories (DB)
    - Database: Usually a large collection of typically quantitative information organized especially for rapid search and retrieval.

- Data Warehouse: Where data are stored after they are cleaned, transformed, and cataloged, and then made available for analysis, data mining, market research, and decision support.
- Data Mart: A subset of data warehouse, usually geared toward a specific business line or team.
- Data Lake: Generally, a large, easily accessible, centralized repository of large volumes of structured and unstructured data.
- Data Repository: A logical partitioning of data where multiple databases, which apply to specific applications or sets of applications, reside.
- Demand Signal Repository (DSR): A database or data warehouse that is used for aggregating and structuring demand data.
- Data Visualization: The graphical representation of information and data.

- Planning and Transactional systems
    - Forecasting System: A system that includes a forecasting feature and also feeds forecasts to various modules for planning.
    - Advanced Planning and Scheduling system (APS): A supply chain management system that analyzes and plans logistics and manufacturing resources during short, intermediate, and long-term periods.
    - Enterprise Resource Planning (ERP): Provides an integrated real-time view of core business processes, using common databases maintained by a database management system.
    - Customer Relationship Management (CRM): A system for managing all your company's data, relationships, and interactions with customers and potential customers.
    - Expert System: A software system that determines an optimal solution based on pre-determined rules.

All of these can play a part in an overall demand planning and predictive analytics system. Knowledge is power when it comes to choosing software solutions. Therefore, it's a good idea to do your research and read up on the most popular providers. It is also important to do your due diligence and come prepared with what exactly you need and understand the process and how it should work for you.

Regardless of which database or system you select, make sure that it offers robust solutions, automates various tasks, and is flexible enough to allow for necessary enhancements in the future. The most frequently heard complaint is that a system takes too long to complete even a small request. This happens because at the time of designing and implementing the system, the developer did not fully understand the needs of the users.

Another important consideration when implementing a system is to take into account your organization's plans for the future. One must anticipate what will be needed if the company grows. Make sure that the system you select can meet most of what you will likely require. It's difficult to foresee the future—as Demand Planners know—but with proper preparation, we can avoid many potential problems.

What Do I Need the Software to Do?

Which software is best for you? It depends. I know it sounds like a cop-out, but it would be truly irresponsible for me to tell you that a particular software will fit your needs without knowing exactly what your needs, maturity, budget, value chains, resources, and data look like. It is also irresponsible for any vendor to sell you anything without understanding your process and business. If they tell you a particular product is perfect for your needs, be very wary. And contrary to popular belief, it is not good enough if a system provides 80% of what you require. You do not need to settle; there are enough options out there for you to get what you need.

AI-based forecasting tools are now able to combine data from multiple sources, allowing for quick demand estimates for a given product. These tools can combine data that currently exists in a company's legacy systems to create comprehensive demand forecasts, far exceeding the capabilities of humans. There are open source technologies we have already mentioned such as R or Python that can be used to augment current processes or systems relatively easily. There are options out there and technology has advanced to the point that what you need may be achievable and affordable.

Map the Process

Before you jump in and throw technology at your problem, it is a good idea to understand the problem and your process. The first step any company should take when looking for new demand planning or predictive analytics software is determining your process, technical, and system needs; your budget and other constraints; and a detailed list of requirements. Most systems will have the usual industry-standard time-series forecasting algorithms, but maybe you also need some of the more advanced tools on the market. These include advanced analytics like machine learning, AI, Monte-Carlo simulation, and Stochastic Optimization.

Going through the design process first gives you a systematic way to work from abstract concepts down to specific technical details and physical designs for the solution; i.e., you start with the benefit you want to gain from the system and work backward until you get down to specific features.

To select the right technology for your operation, map the demand streams and the demand drivers. Consider a process map that helps visualize each step including inputs and outputs, as well as the technology or information you already rely on that will need to be integrated. Techniques like causality, seasonality, top-down and bottom-up forecasting, and forecast-value add analysis are essential to the selection of the technology because whatever system you choose must support them.

Understand Your Internal Customer

Think about your customers. No, not necessarily the end-users of your company's product but the internal users of your forecasting and demand plans. This can be Operations, Supply Planning, Finance, etc. Each internal customer may look at your forecast at different levels of aggregation and different time horizons and may need different levels of forecast accuracy.

From here it becomes easier to develop a detailed functional specification document that provides direction and guidance for what you need and the must-haves for when you start comparing solutions. In this document, simply list what you require. Remember to include the models you use, data and input requirements, and process steps it needs to support, and the metrics and information you need out of it. Address collaboration and process, functionality, as well as technical requirements. Your company's list may be 10 items or 50 items long. Take your time and include the must-haves and the like-to-haves.

System Requirements

Before we lay out what your exact system requirements are, you should understand some overarching principles of what you want to accomplish. Your next system is most likely doing more than just creating a forecast; you will also be enabling predictive analytics. But it is more than that. It is about getting the best forecast you can achieve to save or make your company more money.

As with AI, we should strive to automate and augment our forecasting and demand planning processes and outputs. A system should make things easier and not require endless resources. A good system will automate and perfect routine processes, freeing up planners for more value-added activities. It should also expand a planner's capabilities regarding inputs, processes, and outputs.

Second, we should not forget our primary objectives in developing any forecast:

- Create the most accurate projection of the future with the lowest error; and
- Eliminate or alleviate bias whenever possible.

However, you also need to think about removing latency in the process and being efficient at what you do. All of these should be at the forefront of your mind when determining the system requirements and individual features you may need.

With this in mind, below is a general list of some of the more common features you can find or may want to look for in your next system. Do not think of this as a complete list or that your system needs all of these. I have separated them according to three maturity levels to help you understand what you need according to where you are in your planning evolution. "Essential" should be considered just that—this the first stage in the planning journey and the foundation everything else rests upon. "Next Level" enables predictive analytics, but you may find you do not need or cannot get everything at this stage. Finally, "Vanguard" is for mature demand planning organizations looking to push the envelope. Here you may find some of (but not all) your requirements in a single system.

On a final note, this is a sample for you to use, expand on, and, most importantly, make your own. Remember this needs to be your list to meet your company's needs and resources. Typical requirements may include but are not limited to the following:

Essential

This is the first stage of a demand planning and analytics journey. This is what your system should have as standard. For some organizations, this may be all that you need.

- Full spectrum of time-series forecasting methods available (e.g., ARIMAX, Winters, Moving Average, etc.)
- Intermittent demand function methods
- Events and promotional planning capabilities
- Like products, market opportunity analysis, etc., to drive better NPI plans
- Manages demand planning consensus workflow
- Demand forecast error measured at different lags (e.g. MAE, MAPE, WMAPE, RMSE, Bias)
- Identification of outliers and data pruning
- Variety of standard reports, as well as a report writer for *ad hoc* reports from standard fields
- Ease of integration and reliability, and a high degree of support
- Simple to use—that doesn't mean a system should be simple, but it should be simple to *use*
- Languages/global presence and support
- Supports multiple calendars (production, fiscal, etc.)

Next Level

This is the next phase of demand planning and is where predictive analytics begins to be enabled through technology. This is more advanced software that provides more flexibility in inputs and processes.

- Regression methods (Linear, Ratio, Survival Analysis, etc.)
- Ability to utilize POS and external data signals
- Ability to run segmentation on multiple attributes
- Forecast generation using scalable dynamic multiple hierarchies
- Ability to perform simulations with complex event or pricing models and what-if scenarios
- Ability to dollarize forecasts and plans
- Overrides performed at varying levels by different users and then reconciled
- Handling of omnichannel, multi-region, or large product portfolio complexity
- Measurements to improve the efficiency and value of the demand planning and forecasting process instead of just the output (e.g., FVA, tracking signals)
- Facilitate comparison of multiple forecasts
- Point and click data visualization capabilities
- Interactive dashboards and reports that export to different channels (e.g., Microsoft office or other systems)
- Segmented and graphed results based on differentiating lags, hierarchy, segments, and inputs or process steps
- Web interface and mobile capabilities

Vanguard

A mature organization that fully embraces the possibilities that demand planning, predictive analytics, and data science can offer needs additional system requirements to support it. While these are not all necessarily core requirements for a Vanguard organization, a combination of these can be leveraged to reach the final level of maturity.

- Classification methods (Naïve Bayes, Logistic Regression, Decision Trees, Random Forests, etc.)

- Supports cluster analysis (centroid, K-Means, Nearest Neighbor, etc.)
- Can create a scalable multi-layer artificial neural network
- Automated new product forecast capability using data mining and other techniques
- Generate variance reports of budget, actual and forecasted numbers
- Leverages demand sensing to gain early insight into potential new patterns
- Open APIs and supports R or Python that can be used for extension modeling capabilities
- Provides support and functions for various applications of machine learning such as NLP and Reinforcement Learning
- Can optimize model performance through bagging, boosting, and building the model ensembles
- Allows the users to intuitively build data processing workflows
- Provides expressive Scala DSL and a distributed linear algebra framework for deep learning
- Can easily integrate any Hadoop or similar source to work seamlessly

Here we have only highlighted demand planning and forecasting packages. **Forecasting Package:** *A standalone package that generates forecasts either by a model selected by a forecaster or by an automatic feature (called an expert system) that is built into a software package.* If you are looking at an Advanced Planning System (APS) that does forecasting as well as supply planning, inventory optimization, and more, you will need to be even more comprehensive and include other functions as well. To this point though, with demand planning being more than just a supply chain process and with advancements in technology and integration, do not assume it must be part of a supply chain or ERP system to get what you need.

You no longer need a single solution and may be able to meet your organization's needs with a standalone forecasting package. Planning systems can now be homegrown and open source or part of a BI software, or even an external Cloud-based system. Regardless, the results are the same and a separate system provides valuable benefits as long as you know what you need.

System Cost and Resources

A good vendor becomes a long-term partner committed to the success of your business. The software vendor (or other consulting partner) can provide predictive analytics expertise you may not have in-house and should be a source of objective advice on addressing your business problems. All of this, however, comes at a cost.

When it comes to software, spending more does not guarantee you get more. We demonstrated this with the section on open-source software that provides a tremendous benefit. It should also be noted that popular doesn't always equate to quality, and an ERP or an APS that claims to do it all may not have the forecasting tools you need. There are plenty of specialized and lesser-known products that deliver brilliant results. But how do you narrow them down, and what does something like that cost?

What Is This Forecasting Software Going to Cost Me?

The cost can be determined by the users, size, or complexity of your processes and data. You'll pay either via a subscription or have an annual service contract that provides access to the software along with support. In addition to these annual or monthly fees, there is generally an upfront consulting or installation fee that should include project design, configuration, help with data extracts, and education. While sometimes this is a flat rate, it is usually on a per-hour or per-project phase basis. The scope of the project with key deliverables should be provided by the vendor before you start, and an indication of what it will cost.

Typical Cost May Include:

- Typical software costs (assuming data repository has already been licensed) anywhere from $5,000 to $30,000 per user or very roughly about $2,000-$6,000 for every $100,000 of revenue. These are ballpark numbers and vary based on packages, features, and other costs over and above basic systems.
- Typical consulting service costs range from $110 to $220 an hour per resource depending on the collaborative process and you will require anywhere from 600 to 2,000 hours depending on the complexity (these costs exclude travel and other expenses). This information can be difficult to get from some vendors upfront because they know costs can add up when dealing with teething problems following installation.

Never rush into a deal. If you try to do things as quickly as possible, you will likely miss the full scope of what you need and end up with a solution that fails to deliver the functionality you need, putting you in a position where you have to spend more money down the line. With all of this said, cost should be based on what you get out of it—it is important to understand what your benefits will be before you look at what vendors are charging. The benefits derived from an automated demand forecasting solution can be realized in both soft and hard cost savings, as well as overall process improvements.

Another critical question is: Do I have the right staff in place both from a planning and technical perspective to get the most out of this application? The resources you have at your disposal should directly influence the kind of package you'll buy.

Typical Internal Resources Include:

- Project Sponsor/Manager (full-time employee, 16-28 hours per week): Executive oversight, provides guidance. Works with a software provider to develop project plans and manage day-to-day priorities. Reviews deliverables for quality and completeness.

- Functional core team members (full-time employee, 6-18 hours per week each team member): Represents end-user and voice of the customer, validates business requirements, defines user workflows, validates functionality, provides testing.
- Technical core team members (5 – 15 days IT resources): Develops automated programs to extract and import data, acts as SME as required in support of a core team.
- Functional end-users (3 – 10 days per member): Functional end-user testing and training.

Good forecasting software can be a big investment—hundreds of thousands or even millions of dollars. But the payback in automation, efficiency, and forecasting performance can make a very real difference to both the top and bottom lines. When seeing the demonstrations and hearing the promises, remember that fitting a model to history is easy, but generating a good forecast is not. When selecting software, it is worth taking the time and effort to arrive at an informed decision.

A demand forecasting system lives and dies by how well the system implementation is handled. As the saying goes, "the devil is in the detail," which most certainly applies to a forecasting project. The essential message for every buyer is be skeptical of marketing hype and require demonstration of all vendor claims about performance, scalability, flexibility, and—especially—forecast accuracy.

Building a Business Case

The potential improvements in analytics, integration, communications, performance measurement, and visibility afforded across the business can greatly streamline decision-making processes, create new insights, and save several business functions a huge amount of time and money. This is so simple and obvious to you that you can't understand why your company does not invest in it already. But leadership doesn't always get it and will need convincing, which is why you need a business case.

Remember that your company will most likely invest in a new a system to solve pain points, drive quantified savings, or to deliver other clearly defined improvements. They need to be sold on the idea and you need to be the salesperson. To successfully build a business case, you need to both help the organization understand the need and see the benefits.

Most companies that decide to move to a new forecasting/planning system are primarily driven by one or more of the following:

- Obvious forecast accuracy challenges,
- A highly variable process that requires dedicated technology to support it,
- Detail-level forecasts that are required to support a more efficient manufacturing or distribution system,
- Downstream inventory problems that are clearly driven by demand variability, and

- An attempt to drive more cooperation between Sales and Operations through a consensus-based forecast.

A mountain of research today shows that improving forecast accuracy delivers a high ROI. Improved forecast accuracy, when combined with software that translates the forecast into meaningful actions, will decrease inventory and operating costs, increase service and sales, improve cash flow and GMROI (gross margin return on inventory investment), and increase pre-tax profitability. The forecasting error, no matter how small it is, has a significant effect on the bottom line. In our experience, a 15% forecast accuracy improvement will deliver a 3% or higher pre-tax improvement.

In a previous IBF study of 15 U.S. companies, we found that even a one percentage point improvement in under-forecasting at a $1 billion company gives a saving of as much as $1.52 million, and for the same amount of improvement in over-forecasting, $1.28 million.[66]

Indirect Cost Savings from Forecasting Software

Forecast process automation will reduce the time spent on creating and managing the overall forecast process but rarely results in hard labor cost savings due to redeployment. There should be operational efficiency gains from planning and scheduling improvements resulting from more accurate and (sometimes more detailed) forecasts. You can expect more predictable financial planning resulting from a more accurate forecast, as well as better consensus planning driven by the collaborative process changes.

Other soft benefits include saving time and energy by focusing resources on the right items. Do I really need to forecast hundreds of C items, or can they be grouped into more natural segments, allowing me to focus on the highest revenue/margin products and customers? This is a soft, non-quantifiable benefit. What ROI would you put on having a system that captures the planning process and BI of your teams? Most companies have this spread across hundreds of spreadsheets owned by just a few users—it is impossible to dollarize improvements like this, but they are valuable.

Hard Cost Savings from Forecasting Software

The reduction in downstream finished goods inventory resulting from forecast accuracy improvements

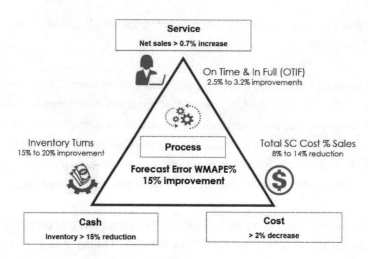

Fig y | Graphic showing typical benefits from a 15% improvement in forecast accuracy

provides a one-time saving, as well as recurring savings arising from reduced carrying costs. In a pure make-to-stock or distribution company, the downstream inventory reduction could range from 10% to 20% since forecasting inaccuracies typically drive around 75% of the required safety stock.

Many companies are leaving money on the table with lost sales or poor service levels. Forecast accuracy can translate to increased revenue of 0.5% to 3% with improved inventory availability or demand shaping capabilities. Total annual direct material purchase, along with logistics-related expenses arising from demand variability, can see direct improvements of 3% to 5%. We can also benefit from a 20% reduction in airfreight costs. Fig y shows the anticipated benefits from a 15% improvement in forecast accuracy (these are averages and individual results for organizations are dependent on many other variables and can be higher or lower).

It is important to understand these average savings amounts and you should determine what savings you believe you can drive with technology. Sometimes you need to know what finance and executive leadership anticipate in terms of benefits; you need to be on the same page in terms of expectations. It is here that many software providers can shed some light on what is realistic based on past implementations (keep in mind they are trying to sell you a product). Do your own analysis and reach a consensus with key people in your company before signing on the dotted line.

When to Expect a Return on Investment

Most technology should reasonably have a payback in less than 24 months with many showing ROI in under 18 months. If you're looking at a particular solution and the numbers are not adding up, you may consider a less expensive solution that meets your company size, and reconsider some of your functionality requirements. Remember not to settle. You just may want to keep looking for other providers that will not only give what you need but also at the price you can afford, complete with the benefits you want. Shop around, there's a lot out there.

Should You Use a Consultant?

So, you've got a long list of possible options for when you decide to upgrade or replace your demand planning and predictive analytics software. In the previous sections, we looked at the functional, service, technical, and implementation requirements of your new software. We have carefully calculated likely benefits and improvements and created our budget to look for an 18-month return on investment. Now it is time to find that perfect match and seal the deal.

Unfortunately, there is no perfect dating app for this. You can't just say what you want and when you and the solution provider both find a connection, you both swipe right.

From here, the next step is to begin conversations with the various vendors that meet your needs. A great place to start—outside of some simple internet searches—is by attending an IBF conference. Many of the top solution providers exhibit at these conferences, allowing you to find all the major vendors under one roof. This provides the opportunity to ask questions and even the opportunity for demos to see the functionality they offer.

For some, this is where things get even more confusing. How do you narrow down the list, scheduling demos and ensuring the right points are covered? Are you missing anything? Are you asking the right questions? If what you need is not overly complicated, many people can sort through the next steps of the process to a final selection. If done right, you'll have all the necessary information to make an informed choice and get the solution you need. But there is another potential option that may help save time and money.

Should I Use a Third-Party Company?

Many companies believe that going directly to a software manufacturer to obtain new forecasting or demand planning solutions is the best way to get exactly what they are looking for. For many companies, this will work and there are good solution providers that will help you get what you need. Unfortunately, the reality is that no matter how good you or the software provider is, there is still bias and you have no way of knowing if the software gives you exactly what you need unless you have used it before. What's more, you may not be completely confident you know what you need and want an independent, second opinion before you commit a big chunk of your department's budget.

Rather than relying on the biased opinion of a specific software developer, it may be best to involve a third-party, such as a software consulting company or even something like a trade organization like IBF, which offer advisory services to help with such problems. These businesses exist with the sole purpose of helping companies sort through their specific needs and budget, and navigate all available software options to find the best solution. They can also provide you with an in-depth analysis of the pros and cons of each of your options, along with an estimate of the likelihood of a specific software platform to stay at the "top of the heap" based on current software trends.

Beware the Limitations of Consultants

Consultants are not all-knowing though. You still need to do your own homework and due diligence. Just because you pay someone $650 an hour does not mean they know everything. Many naïvely assume all consultants are geniuses and later find out they are far from it. It is vital you still understand your own needs and requirements, budget, and estimated benefits; and stay heavily engaged. No matter how much analysis consultants do, they will never know the full details of your unique business or your employees.

There are many things good third-party consultants can do for you. Because a software consulting company needs to know the ins and outs of the industry, they are able to help you assess your needs and requirements too. Many consultants can facilitate process mapping exercises and drill down to better understand current and recommended future processes.

Although no third-party company can guarantee you the best package or a glitch-free roll out, they can help you avoid the potentially serious issues that companies face when they decide to implement a new software package. In addition to helping you locate the right software, a software consulting company can help you obtain a fair contract. They will have the necessary industry experience to know which contract terms to insist upon and which ones to avoid.

How Much to Pay a Consultant

All of this will come with a price tag. Many factors contribute to the total third-party consultant cost. The greatest aspect is the time investment. Generally, you are looking at anywhere from $150 to $650 an hour plus travel costs; however, some do charge flat project rates, which are highly dependent on the scope and everything they will be doing. The time or scope can be as basic as the software selection to full-service project management, so it is difficult to put a number on it.

Let's be clear though, hiring a consultant can be expensive. At the same time, with the many software vendors to choose from and potential pitfalls of the selection process, a good consultant can pay for themselves in project or contract savings alone. Additionally, if you are unable to do the implementation with your internal resources, the benefits of having an implementation consultant can be huge and ensure you launch your system as effectively as possible.

Is it expensive? Yes. Is it worth it to have the job done right? Absolutely!

Remember though, third-party consultants will not make us successful. Consultants can educate, suggest, coach, and help choose the right software, but they cannot make your company forecast better than your people and processes are capable of. Focus first and foremost on the right talent, culture, processes, and best practices that allow you to get the most out of the technology.

Digital Transformation

The transformation from traditional planning to predictive analytics is not about updating the demand planning function but about changing the culture of the company to drive benefits across the entire organization. For many companies, it is even wider than that, using predictive analytics to position them in their industry and driving strategic decisions. Companies no longer operate linearly with isolated departments; there is a whole new business framework we need to understand to successfully implement predictive analytics.

For many mature organizations, the journey of implementing new technologies for demand planning and predictive analytics is less about the system and more about company-wide digital transformation. It is about analytics, data, and visualization, as well as how you utilize that information. It is also about the people, culture, and processes, and how everything fits together.

Digital transformation is rethinking how an organization uses technology, people, and processes to fundamentally change the way we do business. This is substantially different than change, which may be incremental. Instead, this is a giant leap forward that is almost inconceivable until the transformation is fully achieved.

Change: Can be small and incremental, or it can be large and complex. But it is something that needs to be constantly monitored and maintained.

Transformation is almost always large and significant. Transformation is an internal fundamental change in your beliefs of why you perform certain actions. Transformation does not require any external influence to maintain, and because of its fundamental nature, transformation is more likely permanent.

The phrase digital transformation has become ubiquitous in the age of digitization and every company seems to be doing or preparing for a digital transformation project. That's because every organization—regardless of its size or industry—increasingly relies on data and technology to operate more efficiently and deliver value to customers. At the core of these transformation projects is a move towards insights and analytics that drive strategy and decisions for organizations.

This makes your predictive analytics process and technologies a critical component and driving force of many transformation projects. A good digital transformation project is truly a union of data, predictive analytics capabilities, and culture (people, processes, and technologies). Together they form the business ecosystem and canvas for fundamental change to meet tomorrow's business needs.

Data

In transformation projects, this is a foundational and primary concern. This is why I always start with data. Not only because it is essential but also because it shines a light on other issues. In transformation projects consider:

- Data transparency: In this age of digital transformation, optimizing predictive modeling requires the consideration of an increasingly complex web of variables. Factors like consumer sentiment, average hourly earnings, and even POS data, all need to be examined. A keystone of many digital transformation initiatives, data integration across the organization provides visibility to data previously siloed within various departments.
- Processing large data sets: When big data initiatives are included in a company's transformation efforts, predictive analytics has a goldmine of data that can be used for forecasting. With machine learning and predictive analytics, you can create better predictions with data from across the company that can be married with other data—like social media, environmental, historical industry data, and the like.
- Data visualization: Some team members are highly skilled in data analysis. Unfortunately, those

resources are in high demand and not everyone who needs to review data and contribute to decision-making can extrapolate decision-critical information from a spreadsheet of numbers. Data visualization tools and dashboards, however, simplify the meaning behind the numbers so that data-driven decisions can be made across the organization. It improves forecasting, as everyone involved can have a clear understanding of the critical data involved in the forecasting process.

Predictive Analytics

Emerging technologies like AI and IoT, as well as foundational technologies like data management and analytics, are important. A digital transformation strategy aims to establish a foundation upon which companies can leverage new technologies, both now and into the future. Success comes in transforming the data through technology and process into insights that enable business change to occur dynamically.

Business culture

Digital transformation is not about technology alone. It occurs at the intersection of people, business, and technology—and is guided by a broader business strategy. It is about creating and changing—no, better yet—it is about transforming the culture to be more analytically driven. With digital transformation, it is not only impacting all functions of an organization but democratizing data and predictive analytics so that foresight and insight drive decisions and strategy.

Five Pitfalls of Transformation Projects

Excerpts of the following originally appeared in a presentation by Eric Wilson on May 10, 2019. It was then developed into an online article and written and distributed by Arkieva: Key Supply Chain Digital Transformation Pitfalls to Avoid, May 23, 2019, https://blog.arkieva.com/supply-chain-digital-transformation/[67]

Predictive analytics and digital transformation have the potential to be, for want of a better word, transformative; when done right, a transformation project enables your business to reap significant and well-documented benefits. On the other hand, if executed poorly, these can cost companies millions of dollars, go on for years, fail to deliver the expected (or any) benefits, and ultimately end up costing the CEO and CIO their jobs.

Part of the reason for this is that transformation is more than technical. It's procedural and cultural. It can change how thousands of employees do their jobs, make business decisions, and collaborate across the company. It is not just a thing that you can buy and plug into the organization. It is multi-faceted and diffuse, and it requires foundational investments in skills, projects, infrastructure, and, often, in cleaning up current systems. It requires mixing people, machines, and business processes, with all the messiness that entails. It also requires continuous monitoring and intervention to ensure that both digital leaders and non-digital leaders are making good decisions about their transformation efforts. Predictive analytics and digital transformation can change everything.

A mountain of research today shows that improving forecast accuracy delivers a high ROI. Improved forecast accuracy using predictive analytics software that translates the forecast into meaningful actions will decrease inventory and operating costs, increase service and sales, improve cash flow and GMROI, and increase pre-tax profitability. The journey to digital transformation is no longer an option; it's a strategic mandate to stay relevant and ahead of your competition. Still, the unfortunate reality is that 70% of all transformation initiatives fail.[68]

So, what are the top 5 reasons that 7 out of 10 transformation projects fail?

1. Not Having a Vision

Building the business case for change is crucial to compel leadership and the entire organization to transform. Lack of a clear strategy and vision was cited by 35% of executives as a key barrier to achieving its full transformation potential.[69] By its very name, part of transformation is envisioning an unforeseen end state that is difficult to imagine. Companies struggle enough with assessing the current state of their supply chains, so asking them to envision a new one that is required to support the future state—from technologies and processes to human resources and governance—is even more difficult.

Before you start any transformation project, it is important to understand the why, what, and how, and then articulate a clear vision and path of the future state. Three steps should be followed in developing the case. First, articulate a need for change based on the company's current situation and market opportunities. Second, quantify the expected benefits and highlight how to achieve one or more corporate goals like growth or customer service levels, and calculate the return on investment (ROI). Third, explain how to show progress and measure success, which metrics will be improved, what the new performance targets and deadlines will be, and who will accountable.

2. Not Aligning to Business Strategy

Many failed forecasting and predictive analytics implementations can be traced back to a failure to properly understand and align with the business strategy. Sometimes we get caught up in the change process: the cool technology, the fancy optimization, and the improved processes that enable the flow of work. They often forget how these changes need to improve customer relationships, improve shareholder value, and help other functions to succeed. These results are a siloed approach to change and while the results may be an improvement on what was there before, they rarely lead to true transformation for the organization.

To help avoid this, any transformation project needs to be explicitly linked to the specific features of the business strategy. This could be a cost, cash, or service strategy with strategic features focused on a specific area. A great example is a company that plans a growth strategy by acquisition. For them, it may be important to focus more on the cash piece of the strategy with technology and processes that would be scalable across multiple different business models and can be quickly implemented in an acquired business.

3. CEO Is Not Engaged

The problem for most transformation projects is not that they lack executive sponsorship; rather, they do not have executive engagement. There is a difference between sponsorship and engagement. Digital transformation needs engaged leaders and stakeholders rather than seeking just sponsorship where the sponsor's role is open to interpretation. Engagement is a process of being actively involved and being seen participating in the process at every level.

Digital transformation is about sweeping change. It changes everything about how products are designed, manufactured, sold, delivered, and serviced—and it forces the company and CEO to rethink how companies execute, with new business processes, management practices, information systems, and customer relationships. Because of this, such projects cannot just be flavor of the month. A transformation project needs to be properly resourced and continually supported by actively engaged CEOs.

4. Not Having a Proven Change Management Methodology

Change is easy until you are asked to do it. In business, people build their careers on what they know and with any transformation project, it is hard for people to let go of what they're familiar with and embrace something new. Indeed, 43% of the 4,500 CIOs surveyed for the 2017 Harvey Nash/KPMG CIO survey cited resistance to change as the top impediment to a successful transformation strategy.[70] Resistance to change can grind transformations to a halt. For transformation programs to work, there must be convergence between the new process, new technology capabilities, new skills, and new organizational alignment.

Having a structured and proven methodology to show the way is a must. Any significant transformation program creates uncertainty and resistance. New leaders emerge, job descriptions are changed, and new skills and capabilities must be developed. Dealing with these change management issues on a reactive, case-by-case basis puts timeline, morale, and results all at risk. A structured and formal plan for managing change—beginning with the transformation team and then engaging key stakeholders and leaders—should be developed early and executed effectively as changes move through the organization. The plan should be comprehensive enough to cover planning, implementing, and sustaining the transformation changes.

5. Realistic Expectations

A major cause of predictive analytics failures is the mismanagement of expectations for what forecasting can realistically deliver. Some expect that you can just get customer data and a new system forecast should be close to perfect. The problem is that fundamental variability of the product or industry still exists, and a perfect forecast is unrealistic. Transformation can greatly improve accuracy, free up resources, and automate or augment processes or outputs. But even the best of these systems can only forecast as accurately as the nature of human behavior allows. No software can forecast with 100% accuracy every time, no matter how costly or complex.

Setting these expectations in advance is important for the success not only of the transformation project but also the longevity of predictive analytics and business forecasting. Hope is never a good strategy and even if executives hope for 99% accuracy from the implementation of a new system, it is your responsibility to bring them back to reality. I am not saying under-promise and over-deliver, but identifying realistic advantages and a timeline for the implementation of a system will stop executives from perceiving an implementation initiative as failure when it is anything but.

Building the Right Training and Development Program

The sixth reason why technology implementations fail is not in the vision or strategy, or even the level of CEO engagement; rather, it is adoption. No matter how great and intuitive the new tools are, implementation does not equal adoption. For success, you need to ensure that users are properly trained to facilitate acceptance and adoption of the new system. Without positive engagement around the product, you risk adoption falling flat and ruining the whole software implementation plan.

Unfortunately, far too often training is neglected or not properly budgeted. It might seem like an unnecessary cost but be assured—it is most definitely worth the investment. The cost of not properly using a great tool is likely much higher. Even some of the most experienced professionals can benefit not only from technical training of the software but also from professional training on best practices and processes to help them use it.

To prepare users and companies, training needs to be part of your implementation strategy. More than that, training needs to be a central pillar in your digital transformation. But much like implementation as a whole, the right kind of training done at the right time is better than poor training done often. Proper training consists of not only telling people what buttons to push but also revealing to people how their roles fit into the overall ecosystem and what they can do with the new technology. The technology will likely change or expand their roles, giving them the opportunity to do new things and the ability to add more value.

Train the Trainers

During the project—or even better, at the onset of a software implementation—you should identify someone who will be the subject matter expert (SME). This SME can not only help with implementation, but can also act as an internal trainer. When most people think of training, they think of a classroom and structured materials—this may be part of it, but just as important is someone people can turn to when they have a question or an issue they need to work through. Ensuring you have an in-house SME that is trained in the system, knowledgeable about the process, and aligned to the strategy is an important first step.

Learn the Tools

Your vendor is a key stakeholder in your software implementation plan. The extent of implementation support that vendors provide, and how much that costs, varies. You need a strong software provider that offers the right level of technical training on their system. The training is just as important as after-sale support. A lot of software providers have an onboarding program where they teach you how to get the most of the system. Make sure to understand what training they offer at the selection stage and make use of all the training they provide.

For the users, it is best to involve teams at the beginning of the project. Inevitably, there will be gaps in the vendor training, such as company policies and procedures as well as any customization you plan to do. Different roles will have varying levels of access to the same features, and how your team uses those features in their day-to-day jobs will vary. Take the time to define all your audiences by role, seniority level, and skill level. Define training requirements for each of these attributes and consider asking the vendor to supplement the standard training and deliver this more specific training.

Train Beyond the Tool

A strong training program will also include external or customized internal training that supports not only the technical aspects of the software but also the professional aspects of the role. New software implementation comes with a host of challenges. To fully realize the benefits of large-scale software initiatives, comprehensive training is critical; a lack of training can be a major setback in recovering the cost of implementation. Unfortunately, off-the-shelf vendor training packages don't always align with your company's business model, and customization can be expensive.

Remember, the goal is to prepare your team for the first day of go-live, which means training must go beyond system features to connect employees to the new way they will work individually and as a team. This internal customized training doesn't have to be expensive or drawn out. There are resources available that help fill these gaps so you don't need to reinvent the wheel.

Combining this with external professional training helps ensure you get the most out of your system. It works together with new software and enables users to take advantage all the features of the system and exploit all its capabilities. Training programs like the boot camps provided by the Institute of Business Forecasting (IBF) provide an excellent foundation. One of the main advantages of programs like these is that they reduce the learning curve and speed up ROI.

- It's in the interest of software providers that users maximize their system's capabilities, which is why many include external training as part of their implementation packages.
- For users, training is invaluable because it helps build confidence and allows them to understand the principles behind the features of the new system.
- For companies, training is invaluable because it extracts maximum value from a new system and, assuming the appropriate planning processes are in place, will provide an ROI.

Learning Should Not Stop at Implementation

To support the long-term ROI of your new system, put together a long-term strategy to keep professionals engaged and encourage continuous learning. Through groups like IBF, professionals continuously learn new processes and keep up to date on best practices. Returning to conferences and through reading articles and research, practitioners get a constant refresher course, reinforcing what they learn and keeping their knowledge current.

Cloud

At this point, the Cloud has gone way beyond being a buzzword and has shaped the way business is being done today. **Cloud Software**: *A metaphor for an application or process that operates outside of your own personal or company's storage or servers.* It has become one of the most powerful tools in modern businesses. Over the past decade, the Cloud has changed the Internet beyond recognition. Lower costs, flexibility, and stability are the basic benefits of cloud computing. These benefits help Demand Planners provide their organizations with better insights faster and more efficiently.

The opportunities and possibilities of the Cloud are bigger than the platform itself. It is the Cloud that has made possible the creation of millions of apps used by billions of people. This is just one feature of the Cloud; it also greatly amplifies computing power because programs running on the Cloud can be powered by far more powerful processors and software than those found on individual servers, desktops, or laptops. Hence, the Cloud allows smaller businesses to use data as easily as larger businesses can. Furthermore, it has allowed demand planning and forecasting functions to tap into new data sources, run multiple complex advanced models at the same time, and collaborate and share information like never before.[71]

The Cloud has reshaped the Internet into a more clear, friendly, and easy-to-use platform. Its benefits and importance to organizations are various and complex. Those familiar with the Cloud have already discovered its rewards; others are just getting on the Cloud and are uncovering its vast potential.

Cloud Computing—The Great Equalizer

With the increase in the amount of data, it is becoming problematic to keep all this data in-house and manage it yourself. We're talking about terabytes of data that are refreshed daily. At the same time, these data can provide extremely valuable insights when organized and analyzed. They help us to increase sales, create better forecasts, generate leads, and develop valuable market intelligence.

Today, small and large companies alike are taking advantage of the Cloud to tap into the gold mine that is big data and remain competitive. What could previously only be done with a large bank of servers and supercomputers is now being performed easily and cheaply with the Cloud. It has leveled the playing field when it comes to storing and using new forms of data.

Often, it is fundamentally cheaper to store data on the Cloud than on servers and the process time is typically faster. When demand planning is hosted within the Cloud, the costs of IT management are diminished. This includes the cost of upgrades, patches, and any form of general management. We are now realizing that data can be stored externally and manipulated virtually on the Cloud, at low cost, giving small companies the kind of insights previously available to only the biggest of companies.

The Cloud Enables Collaboration

Companies live on information, much of which is stored and shared on spreadsheets inside organizations. We have always preached the benefits of collaboration, but a perennial problem was that the data and information of one function were never in the right format for another. Demand planning often needs to provide data to sales teams around the globe and to get feedback. Meanwhile, Marketing needs the same information but presented in a different way. The Cloud makes all this possible.

With cloud computing, a Demand Planner need not be tied to their desktop because they can access this information and provide inputs from a tablet or even a smartphone. Collaboration through the Cloud opens up more information in more ways and allows more people access to the same data when and how they need to see it—without having to share large spreadsheets and emails. Your team accesses the exact data they need, when they need it, without worrying about how timely or accurate the data is because it is always up to date.

No business is an island. Businesses work with suppliers and customers with whom data must be regularly shared. The Cloud makes this easier too. Sharing data with customers can be done in the Cloud and providing or getting access to the right information can be as easy as a couple of clicks. Whether you're dealing with suppliers or customers, you can have access to valuable information in seconds, whereas previously it would often take a long series of emails.[72]

The Cloud Keeps Data Secure

Safety has always been an underlying concern when it comes to moving demand planning to the Cloud. Can you trust that it will safely store your data? The truth is that many companies are finding the Cloud to be safer than housing their data internally. Instead of shying away from the Cloud because of security, organizations today are migrating towards the Cloud because it keeps data more secure.

Most data stored on the Cloud is protected behind multiple layers of safety, meaning business and customer data are as secure as possible. Companies like Amazon (AWS) and Google Cloud have an incredible incentive to keep data safe and spend millions, even billions, on security. These and other companies are the data centers people are trusting when they refer to "the Cloud."

While a server may fail, the Cloud never does. Data stored on the Cloud is safer than data stored anywhere else. Data centers spend millions or billions to make sure data loss never happens because it can cost them much more if it ever does. Everything is backed up. Everything is duplicated. The chances of you losing data are minuscule and are shrinking every day as data centers add more redundancy (the act of duplicating data) and new layers of security using better technology.

Cloud Is More Up to Date

Your software may need to be updated with patches or version updates. When this happens on your server it takes resources and time, and hampers productivity. **Software as a Service (SaaS):** *A method of software delivery and licensing in which software is accessed online via a subscription rather than bought and installed on individual computers.* Compare this to the type of software on the Cloud that is updated automatically, eliminating the need for organization-wide software blackouts. And there is no waiting for the next release because being on the Cloud allows you to be up to date with the most recent version at all times.

The cloud removes latency in other information systems that previously needed to collect data through other means to store on your own servers. Real-time integration gives us real-time insight into demand. With access to real-time demand signals, the company can quickly and efficiently respond to any spikes or drops in demand, even when conditions are constantly changing.

Data Visualization and BI

The brain devotes up to 30% of its neurons to visual processing, compared with 8% for touch and just 3% for hearing.[73] It stands to reason then that research reveals that visual presentations are remembered 43% more of the time compared with other forms of information delivery. They're also more persuasive, with the presenter being perceived as more concise and clear, making better use of supporting data, as well as being more professional and interesting.[74] Visualization is key when we are trying to understand and interpret data or when we are looking for relationships among hundreds or thousands of variables to determine their importance.

One of the most effective ways to discern important relationships is through advanced analytics and easy-to-understand visualizations. **Data Visualization:** *The graphical representation of information and data.* By using visual elements like charts, graphs, and maps, data visualization tools provide an easy way to see and understand trends, outliers, and patterns in data.[75]

Demand forecasting and predictive analytics rely on data. Collecting and storing data in a single location and in a format that allows you to actually use and clean them, is critical. To understand the data, most companies adopt a BI solution to assist with data preparation and consolidation, analysis, visualization, and reporting.

Business Intelligence Tools: *Software that collects and processes large amounts of data from internal* *and external systems.* While not as flexible for planning as business analytics and forecasting tools, BI tools provide a way of amassing data to find information primarily through queries. These tools also help prepare data for analysis so that you can create reports, dashboards, and data visualizations.

Typically used for more straightforward querying and reporting of business data, BI tools are seeing a revolution in what they can do and what they can offer organizations. BI tools are changing fast to adapt to the user's needs regarding big data.

BI tools can:

- Combine a broad set of data analysis applications (*ad hoc* analysis and querying, enterprise reporting, online analytical processing (OLAP), mobile BI, real-time BI, operational BI, Cloud and Software as a Service BI, open-source BI, collaborative BI, and location intelligence).
- Include data visualization software that allows you to design charts, and tools for building BI dashboards and performance scorecards that display business metrics and KPIs.
- More recently, be used to forecast. Using open-source analysis tools like R or Python, BI tools have the capability for modeling and predictive analytics.
- Find new relationships in new data. It can be used to find previously unknown relationships in internal data, and some software offers access to large external data sets to find other leading indicators and predictive variables.

The rapid growth of data won't be slowing anytime soon. BI tools help you find new data, manipulate them, and visualize them. And then business decisions can be made, which drive value. Here are the five major areas where BI tools help you leverage the power of predictive analytics and data analysis:

Data Consolidation

BI software is built to collect, unify, sort, tag, analyze, and report on vast amounts of data. Most companies' data do not come from a single source nor are they held in the same place. A data warehouse can help you collect business data from multiple sources and use them for accurate reporting and analytics. BI tools working with data warehouses can better collect data from disparate systems and provide greater insight into the supply chain, sales, and financials, etc.

Data Preparation

What most organizations find when collecting data or trying to transform them into something meaningful is that data in the raw form are messy. Planners and companies spend hours and hours cleansing data, finding missing data, discovering outliers and irregularities in data, and formatting data for use. Most of the data companies have are inaccurate, incomplete, or unavailable. BI software can be used to organize and clean your data. This helps planners manage their data using just one solution, and build their analytics off more accurate data.

Data Visualization

One of the more powerful advantages provided by BI tools is being able to visualize your data. It allows you to use data visualization not only as the final step of the analysis when we want to share our findings with the team, but you can also quickly make sense of large amounts of information. BI tools visualize your outputs in formats that are easily understood and reveal more insights. Contrary to popular belief, data visualization is not simply the last step of an analysis. There's more to it than simply creating a quick chart for a presentation to management; it's part of visual analytics. Data visualization and BI software can help planners see relationships in data before they model them to help determine which data sets, clusters, attributes, and models to use.

Data Analysis

BI software is designed for complex analysis and calculations of large data sets. BI software that allows users to make queries and generate a report to answer a specific question often uses an online analytical processing (OLAP) "point and click" dashboard. **Online Analytical Processing (OLAP):** *A computing method that enables users to easily extract and query data for analysis from different points of view.* OLAP can be used to analyze large volumes of historical data with drill-down functionality. Information is stored in OLAP cubes and provides a multidimensional view of data. Many BI solutions now come with advanced analytical features that allow you to integrate open-source data analysis tools for constructing predictive and prescriptive analytical models.

Data Reporting

BI software gives you a single view into performance, complete with dashboards and reports for quick sharing and dissemination of real-time information. It also allows you to prepare a report and share it with your team in one click and to compare forecasts to see how you're tracking against actuals, budgets, previous forecasts, and KPIs. These reports provide a visual representation of data that is extracted in a query such as charts, maps, and graphs. This allows for better planning and more collaboration, both internally and externally.

SPOTLIGHT

Escalade Sports Transformation

The "Amazon effect" has already changed shipping, logistics, employment, and consumer behavior, not to mention giving a good kicking to brick-and-mortar stores. As a result, demand planning and forecasting are very different from how they were just a few years ago, and our jobs have evolved drastically.

When it comes to demand planning and forecasting, Amazon—and eCommerce generally—has been a phenomenally disruptive force. In today's business environment, changes in the marketplace are swift and sudden and may not follow the historical pattern, meaning time-series models cannot always be relied on for accurate forecasts. The new e-Planning environment is not just dynamic; it operates on the power of technology and innovation.

A small publicly traded company headquartered in Evansville, Indiana had seen the marketplace change over the past few years and the need to adapt and change to stay competitive. They understood the winners in this new era will be the ones that can see, interpret, and act on data the most efficiently. Like many companies, they embarked on a large predictive analytics and digital transformation initiative to totally change the way they consumed and interpreted data to create insights and respond to this new eCommerce world.

While you may not have heard of Escalade Sports, you may be familiar with many of the brands they own or distribute. Escalade Sports (ESCA) manufactures, imports, and distributes over 47 widely recognized sporting goods brands in basketball, archery, indoor and outdoor game recreation, and fitness products through major sporting goods retailers, specialty dealers, key online retailers, traditional department stores, and eCommerce.

Over the past few years, Escalade Sports, along with many similar companies, have witnessed a changing landscape in the way consumers are making purchases and how they need to go to market. Direct-to-consumer was less than 10% of all sales just a few years ago but now represents 25% of most companies' business and is estimated to grow at double digits over the next few years. With this, expectations change; companies have gone from delivering in two weeks in the BTB channel to having to deliver in less than 36 hours to satify consumers in the direct to consumer (DTC) channel.

All of this added up to more inventory, increased expediting and supply chain costs, and a steady decrease in customer service levels. Escalade realized they were nickel and diming themselves to cover planning and execution issues; that the market was shifting to eCommerce and DTC; that they were quickly outpacing their ability to stay in control; and that money was being left on the table by not having what online customers wanted.

To help focus the company's attention and work towards fixing the problem, the CEO highlighted three major initiatives:

- Digital transformation (we need to become more analytically driven and establish technology to enable our future needs)
- Consumer Direct (we need to ship every order on time and in full within 48 hours), and
- eCommerce (we need to grow this percentage of the business by over 20%).

Escalade Sports kicked-off a comprehensive digital transformation project whose goal was to standardize the planning processes to improve customer satisfaction and create competitive advantages with go-to market strategies while improving total cost and enabling inventory optimization by integrating forecasts, planning, and perpetual inventory. Over an 18-month time horizon, they would totally revamp their planning process, implement new platforms and technology across the entire organization, and introduce an SKU-rationalization initiative and predictive analytics capabilities.

Their initial focus was data and within the first few months, they went live with a new data warehouse and central data storage repository (DSR) as well as BI software. These critical first steps helped them find previously hidden issues in their data structure and in the information that was being used to make decisions. It provided visibility into data and was important for ensuring they had the right data for planning and to create insights. It also allowed them to begin looking at new attributes using web crawlers that extracted consumer and other information from the eCommerce channel they could use in modeling.

By the end of the first full year of the project, they defined and created specialized roles and hired new planners and a data architect to augment the current team and went live with an advanced planning system (APS). They used clustering methods to help segregate their items and customers, which allowed them to not only focus their planning resources on the most important items but to also contribute to SKU rationalization to eliminate poor performing items. They now had a planner focused on eCommerce and began forecasting this channel weekly, using a combination of traditional methods and new models, such as decision trees, using new external data. One example of this was using the number of customer comments in their modeling to predict online sell-through of new items.

The results came with much coordination, collaboration, challenges, and success. Due to these efforts, by the end of the second year, Escalade Sports saw a 10% improvement in fill rates to customers, a 26% improvement on forecast accuracy, a 19% reduction in some supply chain costs, and an 11% reduction in excess inventory. Add to this the automation of key processes, real-time visibility of data, and new business insights, and the company was transformed. Perhaps even more importantly, they laid the foundation to see, interpret, and act on data in the most efficient way possible, allowing them to maintain their position as a leader in their industry for years to come.

Digital transformation, making the leap to becoming more analytically driven and enabling predictive analytics may seem overwhelming. Escalade Sports saw an ROI in less than 14 months and continue to benefit by taking advantage of the changing consumer landscape. Transformation requires step-by-step changes over an extended period which is time-consuming and challenging but ultimately results in a significant advantage for the business.

Summary—Building the Perfect System

For the longest time we have been proclaiming "People then process then technology"—in that order. While this is still true, it almost discounts the need, importance, and urgency for the right technology. It is no longer a question of *if* you need technology but *what* technology you need. Then it's a question of how you integrate it into your organization.

It used to be that you could manage data in spreadsheets and, using the judgment of a few experts with tribal knowledge, you could get by. But times have changed. As you have seen throughout this book, we are no longer in an era of just extrapolating history to forecast demand. Forecasting is about people and competencies, as well as processes and principles; but more than that, it is about data, models, and understanding drivers. Excel is not enough in the predictive analytics revolution and we need better tools and technology to enable the future of demand planning.

As you embark on this predictive analytics journey or refine what you already have, technology will play a critical role. We're not saying that technology comes first, but it is equally important as any other step. To fully achieve the benefits of predictive analytics and build an analytically driven organization, technology is not just a component but a cornerstone.

The Key is to Design a System, Not Just Install Technology

A system is a set of things working together as parts of a mechanism or an interconnecting network. Technology is one of those things. People and process are another and, together, they make up the mechanism of predictive analytics. The goal is not to fix your problems with one of them but to interconnect all of them (and everything you have read in this book) to create a system.

Whether it be people, process, or technology, you must align it with strategy. Technology implementations will never succeed unless they are aligned with processes and have the right people involved. None of your analytics ambitions will go anywhere if they are not aligned to strategy. You need an overarching organizational objective, one that seeks to drive the business with data-driven decision-making. With that in place, everything else follows.

You need to think beyond your function and develop an ecosystem mentality. This means you are not Supply Chain or Finance or Sales. Instead, you're building a system of people, processes, and technology that is collaborative and supportive. Every decision works towards the desired future state, aiming to provide insights across the organization and not just your own function. Stop thinking only in terms of a demand or sales plan and start thinking in terms of enterprise-wide analytics and insights.

Invest in technology and build systems to consolidate data and provide predictive and prescriptive analytics. If we have the right ecosystem mentality, we will find ways to provide greater visibility of data and information and new ways to translate and turn that data into insights.

Find ways to automate and augment processes or outputs. This was our original definition of AI and a critical part of the future of demand planning and predictive analytics. We should continue to strive for this, improving processing and outputs using machines and proven techniques. Automation frees us up to focus on value-added work. Integrating demand sensing and real-time operational execution removes latency in processes and speeds up delivery of insights. Augmenting outputs using technology allows us to examine more variables and take advantage of more advanced modeling.

As I said at the beginning of this book, demand planning and predictive analytics will become the top priority and key area of investment in the next few years. The sheer volume and complexity of today's data are challenging, but the top organizations of tomorrow will successfully turn data into useful insights more quickly and for better decision-making, establishing a very real competitive advantage.

We are on the verge of a revolution in business. Companies need a new breed of talent, updated processes, new strategies, focus, and more advanced technologies. We cannot simply cobble together existing pieces. We need to think about what this new ecosystem looks like and change how we perceive demand planning and predictive analytics.

So, ask yourself the same questions with which I ended the first section:

- Are you ready?
- Are you embracing disruptive innovation?
- Are you challenging the status quo and the processes that exist in your organization?
- Do you have an agile workforce that can embrace the coming change?
- Are you leveraging big data and predictive analytics to the fullest extent?
- Do you know where and how analytics will play out inside your organization?
- Do you have the right tools and technology to enable your journey?

Only companies that can see, interpret, and act most efficiently and have a system for predictive analytics inside their organization will succeed in the future.

Section Review

Multiple choice: Identify the answer that best completes the statement.

1. A forecasting system is most effective when it is:

    a) User friendly.
    b) Complex in design and use.
    c) Designed for use by a specific demand planning process.
    d) Has many complex and advanced forecasting models.

2. Changes in software, hardware, forecasting process, and forecast training should be reviewed:

    a) On an *ad hoc* basis as problems and complaints arise.
    b) Periodically to ensure continued good performance.
    c) By external groups only with expertise in the field.
    d) None of the above.

3. A good forecast system:

    a) Is a substitute for a poor forecasting process.
    b) Provides answers and insights that never need interpreting.
    c) Eliminates the need for judgment in planning.
    d) None of the above.

4. A primary function of an expert system will:

   a) Suggest the variables to be forecasted for your industry or business.
   b) Select the best model for your data and then forecast with it.
   c) Evaluate the business assumptions being used in your projections.
   d) All of the above.

5. A feature built into a forecasting package that automatically analyzes the data, selects the best model, and then prepares a forecast is known as:

   a) A data best pick system.
   b) Unsupervised machine learning.
   c) An expert system.
   d) All of the above.

True or False?

6. ☐ Excel is open source in that it allows you to create formulas and models yourself.

7. ☐ Not considering a change management strategy is one of the key reasons why transformation projects fail.

8. ☐ You should be careful implementing cloud software because data is always less safe than if you stored it internally on your own servers.

9. ☐ BI tools cannot be used to forecast but do provide the ability to visualize data.

10. ☐ The best predictive analytics system considers people, process, data, and technology.

SECTION REVIEW ANSWERS

SECTION REVIEW ANSWERS

PART I

1. Which is a stated principle of predictive analytics?
   C. Predictive analytics is a process.

2. Business intelligence is:
   D. All of the above.

3. What type of analytics does machine learning support?
   D. All of the above.

4. If I am trying to understand what we can make happen, what type of analytics is this?
   B. Prescriptive analytics.

5. Predictive analytics and machine learning enable us to:
   D. All of the above.

True or False

6. **(False)** Diagnostic analytics is used to help understand what should happen.
7. **(False)** Predictive analytics only uses machine learning whereas traditional planning uses time-series methods.
8. **(True)** Predictive analytics is more forward-looking based on attributes whereas traditional planning is more static and based on the past.
9. **(False)** Machine learning works to automate the traditional forecasting process.
10. **(True)** Supervised machine learning is characterized by learning a model based on a data set that contains the answer or target.

PART II

1. What is NOT a process step in predictive analytics?
   C. Constraining outputs to match targets.

2. If the data has an outlier you can:
   D. All of the above.

3. Which of the following is NOT a data cleansing process?
   B. Building dimensions.

4. What kind of modeling technique would you use for describing past behavior?
   D. Descriptive analysis.

5. Training a model to fit the training data set may result in:
   D. All of the above.

True or False

6. **(True)** Data cleansing includes finding errors in completeness, correctness, and timeliness.
7. **(False)** An algorithm is a mathematical model with an endless number of possible steps.
8. **(True)** Time-series models need to be trained or rerun every time you get a new data point.
9. **(True)** The training data set will contain the answer to the problem.
10. **(False)** It is important to present just the facts and data so people can make their own decisions.

PART III

1. A data set is generally explained as:
   B. An organized stream of information.

2. The number of people that clicked on a product on your website is an example of:
   A. Internal structured data.

3. To be big data, it must:
   D. None of the above

4. Which of these are NOT data mining techniques?
   C. Predictive analytics.

5. A clustering technique where you sort objects into a pre-determined set of clusters based on a mean is an example of:
   A. Centroid-Based Clustering

True or False
6. **(True)** To do predictive analytics, you must first do some type of data mining.
7. **(False)** Unstructured data is data that is external to the planning system.
8. **(True)** Big data is relative to a company and its ability to store and process it.
9. **(False)** More data is always better for predictive analytics so models can learn.
10. **(True)** A dendrogram can be used to visualize Connectivity-Based Clustering.

PART IV

1. A forecasting method that relies on quantitative predefined models may be best categorized as:
   A. Deductive Logic (numerical-based) methods
2. A multiple regression is called "multiple" because it has several:
   C. Independent variables.
3. What is a decision tree commonly used for?
   B. To classify and group like attributes
4. In ARIMA modeling, data series are stationary, if:
   D. All of the above.
5. A _____ model is usually the gold standard for most forecasts.
   D. None of the above

True or False
6. **(True)** Traditional time-series and causal modeling are examples of Deductive Logic (Numerical-Based) methods.
7. **(True)** Logistic and linear regression work very similarly where the dependent variable is a binary value.
8. **(False)** Regression can be used to predict numerical or categorical values.
9. **(False)** Maximum Likelihood Estimation will tell you the likelihood that your model will perform well.
10. **(True)** ANN can be used for deep learning and to enable AI.

PART V

1. The following is NOT a pillar that enables a demand planning organization:
   C. Benchmarking MAPE to industry or competitors

2. Which are the competencies of a good Demand Planner?
   D. All of the above

3. Which of the following are the most common technical core competencies?
   B. Seeing connections in things.

4. The advantages of attending or sending your team to a conference are:
   D. All of the above.

5. Centralized demand planning and predictive analytics functions can:
   A. Improve the accuracy of forecasts.

True or False

6. **(False)** When hiring for demand planning roles it is always better to find someone in a similar industry and to prioritize analytical skills over other skills.
7. **(False)** A core competency is what you teach if the employee already has basic technical skills.
8. **(False)** Demand planning works best if it is a Supply Chain role.
9. **(True)** Data interpreters, data scientists, product analysts, and launch leaders are all variations of the demand planning role.
10. **(True)** Part of selling the idea of a predictive analytics function inside your organization is being able to accept and understand why they might say no.

PART VI

1. A forecasting system is most effective when it is:
   A. User friendly.

2. Changes in software, hardware, forecasting process, and forecast training should be reviewed:
   B. Periodically to ensure continued good performance.

SECTION REVIEW ANSWERS

3. A good forecast system:
   D. None of the above.

4. A primary function of an expert system will:
   B. Select the best model for your data and then forecast with it.

5. A feature built into a forecasting package that automatically analyzes the data, selects the best model, and then prepares a forecast is known as:
   C. An expert system.

True Or False?

6. **(False)** Excel is open source in that it allows you to create formulas and models yourself.
7. **(True)** Not considering a change management strategy is one of the key reasons why transformation projects fail.
8. **(False)** You should be careful implementing cloud software because data is always less safe than if you stored it internally on your own servers.
9. **(False)** BI tools cannot be used to forecast but do provide the ability to visualize data.
10. **(True)** The best predictive analytics system considers people, process, data, and technology.

PREDICTIVE ANALYTICS GLOSSARY OF TERMS

GLOSSARY

Activation Function: A function that takes the weighted sum of all of the inputs from the previous layer and then generates and passes an output value (typically nonlinear) to the next layer. In neural networks, these can be used at nodes in a hidden layer to squash the input.

Algorithm: Any detailed operation or set of rules used to carry out an operation, solve a problem, or express an outcome using a finite number of steps.

Analytics Translator: An analytical and collaborative role whose job it is to manage the inputs and outputs and interpretation of predictive and data analytics. An analytics translator is a conduit between data roles and planning roles and executive decision-makers.

Anomaly Detection: Detecting the outlying values or items in a data set with differing characteristics and separating them from the rest of the data to identify noise and improve predictions.

APS (Advanced Planning System): A supply chain management system that analyzes and plans logistics and manufacturing resources for short-, intermediate-, and long-term periods. APS software uses advanced math and heuristics to perform simulations and optimizations for such things as finite capacity scheduling, demand planning, S&OP, logistics resource planning, and so forth.

ARIMA Model: Part of the group of time-series models that assume that future sales depend on previous values of the same series. ARIMA or ARIMAX are acronyms that stand for (AR) AutoRegressive (I) Integrated (MA) Moving Average (the X is an explanatory variable).

Artificial Intelligence (AI): The capability of a machine or system to augment or automate any process or output that normally requires human intelligence or intervention. By system we mean a collection of algorithms, hardware, software and/or connect ware.

Artificial Neural Network (ANN): A class of supervised learning and pattern matching methods and a computational model based on the structure and functions of biological neural networks. Information that flows through the network consists of units (neurons), arranged in layers, which convert an input vector into an output.

Association: A type of statistical technique that helps find associations between two or more variables.

Autocorrelation: In time-series forecasting, this refers to the correlation an observation has between itself and another observation.

Autocorrelation Function (ACF): The pattern of autocorrelations at different time intervals. In ARIMA modeling, it is used, among other things, to determine the appropriate model.

Autoregressive Model (AR): Part of an ARIMA model that assumes that the sales of the current period depend on the sales of the past values of the same series at different time lags.

Backpropagation: The primary algorithm for performing gradient descent on neural networks by measuring the margin of error of the output and adjusting the weights accordingly to decrease the error.

Bayesian Model: A class of supervised learning methods that explicitly apply Bayes' Theorem to solve problems such as classification and regression. It is a classification technique with an assumption of independence among predictors.

Bias: In forecasting, bias occurs when there is a consistent difference between actual sales and the forecast, which is manifest as over- or under-forecasting.

Big Data: An amount of data that is so large, it exceeds your company's ability to store, process, or use it.

Business Forecasting: The process of using analytics, data, insights, and experience to make predictions and answer questions for various business needs.

Business Intelligence: An umbrella term that covers architectures, databases, analytical tools, applications, and methodologies used for applying data analysis techniques to support business decision-making.

Business Intelligence Tools: Software that collects and processes large amounts of data from internal and external systems.

Categorical Variables: Contain a finite number of categories or distinct groups. Categorical data might not have a logical order. For example, categorical predictors include gender, material type, and payment method.

Causal Model: A collection of values observed cross-functionally and based on the cause-and-effect relationship.

Centroid-Based Clustering: A statistical method for finding relatively homogeneous clusters of cases based on areas of higher density than the remainder of the data set (the most commonly used is K-Means).

Churn Analysis: The evaluation of a company's customer loss rate with the aim of reducing it. Also referred to as customer attrition rate, churn can be minimized by assessing how people use your product.

Classification: An approach or combination of methods where the primary objective is to predict the target class using observed values. Classification helps in deriving important information about data and metadata (data about data).

Click-Stream Data: Such data include page visits and associated clicks executed by website visitors while navigating through a site.

Cloud Software: A metaphor for an application or process that operates outside of your own personal or company's storage or servers.

Clustering: An approach or combination of methods where the primary objective is to group related data points together. This is often used to create clusters or segments that are used as inputs in other analyses. This process involves grouping chunks of data together based on their similarities.

Cognitive Analytics: A process and strategy that brings together several intelligent technologies including semantics, AI algorithms, and many learning techniques such as deep learning and machine learning to accomplish self-healing or semi-autonomous analytical cognition.

Conjoint Analysis: A survey-based statistical technique and optimal market research approach for measuring the value consumers place on features of a product or service.

Connectivity-Based Clustering: A statistical method for finding relatively homogeneous clusters of cases based on dissimilarities or distances between objects (the most commonly used is hierarchical clustering).

Constraint-Based Clustering: A process for finding any classification scheme that makes use of IF-THEN rules and user-specified preferences or constraints to find and determine clusters (the most commonly used are rule-based classifiers).

Continuous Variables: Numeric variables that have an infinite number of values between any two values. A continuous variable can be numeric or date/time, for example the length of a part or the date and time a payment is received.

GLOSSARY

Correlation Coefficient: A standard measure of the relationship between a dependent and independent variable. Its value varies between -1 and 1. Zero means there is no correlation between them, and 1 means a perfect correlation. A positive value means that the relationship is positive; that is, when one goes up, the other also goes up. A negative value means they are negatively related.

Customer Lifetime Value (CLV): Represents the value of a customer to your business over the entire length of your relationship with that customer. At the heart of CLV is the probability of churn as well as the dollars the customer may spend.

Customer Relationship Management (CRM): A system for managing all your company's data, relationships and interactions pertaining to customers and potential customers.

Data Cleansing: The process of finding and eliminating errors in the completeness, correctness, and timeliness of the data.

Data Lake: Generally, a large, easily accessible, centralized repository of large volumes of structured and unstructured data.

Data Mart: A subset of data warehouses, usually geared towards a specific business line or team.

Data Mining: A process that includes the collection, exploration, pattern identification, and deployment of data to gain insights and extract useful information.

Data Repository: A place where logical partitioning of data of multiple databases that apply to specific applications or sets of applications reside.

Data Set: A collection of data organized as a stream of information in logical record and block structures.

Data Visualization: The graphical representation of information and data. By using visual elements like charts, graphs, and maps, data visualization tools provide an accessible way to see and understand trends, outliers, and patterns in data.

Data Warehouse: Where data are stored after they are cleaned, transformed, and cataloged, and then made available for analysis, data mining, market research, and decision support.

Data: Information in its raw form.

Database: Usually a large collection of typically quantitative information organized for rapid search and retrieval (normally by a computer). Models and forecasts may be based on databases that contain sales information that has dimensions such as product, geography, period, and measure.

Decision Trees: A type of classification and regression method that constructs a model of decisions made based on actual values of attributes in the data. Decision trees build classification or regression models in the form of a tree structure. It breaks down a data set into smaller and smaller subsets while at the same time an associated decision tree is incrementally developed.

Deep Learning: A subset of machine learning based on algorithms that attempt to emulate human thought and behavior to solve complex problems. Instead of organizing data to run through predefined equations, deep learning sets up basic parameters about the data and trains the computer to learn on its own by recognizing patterns using many layers of processing.

Demand Orchestration: Determines the best solution or outcome among various choices, given the known parameters.

Demand Plan: A projection of the future that combines the knowledge of the past with the best assessment of the future need of a product or service.

Demand Planning: The process and techniques used to create a demand plan and other data analytic outputs used in the planning process or to enable business decisions.

Demand Sensing: The sensing of demand signals, and then predicting demand. Demand signals include who is buying the product or service and how sales and marketing activities are influencing demand.

Demand Shaping: The manipulation of demand of a product to achieve a desired goal.

Demand Signal Repository (DSR): A database or a data warehouse that is used for aggregating and structuring demand data.

Demand Translation: Translating demand from the market to each role within the organization.

Density-Based Clustering: A statistical method for finding clusters according to the high density of members of a data set, in a determined location (the most commonly used are DBSCAN and OPTICS).

Dendrogram: A tree-like visual diagram used as a main output of hierarchical clustering that gives a visual snapshot of relationships between clusters.

Dependent Variable: A variable that we wish to forecast or output of a model. In regression modeling, the variable to be predicted is called the dependent variable.

Descriptive Analytics: A process and strategy of gathering and interpreting data to describe insights into the past and what has occurred.

Diagnostic Analytics: A process and strategy of gathering and interpreting different data sets to identify anomalies, detect patterns, and determine relational insights into the data and what is occurring.

Discrete Variables: Numeric variables that have a countable number of values between any two values. A discrete variable is always numeric. For example, the number of customer complaints or the number of flaws or defects.

Distribution-Based Clustering: A statistical method for finding clusters based on how probable is it that all data points in the cluster belong to the same distribution (the most commonly used are Normal or Gaussian).

Dynamic Regression: A regression model that includes lagged values of independent variables, dependent variables, or both. For example, if certain promotional activities affect sales only after one or two months, the model will become more efficient if the promotional spending is lagged.

Early Stopping: A method that involves ending model training before overfitting occurs. In early stopping, you end model training when the loss on a validation dataset starts to increase; that is, when generalization performance worsens.

Ensemble Models: A merger of the predictions of multiple models.

Enterprise Resource Planning (ERP): Provides an integrated real-time view of core business processes using common databases maintained by a database management system. It tracks business resources such as cash, raw materials, and production capacity, and the status of business commitments such as orders, purchase orders, and payroll. In other words, it provides totally integrated suites of software that support all functions within the organization including Finance, HR, Supply Chain Planning, and Procurement.

Entropy: As it relates to machine learning, a measure of the randomness in the information being processed. The higher the entropy, the harder it is to draw any conclusions from that information. Entropy is often used to determine how the direction of travel and split values are chosen.

Expert System: A software system that determines the optimal solution based on pre-determined rules. The solution may be finding the best production schedule, the most desirable demand plan, or the best forecast.

Feature: An individual measurable property of a characteristic that is being observed.

Feature Engineering: The process of determining which features might be useful in training a model, and then converting raw data from files and other sources into features models may use.

Forecasting Package: A standalone package that generates forecasts either by a model selected by a forecaster or by an automatic feature (called an expert system) that is built into the software package.

Forecasting System: A system that includes a forecasting package and feeds forecasts to various modules for planning.

Forward Propagation: The primary algorithm for performing gradient ascent on neural networks by applying a set of weights to the input data and calculating an output.

Gradient Descent: A technique to minimize loss or error to help refine machine learning models and operations. The gradient descent algorithm works toward adjusting the input weights of neurons in Artificial Neural Networks and finding local minima or global minima in order to optimize a problem.

Hidden Layer: The synthetic layer in a neural network that is a collection of neurons that has an activation function applied on it. It is an intermediate layer found between the input layer and the output layer.

Hierarchical Clustering: See Connectivity-Based Clustering.

Holdout Period: A dataset, separate from the training set or data being modeled but with the same structure, used to measure and benchmark the performance of various models or parameters.

Independent Variable: An observable quantity recorded and used by a prediction model and variable that affects the variable we wish to predict. An independent variable is also called an explanatory variable, predictor variable, and driver.

Information: A collection of data points that we can use to understand something about the thing being measured.

Input Layer: First layer in a neural network that receives the input data and represents the condition for which we are training.

Insight: Valuable information gained by analyzing data and other inputs to understand what is going on with the particular situation or phenomena. The insight can then be used to make better business decisions

Intercept: In regression, it explains what the forecast value would be if all the Xs (independent variables) have a zero value. Also called a constant.

K-Means: A common method used for centroid-based cluster and unsupervised learning algorithms that clusters **n** objects into **k** clusters, where each object belongs to a cluster with the nearest mean. In this method, we compute the distance of each point from each cluster by computing its distance from the corresponding cluster mean.

Label: The target or final output in a machine learning model. You can also consider the output classes to be the labels. When data scientists speak of labeled data, they mean groups of samples that have been tagged to one or more labels.

Lagged Dependent Variable: A dependent variable that is lagged. For example, if Y_t is the dependent variable, then Y_{t-1} is a lagged dependent variable with a lag of one period. Lagged values are used in Dynamic Regression modeling. They are also used in ARIMA modeling where it is assumed that the forecast of the next period depends on past values of the same series.

Logistic Regression: A statistical method for analyzing a data set that is used to model a binary dependent variable that may determine the probability of a certain class or event existing.

Machine Learning: An algorithm or technique that enables systems to be "trained" and to learn patterns from inputs and subsequently recalibrate from experience without being explicitly programmed. Machine Learning is a subset or application of AI and is more of an approach than a process. A learning algorithm differs from most traditional business forecasting methods such as time-series or simple causal models in that it will take information from previous iterations or a training dataset to help build the current or future model.

Market Basket Analysis: A type of analysis that helps companies cross-sell and up-sell products based upon the theory that if you buy a certain group of items, you are more (or less) likely to buy another group of items.

Maximum Likelihood Estimation: A method that determines values for the parameters of a model. The maximum-likelihood estimation is a "likelihood" maximization method, while ordinary least squares are a distance-minimizing approximation method.

Model: A mathematical representation of a real-world process.

Moving Average Model (MA): In the context of an ARIMA model, the model assumes that the dependent variable depends on the past errors (residuals) at different lags.

Multiple Regression Model: A regression model where two or more independent (explanatory) variables are used to arrive at a predictive model.

Natural Language Processing (NLP): A subset of machine learning and a group of models that seek to understand, analyze, manipulate, and potentially generate human language. Similar to human conversations, natural language models use syntax (arrangement of words) and semantics (meaning of that arrangement).

Naïve Bayes: A family of probabilistic algorithms that take advantage of probability theory and Bayes' Theorem. See Bayesian Models.

Online Analytical Processing (OLAP): A computing method that enables users to easily and selectively extract and query data in order to analyze it from different points of view.

Open Source Software: A type of software where the source code is publicly accessible (or open) and grants users the right to modify and share it. R and Python are the most well-known, high-level, general-purpose statistical programming languages.

GLOSSARY

Ordinary Least Squares (OLS): An estimation method that minimizes the sum of squared residuals to arrive at the best model. It is most often used in regression because of its statistical properties.

Outliers: Observations or values that are unusually large or small or outside of acceptable tolerances.

Output Layer: The final layer of a neural network that provides the output to the user.

Overfitting: The use of an overly complex model that describes noise (randomness) in the data set rather than the underlying statistical relationship. As a result, the model trains to predict the target will perform unusually well on its training data.

Parameter: A variable of a model that the machine learning model trains on its own. For example, weights are parameters whose values the machine learning model gradually learns through successive training iterations.

Partial Autocorrelation Function (PACF): The partial autocorrelation describes the correlation between the current value of a variable and the earlier value of the same variable when the effects of all intervening time lags are held constant. In ARIMA modeling, it is used, among other things, to determine the appropriate model.

Pattern Recognition: A statistical technique that relates to the collection and description of data (similar to Association).

Predictive Analysis: The process of collecting, transforming, cleansing, modeling, and managing data with the goal to predict a discrete or continuous value.

Predictive Analytics: A process and strategy that uses a variety of advanced statistical algorithms to detect patterns and conditions that may occur in the future for insights into what will happen.

Predictive Model: An approach or combination of methods where the primary objective is to predict the probability of a discrete or continuous value using a set of predictor values.

Prescriptive Analytics: A process and strategy combining data, mathematical models, probability of future events, and various business rules to infer actions to influence future desired outcomes. Some refer to this as demand shaping but can include simulation, probability maximization, and optimization.

P-Value: Often used in regression models to determine whether a given explanatory variable is significant or not. Often, a variable is considered significant if the P-value is less than 0.05, though this threshold is arbitrary.

Random Forest: A supervised learning algorithm that randomly creates and merges multiple decision trees into one "forest."

Regression Coefficient: Each independent variable in a regression model has a regression coefficient, which is often denoted by the letter "b."

Regression: A class of cause-and-effect models, where the first relationship between cause (independent variable) and effect (dependent variable) is determined, which then is used to prepare a forecast. This helps understand relationships and to predict continuous variables based on other variables in the data set.

Regularization: A broad range of techniques for artificially forcing your model to be simpler.

Recurrent Neural Network: A type of Artificial Neural Network where connections between nodes are used to recognize patterns and sequences. See Artificial Neural Networks.

Reinforced Learning: A subset of machine learning algorithms that learn an optimal policy whose goal it is to maximize return on performance when interacting with a given environment. Such algorithms try different approaches using trial-and-error to decide which actions to take to maximize a reward.

Rule-Based Clustering: See Constraint-Based Clustering.

Segmentation: The process of defining and sub-dividing a large homogenous data set into clearly identifiable segments having similar or dissimilar characteristics.

Sentiment Analysis: The use of statistical or machine learning algorithms to maximize the margin between positive and negative classes. It is broadly used for customer satisfaction or to determine a group's overall attitude—positive or negative—toward a service, product, organization, or topic.

Sigmoid Function: A function that maps logistic or multinomial regression outputs (log odds) to probabilities, returning a value between 0 and 1.

Slope: In regression, the coefficient of a variable is the slope of that variable. It shows how much Y (dependent variable) will change with one unit of change in X (independent variable).

Social Network Analysis (SNA): A process of mapping and measuring relationships and flows between various attributes, locations, and information/knowledge entities to understand social structures.

Software as a Service (SaaS): A method of software delivery and licensing in which software is accessed online via a subscription, rather than bought and installed on individual computers.

Stationary Data: Time-series data are stationary if their mean, variance, and co-variance do not change over time.

Splitting Data: For supervised learning tasks such as classification and regression, data is separated into sub-datasets for training, validation, and testing.

Structured Data: Data that are both highly organized, easy to digest, and generally refers to data that have a defined length and format.

Supervised Learning: Algorithms that try to model relationships and dependencies between the target prediction output and the input features such that we can predict the output values for new data based on the relationships that it learned from the previous data sets. With Supervised Learning Algorithms we rely on experts who act as teachers to feed the training data to help the model know what the right answers should be, so it learns and improves.

Support Vector Machines (SVM): A supervised machine learning algorithm that analyzes data for classification and regression analysis using data analysis and pattern recognition. Support vector machines are used to sort two data groups by like classification.

Testing Data Set: The part of the overall data set you use to provide an unbiased evaluation of a final model fit before putting it into production. Also known as a holdout period.

Time-Series Models: A collection of values observed sequentially over time and used to perform time-based predictions. In these models, it is assumed that the past data pattern will continue in the future. Here, one needs only the data of the series to be forecasted.

GLOSSARY

Training Data Set: The part of the overall data set you use to train the model.

Underfitting: This occurs when a model is overly simple, informed by too few features or regularized too much, which makes it inflexible in learning from the dataset. As a result, it will assume the noise is much greater than it really is.

Unstructured Data: Data that does not have an easily definable structure and is unorganized and raw. It is not typically a good fit for a mainstream relational database.

Unsupervised Learning: Algorithms that learn from plain examples without any associated response, leaving the algorithm to determine the data patterns on its own. Where with supervised learning we may provide a good dataset to use to compare to future inputs, this looks at the dataset provided and finds structures in that dataset on its own.

Validation Data Set: The part of the overall data set you use for evaluation of a model fit on the training data set while tuning model hyperparameters.

Visualization: A technique or process to see, group, and discover patterns in data, and manually wrangle data from its visual representation.

Weights: A coefficient for a feature in a linear model. In neural networks it is the parameter that transforms input data within the network's hidden layers. Weighting places more focus on different nodes or different functions of the same group of nodes.

SUGGESTED READING FOR IBF CERTIFICATION

This book, along with the *Fundamentals of Demand Planning & Forecasting* written by Chaman L. Jain and published by the Institute of Business Forecasting (IBF), form the course content for IBF's Certified Professional Forecaster program. The program comprises 2 levels,

- Certified Professional Forecaster (CPF)
- Advanced Certified Professional Forecaster (ACPF)

The *Fundamentals of Demand Planning & Forecasting* is primarily the textbook for the CPF program, while this book and the *Fundamentals of Demand Planning & Forecasting* book are the textbooks for the ACPF program.

On the following pages you will find the specific chapters and parts that will help you prepare for each exam for both the CPF and ACPF programs. The *Fundamentals of Demand Planning & Forecasting* is available for purchase at **www.ibf.org/books.**

Find out more about IBF certification at **www.ibf.org/business-analytics-certification.**

Suggested Reading for Certified Professional Forecaster (CPF)

Certified Professional Forecaster (CPF)
Exams 1, 2 & 3

EXAM 1
Book: *Fundamentals of Demand Planning & Forecasting* By Chaman L. Jain

Chapter 1	Forecasting: What and Why
Chapter 2	Evolution in Forecasting
Chapter 3	Fundamentals of Demand Forecasting and Supply Planning
Chapter 4	Demand Planning
Chapter 5	Point-of-Sale-Based Demand Planning
Chapter 6	The Process
Chapter 7	Silo to Consensus Forecasting
Chapter 8	The Sales and Operations Planning Process
Chapter 9	Collaborative Planning, Forecasting and Replenishment
Chapter 10	Building Collaboration

EXAM 2

Book: *Fundamentals of Demand Planning & Forecasting* By Chaman L. Jain

Chapter 11   What You Need to Know About Data
Chapter 12   Data Analysis and Treatment
Chapter 13   How Much Data to Use in Forecasting
Chapter 14   Fundamentals of Models and Modeling
Chapter 15   Averages
Chapter 16   Moving Averages
Chapter 17   Exponential Smoothing
Chapter 18   Trend Line
Chapter 19   Classical Decomposition
Chapter 20   Sales Ratios
Chapter 21   Family Member Forecasting
Chapter 26   Performance Metrics

EXAM 3

Book: *Fundamentals of Demand Planning & Forecasting* By Chaman L. Jain

Chapter 27   Reporting, Presenting, and Selling Forecasts

Suggested Reading for Advanced Certified Professional Forecaster (ACPF)

Advanced Certified Professional Forecaster (ACPF)
Exams 4 & 5

EXAM 4

Book: *Fundamentals of Demand Planning & Forecasting* By Chaman L. Jain

Chapter 22   Simple Regression Models
Chapter 23   Multiple Regression Models
Chapter 24   Box-Jenkins

Book: *Predictive Analytics For Business Forecasting & Planning* By J. Eric Wilson

PART IV   Predictive Analytics As An Approach

EXAM 5

Book: *Fundamentals of Demand Planning & Forecasting* By Chaman L. Jain

Chapter 28   Worst Practices in Demand Planning and Forecasting
Chapter 29   Forecasting Software Packages
Chapter 30   Forecasting Systems

Book: *Predictive Analytics For Business Forecasting & Planning* By J. Eric Wilson

PART IV   Predictive Analytics As An Approach

EXAM 6

Book: *Predictive Analytics For Business Forecasting & Planning* By J. Eric Wilson

PART I   The Predictive Analytics Foundation
PART II   Predictive Analytics As A Process
PART III   Predictive Analytics As Data Analysis
PART V   Predictive Analytics As A Function

REFERENCES AND ENDNOTES

1. Bayireddi, M. (2018) 'The Tipping Point for Artificial Intelligence'. Available at: https://www.datanami.com/2018/07/20/the-tipping-point-for-artificial-intelligence/.
2. Wilson, E. (2018) 'Preparing for Demand Planning in 2025', Journal of Business Forecasting (36)4, 16-19.
3. Friedman, W. (2013) 'Fortune Tellers'. Princeton University Press.
4. Institute of Business Forecasting, 'About Us'. Available at https://demand-planning.com/about-us.
5. Orwell, M. (1946) 'Politics and the English Language'. London: Penguin Books.
6. Edwards, J. (2019) 'Ways Predictive Analytics Can Improve Customer Experience'. Available at: https://www.cio.com/article/3387640/7-ways-predictive-analytics-can-improve-customer-experience.html.
7. Henderson, M and A (2019) 'Data Science for Business. Machine Learning and Data Analytics'. Self-published.
8. Power, D. (2017). 'A Brief History of Decision Support Systems, Version 4.0'. Available at: http://dssresources.com/history/dsshistory.html.
9. Institute of Business Forecasting (2018) 'What Is Business Forecasting, And Why Is It Valuable?'. Available at https://ibf.org/knowledge/posts/what-is-business-forecasting-and-why-is-it-valuable-2-43.
10. Wikipedia (2019) 'Machine Learning'. Available at: https://en.wikipedia.org/wiki/Machine_learning.
11. Davenport, T. and Harris, J. (2006) 'Competing on Analytics'. Harvard Business Review January 2006, pp. 200-213.
12. Mehta, A. (2017). 'Four Types of Business Analytics to Know'. Available at: https://www.analyticsinsight.net/four-types-of-business-analytics-to-know/.
13. Dennis, A. (2019) 'Artificial Intelligence, Machine Learning, and Deep Learning Explained'. Available at: https://www.dataversity.net/artificial-intelligence-machine-learning-and-deep-learning-explained/.
14. Techhq.com (2018) 'How Starbucks Uses Data and Insights to Win Big'. Available at: https://techhq.com/2018/09/how-starbucks-uses-data-and-insights-to-win-big/.
15. Wilson, E. (2018) 'Amazon Effect: Driving New Opportunities and Challenges in Demand Forecasting'. Available at: https://demand-forecasting.cioreview.com/cxoinsight/amazon-effect-driving-new-opportunities-and-challenges-in-demand-forecasting-nid-27109-cid-182.html.
16. Donges, N. (2018) 'Data Types in Statistics'. Available at: https://towardsdatascience.com/data-types-in-statistics-347e152e8bee.
17. Davenport, T. and Harris J. (2006) 'Competing on Analytics'. Harvard Business Review January 2006 pp. 31-34.
18. Chase, C. (2009) 'Demand Driven Forecasting'. Hoboken: Wiley.
19. Kotu, V. and Deshpande, B. (2014) 'Predictive Analytics and Data Mining'. Burlington: Morgan Kaufmann.
20. Elite Data Science (2016) 'Data Cleaning' (2016). Available at: https://elitedatascience.com/data-cleaning.
21. Towards Data Science (2019) 'The Ultimate Guide to Data Cleaning'. Available at: https://towardsdatascience.com/the-ultimate-guide-to-data-cleaning-3969843991d4.
22. Chase, C. (2009) 'Next Generation Demand Management'. Hoboken: Wiley.
23. Intellspot (2017) '10 Key Types of Data Analysis Methods and Techniques'. Available at: http://intellspot.com/types-data-analysis/.
24. Alton, L. (2017) 'The 7 Most Important Data Mining Techniques'. Available at: https://www.datasciencecentral.com/profiles/blogs/the-7-most-important-data-mining-techniques.
25. James, G. (2013) 'An Introduction to Statistical Learning: With Applications in R'. New York City: Springer.
26. Armstrong, S (2001). 'Combining Forecasts, Principles of Forecasting: A Handbook for Researchers and Practitioners'. Norwell: Kluwer Academic Publishers.

27. Kasturi, S. (2018) 'Underfitting and Overfitting in Machine Learning and How to Deal with It'. Available at: https://towardsdatascience.com/underfitting-and-overfitting-in-machine-learning-and-how-to-deal-with-it-6fe4a8a49dbf.
28. Brownlee, J. (2016) 'Master Machine Learning Algorithms'. Self-published.
29. Faber, M.; Manstetten R.; and Proops, J. (1992) 'Toward an Open Future: Ignorance, Novelty, and Evolution'.
30. Gilliland, M.; Tashman, L.; and Sglavo, U. (2016) 'Business Forecasting: Practical Problems and Solutions'. Hoboken: Wiley.
31. Bowne-Anderson, H. (2018) 'What Data Scientists Really Do, According to 35 Data Scientists'. Harvard Business Review August 15, 2018.
32. Reddy, C. (2016) 'Wise Step Data Mining: Purpose, Characteristics, Benefits & Limitations'. Available at: https://content.wisestep.com/data-mining-purpose-characteristics-benefits-limitations/.
33. Tan, P.; Steinbach, M.; and Kumar, V. (2005) 'Introduction to Data Mining'. London: Pearson.
34. Grymes, S. (2008) 'Unstructured Data and the 80 Percent Rule, Breakthrough Analysis'. Available at: https://breakthroughanalysis.com/2008/08/01/unstructured-data-and-the-80-percent-rule/.
35. Laney, D. (2001) '3D Data Management: Controlling Data Volume, Velocity and Variety'. META Group Research Note, 6.
36. Byrne, R. (2012). 'Beyond Traditional Time-Series: Using Demand Sensing to Improve Forecasts in Volatile Times'. Journal of Business Forecasting (31)2, pp. 13-19.
37. Mayer-Schönberger, V., and Cukier, K. (2014) 'Big Data: A Revolution That Will Transform How We Live, Work, and Think'. Eamon Dolan Mariner Books.
38. Manickam, H. (2017). 'Predictive Analysis of Production Strategies'. Master's thesis, Rose Hulman Institute of Technology, Terre Haute, Indiana.
39. McKinsey Global Institute. (2014). 'Five Facts: How Customer Analytics Boosts Corporate Performance'. Available at: https://www.mckinsey.com/business-functions/marketing-and-sales/our-insights/five-facts-how-customer-analytics-boosts-corporate-performance.
40. Wood, G. (2016) 'Google's AI Wins Fifth and Final Game Against Go Genius'. Wired Magazine, March 2016.
41. Sayad, S. (2010). 'Naïve Bayesian'. Available at: https://www.saedsayad.com/naive_bayesian.htm.
42. Jain, C. and Malehorn, J. (2005) 'Practical Guide to Business Forecasting'. New York City: Graceway Publishing Company 2005, pp. 371-383.
43. Sayad, S. (2010). 'Logistic Regression'. Available at: https://www.saedsayad.com/logistic_regression.htm.
44. Henderson, M., and Adams, R. (2019) 'Machine Learning and Data Analytics'. Self-published.
45. Henderson, M., and Adams, R. (2019) 'Machine Learning and Data Analytics'. Self-published.
46. McMenamin, S. (2003). 'A Primer on Neural Networks for Forecasting', Journal of Business Forecasting, 16(3,) pp. 17-22.
47. Vandeput, N. (2018) 'Data Science for Supply Chain Forecasting'. Self-published.
48. Nisbet, R., Miner, G., and Yale, K. (2018) 'Handbook of Statistical Analysis and Data Mining Applications'. Amsterdam: Elsevier Inc.
49. Wang, G. (2008) 'A Guide to Box-Jenkins Modeling'. Journal of Business Forecasting, 27(1) pp. 19–23.
50. Chase, C. (2009) 'Demand Driven Forecasting'. Hoboken: Wiley.
51. Wilson, E. (2018) 'Multi-Cluster Time Series Analysis', Journal of Business Forecasting, (37)3, pp. 20-23.
52. Kaggle (2016) 'Walmart Recruiting – Store Sales Forecasting'. Available at: https://www.kaggle.com/c/walmart-recruiting-store-sales-forecasting/data.

53. Dunkelberg, W. and Wade, H. (2017) 'NFIB Small Business Economic Trends'. Available at: https://www.nfib.com/assets/SBET-January-2017.pdf.
54. Brown, J. (2017) 'CareerCast.com Annual Jobs Rated Report'. Available at: https://www.careercast.com/jobs-rated/2017-jobs-rated-report.
55. Covey, S. (2013) 'The 7 Habits of Highly Effective People'. London: Simon & Schuster.
56. Breault, J (2017) 'Lifework Search Employment Situation Report'. Available at: https://lifeworksearch.com/refresh/templates/news_item.php? id = 362&industry = all.
57. Murphy, M (2015). 'Why New Hires Fail (Emotional Intelligence Vs. Skills). Available at: https://www.leadershipiq.com/blogs/leadershipiq/35354241-why-new-hires-fail-emotional-intelligence-vs-skills.
58. Davidson, K (2016). 'Employers Find 'Soft Skills' Like Critical Thinking in Short Supply'. Available at: https://www.wsj.com/articles/employers-find-soft-skills-like-critical-thinking-in-short-supply-1472549400.
59. Strauss, V. (2017) 'The Surprising Thing Google Learned About its Employees — and What it Means for Today's Students'. Available at: https://www.washingtonpost.com/news/answer-sheet/wp/2017/12/20/the-surprising-thing-google-learned-about-its-employees-and-what-it-means-for-todays-students/.
60. Boyatzis, R. (2008) 'Competencies in the 21st Century', Journal of Management Development, (27)1, pp. 5-10.
61. Eichinger, R., and Lombardo, M. (2004), 'Learning Agility as a Prime Indicator of Potential', Human Resources Planning Journal, (27)4, pp. 12-15.
62. Seth G. (2009) 'The Tribes We Lead'. Available at: https://www.ted.com/talks/seth_godin_the_tribes_we_lead/transcript? language = en.
63. Wilson, E., (2017) 'Preparing for Demand Planning in 2025'. Journal of Business Forecasting, (36)4, pp. 16-19.
64. ABI Research (2019). 'Artificial Intelligence: Investment and Technology Trends'. Available at: https://www.abiresearch.com/market-research/product/7777806-artificial-intelligence-investment-and-tec/.
65. Vandeput, N. (2018) 'Data Science for Supply Chain Forecasting'. Self-published.
66. Jain, C. (2018) 'The Impact of People and Processes on Forecast Error in S&OP'. Available at: https://ibf.org/knowledge/reports/the-impact-of-people-and-processes-on-forecast-error-in-sop-research18.
67. Arkieva (2019) 'Key Supply Chain Digital Transformation Pitfalls to Avoid'. Available at: https://blog.arkieva.com/supply-chain-digital-transformation/.
68. Kotter, J. (1995) 'Leading Change'. Available at: https://hbr.org/1995/05/leading-change-why-transformation-efforts-fail-2.
69. Wipro Digital (2017) 'Digital Transformation ROI Survey'. Available at: https://www.slideshare.net/WiproDigital/digital-transformation-roi-survey-from-wipro-digital-76561582.
70. Heneghan, L., and Ellis, A. (2017) 'Navigating Uncertainty'. Available at: https://assets.kpmg/content/dam/kpmg/xx/pdf/2017/07/harvey-nash-kpmg-cio-survey-2017.pdf.
71. Vinit S. (2018) 'Demand Forecasting in the Cloud: Modern Computing Meets the Forecasting Discipline', Journal of Business Forecasting, (37)3, pp. 12–17.
72. Prescient & Strategic (P&S) Intelligence (2017) 'Cloud SCM Market Overview'. Available at: Https://www.psmarketresearch.com/market-analysis/cloud-supply-chain-management-market.
73. MIT Research (1996) 'Brain Processing of Visual Information'. Available at: http://news.mit.edu/1996/visualprocessing.
74. Vogel, D., Dickson, G., and Lehman, J. (1986) 'Persuasion and the Role of Visual Presentation Support'. Minneapolis: Management Information Systems Research Center, School of Management, University of Minnesota
75. Tableau, 'What is Data Visualization'. Available at: https://www.tableau.com/learn/articles/data-visualization.